INDIA ARRIVING

India Arriving

HOW THIS ECONOMIC POWERHOUSE
IS REDEFINING GLOBAL BUSINESS

Rafiq Dossani

AMACOM

AMERICAN MANAGEMENT ASSOCIATION
New York • Atlanta • Brussels • Chicago • Mexico City • San Francisco
Shanghai • Tokyo • Toronto • Washington, D.C.

Special discounts on bulk quantities of AMACOM books are
available to corporations, professional associations, and other
organizations. For details, contact Special Sales Department,
AMACOM, a division of American Management Association,
1601 Broadway, New York, NY 10019.
Tel: 212–903–8316. Fax: 212–903–8083.
E-mail: specialsls@amanet.org
Website: www.amacombooks.org/go/specialsales
To view all AMACOM titles go to: www.amacombooks.org

This publication is designed to provide accurate and authoritative
information in regard to the subject matter covered. It is sold with
the understanding that the publisher is not engaged in rendering
legal, accounting, or other professional service. If legal advice or
other expert assistance is required, the services of a competent
professional person should be sought.

Library of Congress Cataloging-in-Publication Data

Dossani, Rafiq, 1954-
India arriving : how this economic powerhouse is redefining global business / Rafiq
Dossani.
    p.   cm.
   Includes index.
   ISBN-13: 978-0-8144-7424-2 (hardcover)
   ISBN-10: 0-8144-7424-1 (hardcover)
   1. India—Economic conditions.   2. Globalization—Economic aspects—India.
  3. National characteristics, East Indian.   4. India—Social conditions.   5. Political
culture—India.   I. Title.

  HC435.3.D67   2008
  330.954—dc22

                                                  2007026894

Printing number

10 9 8 7 6 5 4 3 2 1

India is arriving: make sure to take me along.

CONTENTS

Preface   ix

1   India: Not What It Seems   1

2   Nehru's India: The Rise of State Power   17

3   The Rise of States' Power   31

4   The Diverse Outcomes of Federalism   47

5   Corruption   63

6   The English Language and India's Future: Mental Workers or Metal Bashers?   83

7   Walking on Water, or Getting into an IIT   93

8   India and the IT Industry   109

9   The Overseas Indian and the Multinational Firm in IT   123

10   Faith and Tolerance   153

11   The ABCD, NRI, and Other Species: Indians Living in America   187

12   The Stock Exchanges of India   199

13   Rural India   219

14   The Media in India   243

15   Different Approaches to Development?   255

Notes   273

Index   279

About the Author   291

PREFACE

INDIA IS A LAND OF oddities, puzzles, and paradoxes. Consider, for instance, the southern Indian state of Kerala. It was long considered an oddity within India: literacy was universal, the male to female ratio was less than one, life expectancy was nearly on par with developed countries—and economic growth was well below average. Given India's social backwardness and Kerala's pre-independence history of severe caste discrimination (including the prevalence of slavery in some districts), Kerala's subsequent era of rapid social development was a paradox. Given the social progress, its economic backwardness was a puzzle.

The economic condition of Kerala began to change in the 1990s. Kerala is now India's eighth richest state and, excluding the tiny western state of Goa, the fastest growing since 1990. Its social development continues to outpace the rest of India.

India offered its own national puzzle: Poor economic and social development coincided for years with a keenly democratic tradition. By certain measures—the state of women's health or children's nutrition, for instance—India fared worse than countries in sub-Saharan Africa. Given its social backwardness, the preservation of democracy was a puzzle. Given democracy, its poor economic performance was equally puzzling.

As with Kerala, some of this began to change in the 1990s. India's economy now sizzles. By some measures, such as the size and depth of its software or telecommunications industries, it is as sophisticated as any other country. Meanwhile, its democratic traditions have strengthened.

How did this economic change happen? And is it sustainable? Will it lead to higher social development? Like Kerala, India is hard to understand, even for Indians. This is because there is no other country with the diversity of India. Consider, first, ethnic diversity. Scholars measure ethnic diversity using the ethno-linguistic-fractionalization index (ELFI). It measures the probability that two randomly drawn individuals from the overall population belong to two different ethnic groups. India's ELFI score of 89 percent is the highest of all countries with a population of more than 50 million people. The diversity helps to explain why the leading national radio station, All India Radio, broadcasts the news daily in 350 languages and dialects. Add in regional diversities, such as in politics, education, and infrastructure, to name just three, and we have a challenge explaining India.

Yet, it is worth the effort for what it can teach us. Understanding India is the "secret sauce" for succeeding in the twenty-first century. As this century evolves, certain institutions like the market economy and, increasingly, democracy, will prevail across the world, but tastes, languages, and other cultural markers will remain far apart. India is an example of that already.

Just as the world must learn from India, India must learn from the world. Until recently, Indians interacted mostly within their local communities. Even exporters, who were necessarily well connected with their clients overseas, were often poorly connected within greater India. For instance, the business connections of a diamond exporter from the western Indian city of Surat were typically in Antwerp, Mumbai, and Johannesburg. A software exporter's business networks were typically in Bangalore, New York, and Silicon Valley.

A measure of this *isolation-within but globalization-outside* phenomenon is that India has 45,000 registered newspapers, most of which have small, local readerships. It shows, compared with America's 1,500 or China's 2,000 newspapers, the dominance of the local community in daily life (not to mention a great love of reading!).

Again, this began to change in the 1990s. For many reasons—economic progress and mass communication, to name just two—India is becoming a *nation*, that is, a group of people who feel connected to each other, even if the connection is more imagined than real. Many of these people share common aspirations and feelings. This is how nations are built, but the process of nation building does not necessarily always have a positive outcome. Learning how to live in harmony as a nation is still new to Indians, and India has much to learn from other countries.

This book is about the changing India. I argue that India is arriving in multiple senses. In one sense, it is beginning to "look familiar" to an outsider. It is becoming like developed countries in its institutions and like East Asia in economic growth. In another sense, it is going its own way. It is charting a unique role for services in economic growth, and maturing as a nation while remaining pluralistic. Meanwhile, to an insider, particularly one familiar with rural India or the slums of urban India, there is great progress, but it often appears chaotic and divisive.

The implications of these changes for Indians are no less than transformative, for the changes come after centuries of social and economic stagnation. Given India's size, the implications for the rest of the world, though less predictable, could be as great.

ACKNOWLEDGMENTS

I have many people to thank for their help. To Henry Rowen, Martin Kenney, V. Ranganathan, and Murali Patibandla, my academic collaborators, I owe the debt of thoughts developed jointly. Too many people read different chapters to thank individually, including my family and my students at Stanford University, so I must thank them collectively. My thanks to Christina Parisi, Louis Greenstein, and Erika Spelman, among others at the American Management Association, who have been a pleasure to work with.

CHAPTER 1

India: Not What It Seems

ONE NIGHT IN THE LATE 1970S, while attending a student-faculty mixer at Northwestern University's business school, a fellow Indian student and I, fresh off the boat, met a young assistant professor. Derek Smith was himself fresh off the boat to Chicago's shores, but from North Carolina. After a while, when we felt comfortable (a generous flow of wine undoubtedly helped), he remarked, "Boy, you two speak real good English!" Taken aback, I was about to retort, "Well, Indians have been speaking English longer than you Americans!" only to be upstaged by my friend's quicker response, "Some day, you will, too!"

With that one sentence, the good-natured Professor Smith, whose comment was made as a friendly gesture, probably deduced that Indians (1) speak good English, (2) are quick-witted, and (3) have prickly egos. A western diplomat dealing with India during the Cold War years might have concluded similarly. As diplomat Howard Schaffer has noted about the early years of India-U.S. relations, "Washington usually (had) unproductive relations at international forums with Prime Minister Nehru and his assertive and talented

Indian colleagues. . . . For many Americans, India seemed to make a practice of biting the hand that might have fed it."[1] Despite constant American attempts to bring India onto its side of the Cold War with generous offers of aid, Indian diplomats regularly rebuffed the United States for no apparent reason other than that the United States seemed patronizing.

Indeed, from an outsider's viewpoint and for many insiders as well, India has for decades seemed to be more preoccupied with its external image than with mustering the will, resources, and collaborations to succeed. There were, of course, isolated successes of global partnerships. A notable one was the Green Revolution, a program for introducing high-yielding cereal crops in irrigated areas. This solved the problem of food security for the urban middle classes but was more than offset by the continuance of deep rural poverty (see Chapter 13). Overall, the outcome was stagnation. As one journalist remarked, "Every time I come back from India, people ask me how India is changing. My reaction is, so far, the same: The phone system is better, the roads are worse, and not much else has changed."

More than thirty years have passed since my encounter with Professor Smith. Since then, (particularly over the past decade) the West has come to know India, but only somewhat. Nowadays, when they interact over the wires or on their home turf, westerners are impressed with Indians' professional skills, technological experience, legal knowledge, and the like. Attracted by lower labor costs, this leads many western businesspeople to consider outsourcing work to India. Yet, when they step off the plane for the first time, often their first instinct is to wonder why they did not take a flight to China instead.

A businessman from Oxford, England, visited Chennai (the capital of the state of Tamil Nadu) some years ago to see if he might set up a copyediting shop. His first reaction upon exiting the airport was that he felt hot. It was over 30 degrees Celsius (86 degrees

Fahrenheit). And it was 3 A.M. The smells of the big Indian city, teeming with people even at that hour, were his next sensations, and they were not pleasant. At that point, he felt like telling his chauffeur to turn back.

However, as the days passed and he met the same professionals with whom he had conversed by phone from Oxford, he realized that a depth of talent was at hand. It made sense for him to set up shop in Chennai, where he now employs 500 copy editors. Apart from their skills, he notes appreciatively that the state bureaucracy neither discriminates against him nor for him. There are no expectations in return for doing business in Chennai. He prefers this to some other parts of Asia, where the infrastructure is specially tailored to foreign investors, but in return the foreign firm is expected to transfer skills or provide subcontracting work to local businesses. And, no surprise, these expectations are usually negotiated through a "must-have" local partner.

And yet visitors to India, as their visits increase in number, usually return home not just impressed but also distressed. Both emotions are caused by how little they really know the country. For instance, many businesspersons returning from Mumbai, the country's commercial center, report that the quality of professional skills excites them even as the slums attached, barnacle-like, to every highrise building upset them. It is quite different from a visit to China, where the overwhelming impression is of a country united, self-reliant, and uniformly hard at work—and moving ahead as a result.

It is very difficult to get a handle on India because it is a land of heterogeneities and contradictions that are complex enough for anyone, not just an outsider. For example, a first-time visitor to Chennai is sure to be surprised at a uniquely Tamil phenomenon: giant fifty-foot cut-outs of politicians dominate the main thoroughfares of the city, and such politicians inspire nearly godlike devotion.

Even more interesting: These politicians come from lower castes and are representatives of parties that are composed of and supported by lower castes. It is proof of the state's progress against a long history of caste discrimination. Symbolically, it is as if the upper castes, after decades of oppressing the lower castes, must acquiesce to passing by at the feet of the lower castes as they drive through Chennai's high street, Anna Salai.

This is a fascinating development given the general failure of public action and politicians to remove caste separation in the rest of India. It was one of the first things that the businessman from Oxford observed about Chennai. Yet, had he visited some of the more rural areas of Tamil Nadu state, he might then have been particularly distressed by the common phenomenon of the *two-glass* roadside café. In such a place, since untouchables are outside the Hindu caste system, they cannot drink from the same glass as a caste Hindu. Therefore, separate glasses are kept for the two groups.

This seems inexplicable considering the cut-outs of lower-caste politicians, until one understands that Tamil Nadu leads the way in a disturbing recent development, that of *majoritarianism* (see Chapter 2). Majority groups (in this case, castes at the lower end of the caste system) have been uniting to ensure the exclusion of other groups (in Tamil Nadu's case, both the upper-caste Brahmins and the untouchables) from civic and political life. So an outsider's cursory glance would reveal the triumph of lower-caste members, but a deeper look reveals a more complicated picture.

Similarly, the perception of poverty is misleading. A much-quoted World Bank statistic is that 80 percent of Indians get by on less than two dollars a day—and 35 percent on less than a dollar. These figures make it appear as though India is a nation mired in deep poverty. The image it projects is of a country where rural labor is mostly landless and indebted, and urban labor is mostly involved in primitive services such as housecleaning and driving the cars of rich employers. Yet this, like many statistics, hides as much as it reveals.

POOR, EXCEPT FOR THE CELL PHONE

While I was on a speaking tour of India in October 2006 organized by the U.S. Department of State, I stayed in the beautiful city of Varanasi on the Ganges River. Our posh five-star hotel charged rates that seemed in line with booming India at $130 per night. When the hotel charged me an additional Rs.760 ($17 at the time) for the one-hour, ten-mile ride to the airport in the hotel's taxi, I was only mildly surprised. However, when I asked the driver what he earned, and he replied that he earned the equivalent of $20 *a month* as salary, my interest was aroused—especially when it emerged that he made two round trips a day, on average, during the year (more during the peak season), each time bringing a return passenger by the inbound flight.

The hotel obviously has a profitable business model! But I was as interested in the driver's budget management. Pushing him a bit on this, I discovered that he earns a few hundred rupees in tips as well, and owns two acres of fertile land (along with his brothers). Including his wife's salary as a teacher, the family of four (including a son, age eleven, and a retired parent) earns $56 per month. Adjusted for purchasing power differences, which makes the rupee roughly five times more valuable than the official exchange rate of Rs.45 to the dollar at the time of writing, the family earns a little over two dollars a day per person.

This puts the driver in the privileged position of being in the top 20 percent of income earners in India! Yet, as he noted, the family barely makes ends meet, and it saves nothing. He is constantly managing debt taken for various purposes, both for the farm and for personal expenses. His biggest worry is also their biggest expense: their son's education. This takes up nearly a third of the family's income. Monthly tuition at an English-speaking school about three miles from their village is five dollars and transportation to and from doubles that. Another five dollars a month goes to hire an English-speaking tutor to help the child with his studies, a necessity because neither parent speaks English. He worries that someday he might

The River Ganges at moonrise.

In Mumbai, slums attach, barnacle-like, to every high-rise building.

not be able to afford to educate his son in English. Yet, he notes he would still be able to afford some luxuries like a cell phone if the hotel had not already given him one.

A few days later, the driver's remark about his cell phone was on my mind as I checked into a hotel in Indore, a poor town of roughly two million inhabitants in the state of Madhya Pradesh. With 60 million inhabitants, Madhya Pradesh is India's seventh largest state by population and the second largest by area.

Aware that by late 2006, Indians were purchasing more than six million cell phone connections a month—exceeding China's rate of about five million—I was eager to see if small towns were as keen on cell phones as the big cities.

Indore's inhabitants earn their living in the myriad small industries and services typical to urban India. Manufacturing is small-scale and low-tech: textile powerlooms, brick making, pipe manufacturing, and so on. Because Madhya Pradesh is the country's primary producer of soybeans, soybean trading dominates Indore's service sector.

With the exception of a handful of government buildings and hotels, there are no buildings more than six stories high in Indore. My room on the top floor of the Sayaji Hotel—the city's best, though similar in quality to a typical roadside inn off a U.S. interstate—provided a panoramic view of the city. Like other such towns in India, small homes and small offices radiated along streets in disorganized spokes from the railway station (the heart of most Indian towns). The streets were crowded and dirty. There were plenty of tin-roofed shacks on view, reminding me of the real India outside my air-conditioned room—where a supplementary generator supplied daytime power because the power grid was down for eight to ten hours a day. Three decades earlier I had visited Indore as a management trainee. It was little changed, except for being more crowded.

There was, however, one significant change in Indore as well as in other small towns I visited: Two years earlier, five-story buildings dominated the landscape; today cell phone towers are everywhere. I counted fifteen towers from my hotel room.

A few days earlier, driving on a pockmarked road through some of India's poorest areas, the road was as notable for its potholes as for its cell phone towers. These twenty-meter-high structures rose above the landscape every quarter mile or so, marking distance and celebrating technical progress. They are a modern reminder of the massive *kos minars* on the Delhi-Agra Road—distance markers from the last great road-building effort in India about a half a millennium ago during the Mughal Empire.

If cell phone affordability is a measure of economic change, it is hard not to conclude that something dramatic is happening throughout India, something that the statistics of poverty are not showing.

DEVELOPMENT VIA A SERVICES ECONOMY

Another aspect that makes it difficult to compare India with other countries is the fact that it is developing via a new path. China, for example, has been growing through massive industrialization. This is the same route to development taken earlier by most other countries. India, by contrast, has globalized by professionally training select people and offering their services to the world. If it succeeds by spreading the method to the rest of the economy, it would be the first case of a country developing via a revolution in the services sector rather than in manufacturing.

It would also be a rare case of success by a former colony. Ever since Britain's industrial revolution in the late eighteenth century, globalization has been almost exclusively a western phenomenon, occurring in countries that were colonizers, not colonies. The two significant exceptions to western success were Japan in the late nineteenth century—but it was a colonizer—and China in the late twentieth century.

It has been particularly hard for former colonies to globalize. Some small ones, such as Singapore and Taiwan, succeeded by determinedly forgetting both their colonial heritage and their precolonial identities and moving on. But larger ones, such as South Africa and Indonesia, have struggled to develop economically through globalization. This is in large part because the recovery of their precolonial identity was a priority. Because the erstwhile colonizers were from the West, there was a natural distaste for western models of development. There was a feeling that "if we ape the West with its promarket and protrade models of growth, why bother to have become independent?"

India is no exception. Perhaps the biggest difficulty in knowing India is the absence of a national identity.

A NATION'S IDENTITY

India's struggle has been harder because of the problems of deep-rooted poverty and illiteracy. A nationally agreed-upon sense of identity behind which all can pull together to get a nation moving is difficult in such circumstances.

The first leaders of an independent India were the educated urban elite, including Mahatma Gandhi. While fighting for the creation of a nation, these leaders realized they did not know the 80 percent of the country who lived in the villages and on whose behalf they were fighting to gain independence. They were equally aware that it was not just that the elite did not know the poor. Even the poor would be hard-pressed to indicate their identity. As Gandhi put it, "Those in whose name we speak we do not know, nor do they know us."

In the absence of a national identity accepted by a majority of its population, independent India's early leaders felt that the fledgling country could fall apart. Jawaharlal Nehru, independent India's first prime minister, often worried about the "fissiparous tendencies" that could undo the nation. Nehru saw such tendencies in every organ of the state, from politicians and the judiciary to nonofficial organizations such as labor unions and other such public bodies (civil society).

Little wonder, then, that Nehru's chosen model of development was based on tight control. We shall have more to say on this in Chapter 2. Suffice it to say here that the Nehruvian model failed to deliver on its promises of prosperity. Worse still, it created vested interests that perpetuated themselves in an endless spiral: a poorly educated citizenry was fit only for employment in the bureaucracy, or *babudom*, as it was called. This, in turn, created the institutions that produced an unfit citizenry.

At the end of Nehru's rule, Indians had as little a sense of national identity and purpose as when his rule began. Nehru's rule failed to create an identity for India because it perpetuated poverty. Indira Gandhi, his daughter, who ruled for the longest period of any ruler in independent India, also had to face the uncertain identity of India. She would often ask Indians to remember Nehru's vision of a country that ought to be united in order to remain free. Her model of development was an intensified version of Nehru's socialist state.

Under Mrs. Gandhi, the state decayed further, plumbing new depths of control and corruption. An extreme example was the forced sterilizations (vasectomies) of over a million mostly minority and low-caste villagers during the period from 1975 to 1977 (the so-called *Emergency*). This was the lowest point in India's postcolonial experience. Yet, and oddly, through it, India finally began to discover an identity.

Mrs. Gandhi called for elections after the Emergency, believing that the electorate, particularly the illiterate rural voters, would vote her back as they always had. When, instead, they voted her out, it marked the first time that rural voters had taken the lead.

A slum named Asha Nagar (City of Hope) in Malabar Hill, Mumbai, where apartment-building space sells for $800 a square foot.

Thereafter, in no election could the rural voter be taken for granted. In all subsequent elections, the urban voting pattern has been more heterogeneous than the rural pattern and urban turnouts have been lower. As a result, the rural vote determines the outcomes. Thanks to its extreme suffering at the hands of leaders it had elected, rural India found a collective voice through the vote.

This is not to conclude that India now has an identity. Instead, it is to conclude that an identity for India cannot exclude rural India, which accounts for more than two-thirds of its population. Finding its voice and, more important, the discovery that the rural voice is collective and unified, is a critical step in that process.

THE ENGLISH OF INDIA

Perhaps nowhere is the struggle to create a unified country better exemplified than over language. The Varanasi taxi driver's son's education raises the family's standard of English. Even if his family must stop his English education at some time due to a lack of funds—something that his father constantly worries about—his destiny cannot be the same as his father's, for his life has already been permanently changed by this education.

The Indians' knowledge of English is a legacy of British rule. Their love for the language is less easy to explain. Indians have a love-hate relationship with most things British. It is common for public speakers to proclaim that various aspects of civic life— bureaucracy, the railways, the post—are throwbacks to British times, implying both that the systems were bad even in 1947, yet that they remain irreplaceable.

One clear proof of India's love of English is the liveliness with which it is used: Hindi is mixed with English seamlessly, showing the malleability of both tongues. English words are translated into

Hindi as they sound, as in the sentence, *"Sauce pass karo,"* which asks the listener to pass the sauce. The reverse occurs as freely. Many Indian words, as a result, have entered standard English, and many more will do so. This has been happening for centuries, at least since the time of Queen Elizabeth I, when traders carried both exotic products and their names across borders. Words of Indian origin, such as *calico, chintz,* and *gingham,* were already part of British vocabulary by then. The average metropolitan dweller of Mumbai or Delhi dreams in a mixture of English and Hindi.

A thriving literature by Indians writing in English seems destined to extend its influence beyond Indian shores, although many of the best-known—writers such as Amitava Ghosh and Salman Rushdie—produced their best work after migrating west. But many, such as Pankaj Mishra, whose *Butter Chicken in Ludhiana* remains the classic introduction to small-town India, lived and did their best work in India. One of the country's best poets, Nissim Ezekiel, lived in India. Stand-up comics thrive on the possibilities of punning between Hindi and English. For example, in one joke, Colonial Officer A tells subordinate Colonial Officer B: "Simkins, this is a peepul tree" (*peepul* is the local name of a type of fig tree sacred to Buddhists), to which the response is, "Yes, sir, I hear it is very popular."

Yet many worry that if all Indians speak only English, they might as well never have become free in the first place. The state buys this viewpoint and emerges with policies that are inconsistent with popular usage. On the one hand, India has twenty-two official languages, one of which, Sanskrit, is not spoken. On the other hand, the official list does not include English, which is the most widely used language at the federal level and is permitted for the purpose of official communication across states and links the country. The most widely spoken official language, Hindi, differs from another official language, Urdu, only marginally in its vocabulary. Neither is as widely spoken as an unofficial language, Hindustani, a mix of Hindi and Urdu vocabulary, written in the Hindi script and based on their common grammar.

The state's second response has been to try to legislate a national language, a purified version of Hindi, stripped of its Persian/Urdu vocabulary and primarily influenced by Sanskrit. On the one hand, such purification is impractical and inelegant because the grammatical structure of Hindi is firmly rooted in a global heritage that includes Sanskrit, Semitic, and European languages. The result is an uncomfortable mix of Sanskrit words and Hindustani grammar. It is, however, slowly gaining currency, at least in north India, under state patronage. On the other hand, a majority of Indians do not speak Hindi. Further, it is still the case that for most citizens and certainly for the more than 35 percent who are illiterate, the Sanskritized version of the language is unusable. Hearing a newsreader on the government-owned channel present the news in Sanskritized Hindi can be a disconcerting experience; the more popular private channels do not even attempt it.

It would be a mistake to assume that integration into a common, "national" language around some variant of English or Hindustani will be a gradual, peaceful, and culturally enriching task, requiring many non-English speakers to learn English. In fact, such a national language is unlikely in the near future. This is not for want of trying. At various times in the past decades, language has been seen as a key tool for identity creation. For instance, both Jawaharlal Nehru and Indira Gandhi tried to enforce the use of Hindi nationally, leading to anti-Hindi agitations and even suicides by protesters.

Hence, language is one aspect of identity that India must face and work through. How urgently India must face this issue is a topic of speculation. Politicians nowadays argue that the nation should focus on economic development first. Perhaps taking a cue from China's single-minded pursuit of GDP growth, they argue that it is the new form of identity building. Their argument is that a rising tide, as it is said, lifts all boats. It also renders harmless the debris at the bottom of the ocean floor. Given a continuing economic boom, the Varanasi taxi driver's son should be able to complete his English education. Then, he can make choices about his future (including choosing which language to speak)—choices his father never had. For the moment, this strategy appears to be working.

IDENTITY AND PLURALISM

Religion in India is another contested area of identity. The average westerner may not realize how religious Indians actually are. Nearly every Indian follows some religious rituals, even in the most developed cities. In Mumbai, during the October Dussehra festival, for example, it is impossible to find a car whose front end does not have a marigold wreath placed on it, a sign of worshipful respect for the forces of good that the car represents. Even locomotives and machinery of all kinds have the wreath placed on them, although I have not observed it on the noses of aircraft, perhaps because they might scare the pilots.

This might make it appear as if the external dimension of worship is the important one. But nothing could be further from the truth. For every external act of faith at a public festival or in the temple, there are millions more observed, with equal devotion, at home, be it the worship of one's personal deity or the supplications on the prayer mat. Some westerners see yoga as a religious practice. However, far from being a type of worship, yoga is viewed as an outcome of a religious principle: A healthy soul requires a healthy mind and body.

What happens when different beliefs collide, as they must when beliefs are so firmly held? Well, the earth must shake, at least a little. Indian history has several examples of clashes over beliefs. Lives have been lost, particularly in conflicts between Hindus and Muslims, even if, in the grand scheme of things, religion more often teaches tolerance and produces harmony.

India, then, has many identities, even as it acquires new ones—all of them evolving at different rates. Many will be influenced by globalization. For instance, the recent history of developing countries suggests that globalization, far from removing nationalistic feelings, strengthens them. This may happen to Indians and may help the country manage its identities that will always differ from one another due to language and faith. It is also possible that globalization will lead to a more aggressive nationalism that does not tolerate such differences.

Before it can move ahead, India must face its identities and decide on those it wishes to retain and promote, those it can suppress for the moment, and those it must change. Though no easy task, it is also necessary because—like many of the smaller Asian countries—Indian culture could crumble in the melting pot and unifying forces of globalization. Some do not see this as a bad thing, given the problems India has faced with managing its conflicting interests. But in such a heterogeneous society, in which economically weak segments are also those with distinct cultural or ethnic identities, there is a risk that they may lose from globalization. If so, they may rebel and subvert the collective will to succeed.

CHAPTER 2

Nehru's India:
The Rise of State Power

THE STRUGGLE FOR INDEPENDENCE was a defining moment for India. It established that a poor and ethnically fractured country could overcome its colonial oppressor without armed conflict.

Mohandas Gandhi (later to be called the *Mahatma*, or great soul), led India's fight for freedom. From his stint in South Africa and the experiences of its Zulu population, and his reading of the Indian mutineers during the previous half-century, he concluded that a violent freedom struggle would fail. If attempted, a massacre of Indians was the most likely consequence. So he chose nonviolence as the primary tool for the independence movement. It was an ingenious choice: It resonated with the Indian character and baffled the British.

Gandhi was assassinated shortly after independence, a tragic end for the seer of nonviolence. His legacy of nonviolence continues to diminish in independent India. When violence breaks out these days, the *lumpen*, often aided by the police, maraud unchallenged. The silent acquiescence of the majority is not what the Mahatma had in mind for the future of nonviolence. As this has happened, Gandhi's iconic status has become diluted.

India's first prime minister, Jawaharlal Nehru, had a momentous task of turning India around. By the time of India's independence in 1947, the British had ruled and molded the country for nearly two hundred years and left it in a state of deep poverty. Nehru, a man in a hurry, did not have the same luxury of time. He had been hand-picked by Gandhi to lead the Congress Party and to succeed him. He was a natural successor to Gandhi: intellectual, committed to peaceful change and democracy, and popular with the masses. He was not shy of energetically using these capabilities. As a result, until his death in 1964, the charismatic Nehru was the person everyone—whether inside the country or outside—most identified with India. Even today, parts of the Nehruvian legacy permeate India.

INDIA'S INHERITANCE

Jawaharlal Nehru recognized that India's condition at independence was due not just to the impact of British rule but also to that of the Mughals (originally from Central Asia) before them, who had ruled for an even longer period. Although there had been many prior empires in the common era, the Mughals and the British were the first groups to rule over an area that generally corresponds to modern India's geography. The difference between them was that the Mughals came to stay, whereas the British came as colonizers and remained that way, choosing never to integrate with the native population. Instead, following policies of divide-and-rule and a parsimonious use of their own subjects, the British ruled some parts of India directly and other parts through locals who came from land-owning and noble classes.

The Mughals had settled in early in the sixteenth century. The stability and longevity of Mughal rule enabled Indians to have their first sense of identity as a nation whose people spanned the geographic contours of the subcontinent. Travel and trade across the subcontinent became possible through a common currency and administration. The Mughals, however, were not interested in imposing a common culture or deliberately creating a common identity, such as through imposing a common language. Different regions saw their own maturing of cultural expressions—codifications of language, dress, dance, music, and the like—over this period. These regions even created and held to their own calendars. According to Nobel laureate Amartya Sen, shortly after independence, a Calendar Reform Committee identified more than thirty calendar systems in use.

The Mughals created a vast bureaucracy that ensured stable revenue through the taxation of agriculture. Over time, this bureaucracy, known as the *zamindari system* (*zamin* is the Persian-Hindi-Urdu word for *land*), began to acquire hereditary powers. During its turn, the British converted the *zamindar* to a feudal landlord, that is, one with hereditary rights over the land that he originally governed. Later on, in a search of ever more revenue, they then converted *zamindari* into an extortionary rent system that impoverished rural India—and even expanded it with the creation of more than five hundred principalities, ruled mostly by British-designated hereditary *princes*.

Like the Mughals, however, the English were not interested in promoting a national Indian identity. As a colony, it was better not to have a unified national identity other than that of a colony subjugated to the English rule.

By the time India began to fight for independence, World War I had begun and financially depleted Britain had already begun a process of disengagement from its colonies. The largest, India, was a prime candidate. The contested issues were primarily the degree of autonomy to be given to India, the timing of disengagement, and, on the Indian side, political boundaries.

The biggest boundary controversy was over the creation of Pakistan as a homeland for the subcontinent's Muslims. This was a particularly difficult issue among Muslims in India's northern latitudes, who had long been discriminated against by the British. They were worried about surviving in independent India and were ambivalent about the Congress party that would rule. They observed that the secular ideals of Gandhi and Jawaharlal Nehru were often sacrificed to the arithmetic of caste, religion, and campaign contributions.

After a battle that was fought, remarkably, among intellectuals rather than foot soldiers (though in the backdrop of the World Wars), both India and Pakistan were created in 1947. Seven million Muslim migrants arrived into newly independent Pakistan from newly independent India, and seven million non-Muslims migrated from Pakistan to India. Most of the migration took place in the western half of the subcontinent. It was a horrifying process in which hundreds of thousands lost their lives and millions their livelihoods due to rampant, uncontrolled violence and landgrabs on both sides of the border.

Pakistan thus began a troubled existence that was to last for the next six decades. A power struggle between the migrants from India's heartland who had led the freedom movement and rural landlords in Pakistan's two most populous western provinces, the Punjab and Sindh provinces, stymied political and economic institutionalization. Gradually, in this political vacuum, Pakistan's army came to be seen as the new nation's only true champion of people's rights. Predictably, this led to the army's first coup in 1958, and there have been three of these to date. The army has been in power either directly or indirectly for most of independent Pakistan's existence. A one-line history of Pakistan, if one may cynically attempt to do so, would read thus: It never got beyond its very first struggle as an independent state, that of rooting democracy.

Nehru's inheritance, then, consisted of a country still in the aftermath of the trauma of partition and internally divided as a result, and deep poverty, especially in rural areas. The disparate identities of Indians, inherited from the Mughals, remained. But, instead of such pluralism being a source of strength, the effect of impoverishment under the British had converted it into a weakness. At least, though, Nehru had the goodwill of the people.

DEMOCRACY 1, LAND REFORM 0

The first priority was to establish democracy firmly in the new nation. This required a constitutional commitment. Of equal priority and, perhaps even necessary for sustaining democracy, was action on land ownership in order to reverse the extortionary rent system.

Nehru's personal commitment indeed mattered a great deal to the establishment of democracy. Largely owing to his unquestioned interventions when disputes arose, the Indian constitutional assembly completed its work in just two years, creating all the organs of state including an independent judiciary and election commission. By contrast, it took Pakistan nine years to accomplish this.

Nevertheless, India remained a politically heterogeneous country. The Congress Party typified this. It was truly a congress of "nations" representing all the varied, often conflicting, interests of India, brought under the Gandhi-Nehru umbrella.

Among them were entrenched landowning interests who, as in Pakistan, prevented any meaningful land reform. This was a critical, near-fatal failure. In India, as in Pakistan, land ownership was heavily skewed due to the zamindari system. Nearly half the country's rural population owned no land at all. More than 75 percent of landholdings were below five acres.

Nehru saw land reform as necessary for both social welfare and democracy. Initially, he was hopeful that his personal backing would make reform successful. In a speech to the U.S. Congress in October 1949, Nehru said:

We have tackled the major problem of India, as it is today the major problem of Asia, the agrarian problem. Much that was feudal in our system of land tenure is being changed so that the fruits of cultivation should go to the tiller of the soil and that he may be secure in the possession of the land he cultivates. In a country of which agriculture is still the principal industry, this reform is essential not only for the well-being and contentment of the individual but also for the stability of society. One of the main causes of social instability in many parts of the world, more especially in Asia, is agrarian discontent due to the continuance of systems of land tenure which are completely out of place in the modern world.

In reality, he was never able to bring about significant land reform. Land reform failed because the Congress Party's wealthier supporters fiercely resisted it. This was especially so in North India, which supplied the Congress's political leadership. Facing threats of a split in the Congress Party over the subject, Nehru ultimately gave up seeking land reform.

The unbalanced ownership of land remains a problem that severely afflicts India even today. For example, in late 2006, despite several years of adequate rainfall and high output, the suicide rate among farmers was distressingly high at four per day. More than three-fourths of the rural population consumes less than the state-mandated minimum calorie requirement of 2,400 calories per day, and the bottom 30 percent consume an average of 1,600 calories per day.

Perhaps to Nehru's surprise, the absence of land reform did not jeopardize India's territorial integrity or democracy—at least in the minimal sense of universal, free, and fair suffrage. Instead, establishing a democratic tradition turned out to be relatively easy in the sense of determining the forms of governance: An elected legislature with limited powers had already been established by the British. But now as a fully democratic system, its power went all the way up to the executive office. After the creation of Pakistan and the general acceptance of the Nehruvian view, many issues that had been contested under British rule—separate representation for different castes and faiths, for example—disappeared.

Another reason for rural stability is that in rural areas, the poor, among whom the representation of lower castes is relatively high, are poorly organized relative to the rich. In some cases, the lower castes are kept repressed through organized violence. For example, in India's second most populous state, Bihar, located in eastern India, upper castes in rural areas have been known to run a vigilante army called the *Ranvir Sena*. It is classified by the Indian government as a terrorist group and has been responsible for thousands of lower-caste killings. Yet, it is beyond the writ of the law, due to tacit support from administrators. This is possible despite the establishment of democratically elected governments in areas where the majority of voters are from the lower castes. Quite simply, democracy in these areas is held hostage by feudal elements with their extensive and ruthless patronage networks.

Even in Tamil Nadu, where the anti-Brahmin movement has been most successful, the lowest castes fare badly in politics because of oppression by castes a few rungs higher. For example, according to Vaasanthi, a contemporary writer on Tamil politics, as part of the government's affirmative-action campaign there are villages where seats are reserved for the lowest groups, the *Dalits* (untouchables), based on population count. And yet, she notes:

> [No Dalit] promoted by political parties dares to contest elections because of the dominant local Thevar [a higher caste grouping] community. Only a Dalit candidate supported by the locals is allowed to contest since it is a reserved constituency, but soon after winning, the Dalit resigns "as it would be embarrassing [i.e., in practice, *untenable*] for a person working as a farm hand for the Thevars to sit on a chair and administer."[1]

It is only in the past decade that the poor in rural areas have elected leaders who represent their interests, a change inextricably linked with rising caste consciousness in India. Whether this will lead to land reform is unknown, but the odds are against it. In the new, market-friendly India, a land reform movement that transfers ownership from absentee landlord to the cultivator would be viewed as against property rights.

A question that faces India today is whether, in response to upper-caste oppression or other factors, democracy will lead to *majoritarianism*—the tendency of the victors to exclude the losers from political participation. In states such as Tamil Nadu, which was the first to see lower castes rise politically, the exclusion of upper castes in highly sought-after medical and state-run engineering institutions through various *reservation policies* is now almost total.

In Nehru's time, whether due to a lack of assertiveness or weak organization by the rural poor, the reality is that democracy survived in India despite the lack of land reforms and despite several years of antidevelopment policies. It also survived, as we shall discuss, several years of antipoor policies in urban areas. This was despite massive protests by labor unions that were far better able to organize the urban poor than the rural poor were ever able to organize themselves. And, finally, it survived because, to his credit, Nehru passed up several opportunities to convert his dominant position in the Congress Party to a personal dictatorship of the whole country—a temptation to which many of his peers in other developing countries succumbed.

Thus, India, like Pakistan, struggled in its early years. But once it passed the hurdle of democracy that has been Pakistan's Mount Everest, India's issues were different.

DEVELOPMENT STRATEGIES

In 1950, with democracy stabilized, Nehru became concerned with how to set in place the institutions that would one day make India a great country. He had observed the country's deep divisions based on language, faith, and caste. His biggest worry was that the new Indian state would not be able to maintain its integrity in the absence of a powerful ruler. He feared that under the weight of its burdens, India would fragment into many small, unviable states. Yet, given his intrinsic faith in democracy, he faced an interesting contradiction of two deeply felt views: the need for centralism to keep the country together and the need for democracy to honestly reflect the people's views. He believed India needed an all-powerful ruler—subject to the will of the people every five years, but unquestioned in the interim. To resolve this contradiction, he defederalized democracy and stripped the Congress Party of opposing points of view. In other words, he created a centralist government with power concentrated in New Delhi on the one hand, while on the other converting the Congress party into a personal fiefdom.

The key features of centralist governance implemented by Nehru were the control of government from New Delhi (rather than a more federal division of powers envisaged by the constitution), state control of economic development, and government involvement in public bodies (civil society), such as trade unions and non-government organizations.

Nehru's centralism was enthusiastically supported by fellow politicians. India's rulers, who came from the Congress Party, attributed the successful campaign for independence to united opposition to the British. Similarly, they felt that India's many castes, faiths, geographies, and deep poverty in the rural areas posed obstacles that could only be overcome by inculcating a feeling of national unity. In their view, only a united India could build and maintain educational institutions, roads, utilities, and other public infrastructure. Of course, this would require citizens to accept, in the short term, sacrifices such as high taxes and a large public administration. The leaders believed that no common cultural bonds existed that could elicit such a unified response—at least none that they could identify and channel.

Nehru and his peers also observed that the poverty of British India had continually increased despite a long tradition of private enterprise. At independence, only 17 percent of the population was literate, and the GDP growth rate had averaged just one percent for the past five decades. How could one trust private enterprise under such circumstances? Should private enterprise stay or go? That would be up to the people. Of course, since the ruling Congress Party (and nearly every other political party) was dominated by upper-caste interests that were sympathetic to private enterprise, it was highly unlikely that the state would take over the assets of the private sector, much as Nehru would have liked to.

Nehru and his successors chose centralized control of economics and politics, as well as state involvement in civil society. The first was done through adopting a Soviet-style model with state ownership of what Nehru called the "commanding heights" of the economy while allowing the private sector to operate at the margins. A system of five-year plans controlling investment was established in 1951 and continues to this day, although it now controls only public investment.

Political control was accomplished by making local politicians dependent on the center for their resources and through the frequent use of constitutional provisions for central control that had been intended for use only in emergencies. New Delhi even controlled civil society by regulating and limiting its organs, such as by becoming the chief patron of the arts, financing religious places, and organizing the unionization of labor.

Most developing countries need foreign capital and obtain it through political alliances. India was no exception. But here Nehru had a problem: On the one hand, he did not trust the capitalist economies of the West due to their promarket stance, which he blamed for India's past failures. On the other hand, the Soviet bloc did not trust India's private entrepreneurs.

Nehru faced another, related dilemma: He was unwilling to accept a subordinate role for India in world affairs. He unambiguously stated (as has every prime minister after him) that India's ambition was to join the world's elite. However, his ambition of playing a key role was thwarted by the Cold War. The United States and the Soviet Union each wanted India on its side, but neither was willing to let

India play an important role. India, ultimately, sided with the Soviet Union. Largely, this was because its economic development was socialistic, whereas western donors and lenders were insistent that development capital be given only to a market-friendly economy.

Some of Nehru's strategies lasted for decades after his tenure even while failing to achieve their objectives. For instance, the politicization of civil society remains prevalent. It emasculated positive public action such as land reform movements or women's rights movements while failing to prevent—and often stimulating—its negative aspects such as trade-union or sectarian violence. The central role of the state in economics failed right from the start yet was continued for several decades.

THE ROOTS OF CORRUPTION

One of the unplanned, though natural, outcomes of Nehruvian centralism was immense corruption in public life. The repeated interference of politicians in bureaucratic affairs (furthered under Indira Gandhi) led to a breakdown of bureaucratic integrity, ironically in the name of national unity. A bureaucrat appointed to a position remained there at the behest of the politician in charge, ready to be moved out once the politician's tenure was over. A public servant in India could not be sacked, so if his political master was out of favor, the servant had to be transferred to a harmless outpost. This, depending on the official's status and networks, might range from the depths of rural India to a posting at the World Bank. Thus, he lost his independence and served at the politician's behest. Because the politician's tenure was equally tenuous, subsisting at the pleasure of a higher minister until the next election, corruption became the way to receive at least some payback for a lifetime of low-paid public service. Corruption thus became an endemic and immutable feature of living in India—and deserving of its own chapter in this book.

Another fallout of centralism was massive inefficiency. It showed itself in the quality of public works. Government offices, for example, all seemed to have been built to a single specification: thick fortresslike grids of concrete beams with tiny windows and dark interiors. This is not the most appealing architecture in any environment, but in a country where electricity frequently fails, especially when it is sweltering outside, it was especially abysmal. Roads were tarred so poorly that they could not survive one single monsoon without becoming hopelessly pitted. Public offices were massively overstaffed while accomplishing very little. And there was never, ever enough trash collection.

THE NEHRUVIAN LEGACY

The nation-building project initiated by Nehru (and continued by the Congress Party after his death) was premised on the danger of India breaking up from within due to its inherent problems. The Congress Party offered political stability, employment, and promises of long-term economic growth in return for the people accepting short-term sacrifices such as high taxes, slow initial economic growth, limited participation in civil society, and centralized politics.

Nehru's developmental strategies asked the people to accept the identity of civic nationalism—that is, that the political boundaries of India also defined the boundaries of the nation. Due to his charisma and role during independence, independent India was probably at its most united during his rule. In the minds of most Indians, the flag and the nation were one. This was evidenced by the near absence of sectarian violence, in sharp contrast to the tenure of all his successors.

The economic stagnation that resulted from Nehru's policies created regular crises, such as food shortages. This reduced the popularity of the Congress Party over time. By the 1960s, the states had elected the first governments led by parties opposed to the Congress Party.

The 1991 collapse of the Soviet Union ended India's free ride on cheap Soviet capital. This, combined with the economic failure of the socialist experiment, ultimately broke the Nehruvian legacy's twin pillars of central control over economics and politics. No doubt influenced by China's rapid break with economic stagnation on the back of the market economy after 1980 (compared to the stagnant Indian economy), Rajiv Gandhi took the nation rightward with his liberalizations of industry. This decisive break reduced the financial levers of central power over state governments, thus breaking the run of the center over state politics as well. Since the 1990s, India has moved steadily toward a market economy and a decentralized polity that brings the key problems of agriculture and education closer to those who should be working on them—politicians in the states rather than in New Delhi.

It is too early to say whether the new institutional structures will be stable and, more important, whether they can solve the problems of development. They have spawned subnationalisms of various types, some of which are undesirable. And there is an unfortunate tendency toward majoritarianism. I shall have more to say on these subjects in Chapter 10. As the Nehruvian legacy of centralism fades, it is worth remembering that India's first prime minister, Jawaharlal Nehru, institutionalized democracy. It is also worth remembering that India, as a nation, may be the world's largest democracy but it is also one of the youngest at only fifty years old. As such, it should still be considered a work in progress.

CHAPTER 3

The Rise of States' Power

BY JAWAHARLAL NEHRU'S DEATH in 1964, India had experienced seventeen years of rising centralism—a rise in New Delhi's power over economic, political, and civic issues. This chapter is about the further rise and ultimate demise of that power.

Nehru's daughter Indira Gandhi took over between 1966 and 1984 (with an interregnum between 1977 and 1980). She was committed to Nehruvian centralism, but with differences that made its dangers manifest. This, over time, weakened both the Congress Party and the logic for centralism. Her son, Rajiv Gandhi, who took over after her death, started differently but ultimately reverted to Nehruvian centralism. Since Rajiv's death by an assassin's bullet in 1991, the public has disfavored centralist parties. Instead, parties specific to individual states became powerful in politics. This was later to have profound consequences on India's economic development, particularly with regard to the sensitivity of politics to development and to the role of private enterprise.

In both economics and politics, Mrs. Gandhi was more centralist than Nehru. In the economic sphere, she expanded social control by creating large, state-owned companies, many of which survived by supporting each other or were given monopoly rights. No field was too inconsequential for the public sector; for instance, her government became the largest owner of hotels, ran the largest engineering consultancy, and produced the most automobiles. These *national champions* then became as important for creating lifetime employment as they were for the products they made. They looked after—and many continue to do so—their employees from cradle to grave, offering housing and other perks, often establishing townships with complete civic facilities around factory sites.

It was a costly approach, because most townships were created in populated areas, often due to trade-union pressure. Combined with the inefficiencies that characterize any state-owned firm anywhere, and worse—poor management, corruption, and overemployment—the consequence was usually high losses. The state-owned enterprises (SOEs) were also responsible for the birth of powerful trade unions that used SOEs as bases from which to branch out to the private sector and influence civic life. During Mrs. Gandhi's tenure, trade-union violence was widespread and often engendered both economic and civic breakdowns. To appreciate the scale of this problem, consider that as late as 2006, largely due to decades of union power, the state-run electric-power sector annually loses a sum equal to a third of its capital!

DRACONIAN TIMES

In politics, Mrs. Gandhi took centralism to a new level altogether, willfully converting Nehru's patiently constructed democracy to an autocracy. After removing all but the most trusted sycophants from the upper echelons of her ruling Congress Party, Mrs. Gandhi's handpicked president, Fakhruddin Ali Ahmed, declared a state of emergency in 1975.

Under the Indian constitution, if there was a state of emergency, the central government was allowed to wield extreme powers. These included powers to suspend civil liberties and elections. Such powers were meant to be used only for short periods during national crises.

No such crisis was at hand. The Emergency was Mrs. Gandhi's response to a 1975 legal verdict against her on charges of misusing state machinery during the earlier national election campaign of 1971. The verdict removed her from her parliamentary seat and banned her from contesting elections for six years. This, in effect, meant that she would not be able to contest the next round of elections, which were scheduled for 1976.

Two weeks after the court's verdict, Mrs. Gandhi declared the Emergency. Once declared, she was able to issue ordinances suspending Parliament and giving the government extraordinary powers over civil liberties.

Mrs. Gandhi used the powers under the emergency laws to interfere in the workings of opposition parties, the bureaucracy, the judiciary, and civil society. Many opposition politicians were jailed and the bureaucracy lost its powers and became corrupt. The judiciary and press followed suit. The labor unions were prevented from calling strikes.

For the average urban resident, the last aspect was a positive change. What most urban residents did not know—thanks to state control over the media—was what was going on in rural areas. The Emergency's most frightening and inexplicable aspect was the forced vasectomies of over a million rural citizens—ostensibly to control population growth, but really designed to terrorize the masses.

Mrs. Gandhi called for elections in March 1977 after releasing all political prisoners in January. She had several reasons for believing that she would win. First, she believed that the opposition politicians, just out of jail, would be ineffective campaigners. She also assumed that the rural masses would support the Congress Party, as they always had. Third, the party's internal polls showed widespread support for the relatively peaceful civic situation caused by the suppression of the unions.

But the opposition surprised her by courageously fighting back. The Congress Party's internal intelligence was also flawed, as the rural vote went against the Congress Party en masse.

In retrospect, the opinion polls were faulty because they were apparently based on urban views. I recall my own experience of the time as a resident of Kolkata. Unaware of the catastrophe being played out in the villages, I enthusiastically supported the Congress Party for promulgating the Emergency. Mine was probably a common urban view. Prior to the Emergency, urban residents had to suffer power and water shortages and constant disruptions from work due to the activities of the trade unions. During the Emergency, for the first time in my experience, the trains ran on time and the power never went off.

Just a few days before the fateful elections, I met an opposition party member in Kolkata. As he recounted the horrors of the Emergency that had occurred in villages just outside Kolkata, it was as if he was talking about a world that I never knew existed. Not for the first time and not for the last time, I realized that there was an India out there that was hard for the urban resident to connect with.

The opposition won the post-Emergency elections of 1977, but constant infighting subsequently botched its chance to rule.

Early elections were held in 1980. Mrs. Gandhi was easily reelected by disgusted voters willing to forgive and forget. Unfortunately, she would not forget her old ways of ruling. She widened her grasp of the country's polity by interfering in the functioning of opposition parties. But she tripped badly in the northern state of Punjab when she supported a radical Sikh group in order to split political opposition. The radicals turned against her and launched a violent agitation for secession. Her violent tactics, in response, alienated many Punjabi Sikhs, one of whom assassinated her.

It is ironic that today Mrs. Gandhi is, to most Indians, a symbol of a successful centralist ruler during a troubled period in India's history. This may be because democracy is so taken for granted these days that Nehru's protection of it and Mrs. Gandhi's attempts to sink it were both forgotten as soon as they died.

It may also be because of another difference between them, that of visibility with the masses. Nehru's popularity arose from his role in the independence campaign. But he was no personal populist. He relied on the Congress Party's networks, including feudal networks in the rural areas, to convey his political messages. Mrs. Gandhi, by contrast, was a populist and tireless campaigner who delivered her messages through face-to-face contact with the people.

In foreign affairs, where Nehru is remembered for defeat in the Sino-Indian war of 1962, his disastrous policy of nonalignment with world powers, and his fruitless attempts to influence world politics, Mrs. Gandhi is remembered for defeating Pakistan in the 1971 war and piloting the creation of Bangladesh. For many Indians, this marked the end of any real Pakistani threat to Indian territorial integrity. It also got India noticed among the great powers for the first time. In 1974, Mrs. Gandhi followed up with another attention-gaining device—a nuclear test.

On the volatile Kashmir issue, over which India and Pakistan had fought a war just after independence, Nehru is remembered as the architect of a failed Kashmir policy that began with the division of Kashmir and continued with the appeasement of its most popular, though unpredictable, politician, Sheikh Abdullah. Mrs. Gandhi is remembered for being tough on Kashmiri dissidence and for destroying Abdullah's National Conference Party.

Although Nehru's disastrous socialist economic policy is widely believed to mark the start of economic stagnation, no one seems to recall that Mrs. Gandhi diligently continued it, strengthened it, and infused it with corruption and intolerance. Instead, she is remembered for assuring food security through the Green Revolution, a program for introducing high-yielding cereal crops, and for getting rid of the privy purses of colonial-era princes, who were symbols of the British colonial divide-and-rule policy.

PHOENIX REBORN

Following Indira Gandhi's assassination in 1984, her son Rajiv Gandhi won a landslide election and ruled for the next five years. By the time he took office, the economic failure of the socialist experiment had become obvious. He realized that attracting votes at the next election required a change in social control of the economy. No doubt also influenced by China's rapid break with economic stagnation on the back of the market economy after 1980, Rajiv Gandhi began liberalizing industry.

After an energetic start during which he raised industrial quotas, removed income taxes on exports, and reduced tariffs on software imports, Gandhi became bogged down in political scandals in his second year in office. The first scandal actually happened during his first days in office but did not taint him: Three thousand Sikhs were killed in Delhi immediately after Mrs. Gandhi's death. A pliant press reported these murders as spontaneous revenge killings by citizens distraught at Mrs. Gandhi's assassination by a Sikh. However, documentation has since emerged showing evidence of a well-planned pogrom, with the support of fascist groups such as the Rashtriya Swayamsevak Sangh under the guidance of Rajiv and the Congress Party. But Rajiv, still in his honeymoon period with the electorate and the media, escaped scrutiny.

His public troubles began in May of 1987 with a pogrom of Muslims under the auspices of a state government ruled by the Congress in Uttar Pradesh. Uttar Pradesh is India's most populous state, in which Muslims account for 20 percent of the population. At least 350 Muslims were killed in Meerut in May, a town of about a million persons in the state of Uttar Pradesh and about forty-five miles from New Delhi. Around the same time, Gandhi was linked to corruption in a multibillion-dollar defense program. It was alleged that he had received bribes from middlemen for the purchase of howitzer guns manufactured by a company known as Bofors.

Rajiv Gandhi's response to public criticism was a return to Mrs. Gandhi's centralism in politics and economics. Several economic liberalizations were reversed. In politics, the Congress Party resumed its interference in the affairs of other parties and the citizenry. Toward the end of 1987, the Congress Party rigged a local election in the state of Kashmir. This precipitated the Kashmir insurgency that was to take several thousand innocent lives over the next ten years. Although it is sadly notable that no one has yet been found guilty for any of the crimes of 1984 and 1987, the public, by the 1989 elections, decided on its own to once again take a breather from Nehru's family.

Historians still debate whether Rajiv Gandhi was merely one more family member in the Nehru–Indira Gandhi axis of centralism and state control and, if so, where to place him. In the early days he differed from his predecessors on centralism and socialism but later reverted to the same policies. In some ways, he was more like Nehru than he was like Indira Gandhi: There was, at least early on, a commitment to democratic values, greater tolerance of opposition, and a sense of freedom under Rajiv Gandhi that had been part of his grandfather's regime but not his mother's. In others, such as the tolerance of corruption in return for personal loyalty, he was like his mother. By the end of his regime, he was hemmed in by so many political problems that he, like his mother, returned to her infamous style of relying only on a few trusted sycophants or, as it was called, *rule by coterie*.

Public memory is, alas, even less flattering. It is interesting that, despite the similarities to Nehru and Indira Gandhi, Rajiv Gandhi is remembered today as a leader who, unlike them, lacked the conviction of his visions. Nehru and Indira Gandhi both pursued misguided policies to develop India. Nehru focused on socialism and Mrs. Gandhi on populist *Garibi Hatao* ("Remove Poverty") strategies that included nationalization of several industries and a massive expansion of the public sector. Their strategies were faulty, but the sincerity with which these were pursued showed both conviction and an interest in India's development. Rajiv Gandhi, by contrast, seemed to have a tepid vision and no interest in following through.

In his speech that marked the centenary celebration of the Congress Party in 1985, Rajiv Gandhi said of his own party,

> We talk of the high principles and lofty ideals needed to build a strong and prosperous India. But we obey no discipline, no rule, follow no principle of public morality, display no sense of social awareness, show no concern for the public weal. Corruption is not only tolerated but even regarded as the hallmark of leadership. Flagrant contradiction between what we say and what we do has become our way of life. At every step, our aims and actions conflict. At every stage, our private self crushes our social commitment.

It seems in retrospect that Rajiv Gandhi was merely describing himself. He, who inspired us (myself included) as youths to sacrifice all for this hitherto benighted country bore out the immortal lines of Yeats that Gandhi himself had quoted: "The best lack all conviction and the worst are full of passionate intensity."

Perhaps the most charitable judgment that history will make of Rajiv Gandhi was that he was so harmful to the country that, after him, not enough voters believed either in the Congress Party or the political centralism it stood for. Even single-party rule by another party became suspect. After him, the country was ruled by coalitions, a trend that continues to this day.

COALITIONS INDIA-STYLE: THE ERA OF NATIONAL–REGIONAL COALITIONS

The coalition that came to power in 1989, like the one in 1977, was an unstable combination, consisting of parties with differing ideologies and national aspirations. However, stable coalitions were formed after the subsequent election in 1991. This is primarily because they were *not* made up of combinations of other national parties. Instead they consisted of a single national party in alliance with several smaller regional parties, which I shall term a *national-regional coalition*.

This was partly due to the prior demise of several national parties. Some of the national parties, such as the promarket Swatantra Party, had suffered under the Indira Gandhi onslaught on political freedom. After the Emergency, they surrendered their separate identities and formed a single party, the Janata Party, with enough combined strength to challenge Mrs. Gandhi in the elections after the Emergency. However, as this omnibus party had no ideological basis other than winning the 1977 election, it collapsed soon after.

Two other national parties were on offer at the 1991 election, notably the Bharatiya Janata Party (BJP; the only real survivor of the omnibus Janata Party) and, to a lesser extent, the Communist Marxist Party. Hence, it is interesting that the political space was filled by regional parties instead. In part, this was because these national parties were identified with ideologies alien to rural voters, the BJP with Hindutva (the politicization of Hinduism) and the Communists with the urban trade-union movement (and with political bases in just two states, the southern state of Kerala and the eastern state of West Bengal).

Perhaps the regional parties succeeded because, bereft of federalism for four decades due to the centralizing politics of the Congress, the people were voting for its return. Although some commentators claim that the vote for regional parties was a rejection of nationalism in favor of a subnational regionalism, this claim must be viewed with caution. All the regional parties, including those most explicitly identifiable as such by name, such as the *Telugu Desam* (Telugu being the local language of Andhra Pradesh) and the *Dravida Munnetra Kazhagam* (the Dravidians in DMK refer to the middle castes of the southern state of Tamil Nadu), call for regional development within the context of a strong Indian state.

For example, the local election manifesto of the All India Anna Dravida Munnetra Kazhagam (DMK), a leading party in Tamil Nadu and an offshoot of the DMK, begins its manifesto with a call for "creating a state of affairs under which Tamil Nadu will be a garden of peace in India."[1]

Regional parties—while willing to work within the Indian constitution—have interests that are primarily local. Even when they participate in national coalitions, regional party leaders usually show a preference for a chief ministerial position in the state rather than a (higher) national ministership. Indeed, they tend to nominate second-rung leaders for central-government posts. Though counterintuitive for many westerners, this should not be surprising. The issues that brought the regional parties to power have been too specific to the region for serious national consideration. Even when the theme is common, there is little cadence across regions. For instance, the middle-caste-based DMK of Tamil Nadu and the untouchable-caste-based Bahujan Samaj Party in Uttar Pradesh both derive their political power by opposing caste discrimination. But the DMK's favored castes are "above" the untouchables and tend to discriminate against them, leaving no political space for working together across regions.

This purely regional focus of the regional parties makes a national-regional coalition government in New Delhi surprisingly easy to manage. Since 1991, the coalitions have consisted of a group of regional parties coalescing around a national party, usually either the Congress or the BJP. As long as the ruling national party allows the regional parties to handle their own local issues, the regional parties will allow their national partner to dictate national governance. Regional parties often show no qualms about switching between the Congress and the BJP as a coalition partner, provided their regional interests are protected.

Outside observers are often baffled to see regional parties competing with national parties in state and national elections and allying with them thereafter. For example, in the western state of Maharashtra (India's wealthiest state), the Congress Party competes in local elections with a regional party, the Nationalist Congress Party (NCP; an ironic choice of name given its regional focus vis-à-vis its competitor). After local elections, they have more than once formed a coalition to achieve a local majority. However, this makes for relatively unstable coalition politics at the state level, in sharp contrast to national politics. Because Maharashtra is the NCP's sole source of political power, it is less willing to accommodate the wishes of the Congress Party in Maharashtra politics. This makes the local coalition far less stable than the Congress-NCP alliance at the central government.

DECISION MAKING IN COALITIONS

The noted political scientist Atul Kohli has spoken of the need for two-track politics in developing countries like India. As he notes, many democracies are likely to want to restrict democratic practices to the political arena, with periodic elections bestowing legitimacy upon new rulers. Once in power, these rulers want government decision-making to be as free as possible from political pressures—especially from the popular sectors. This decision-making autonomy is deemed essential for pursuing the not-so-popular economic reform programs. Kohli argues that, if institutionalized, this two-track polity—democracy in politics but not in government—would offer the best chance of "reconciling" the contradictory goals of democracy and strong executives capable of sustaining *economic rationality*—that is, stable economic growth.

This analysis has the following relevance to India. Had the Congress or the BJP been in power on its own in recent decades, the party would have had to accommodate the inevitable dissensions on economic reforms through debate within its own party. This could have significantly slowed down economic reform. Nehru, for example, experienced this in the case of land reform. However, in a coalition, a regional party may acquiesce to a national party's unpopular policy in New Delhi because it improves the regional party's chances vis-à-vis the national party in state elections. Once the regional allies approve, this makes it easier for the lead reformers in the national party to obtain approval from their own parties.

Another consequence of national-regional coalitions is that it has enhanced the importance of policies that increase the power of state politicians. For instance, the historical neglect of rural employment, primary and secondary education, health, and city roads arose from the inability of local politicians to adopt locally sensitive policies. Under centralism, the national leaders decided how budgets should be spent, even at the local level. In the new era of region-based coalitions, local politicians have the power to obtain financial allocations for local needs. In this way, the federal character of Indian politics, for decades buried under centralism, is making its long-overdue return.

This has had certain positive effects, such as improving basic social services. Civil society, suppressed under centralism, has also been freer to grow. The first noticeable civil society movements after 1989 were subnational movements, such as the Hindutva movement, which followed the Ayodhya agitation in the late 1980s and early 1990s, and the Kashmiriyat movement precipitated by 1987's rigged state elections. We will discuss these in more detail in Chapter 4.

Other important civilian movements, more general in character, such as consumer protection and the right to information, have already benefited the common man through enhanced legal protections and basic rights.

National-regional coalitions have also weakened the power central politicians had over bureaucrats. For example, in 1991, following a financial crisis and under pressure from the International Monetary Fund and other multilateral lenders, bureaucrats under the guidance of Manmohan Singh—an ex-bureaucrat turned finance minister—piloted the first economic reforms of the decade.

The success of bureaucrat-led reforms began a reinstitutionalization of the bureaucracy after a gap of nearly three decades. Once bureaucrats realized that they could survive a change of minister without being shifted to another department, they began to think long-term and to orient themselves to the priorities of the national political party that led the coalition. No longer subject to the whims of the electorate, bureaucrats could recommend liberalizing policies to disinterested regional ministers, who allowed them to go through.

The following tale is an example of this. In the year 2000, the Ministry of Communications sought my advice regarding reforms in the telecommunications sector. The person I dealt with most often was the secretary of the department, the senior-most bureaucrat. Some months after we began our discussions, his minister arrived at Stanford University (where I teach) to discuss the reforms I had proposed. I found him completely uninterested in the details of what was to become a key national telecommunications policy.

As I learned later, the minister had been appointed to his important position primarily because he represented a regional party from the state of Uttar Pradesh, India's most populous state, and a key swing state in national elections. As a regional leader interested primarily in the affairs of Uttar Pradesh, he had little interest in national issues. A year later, when he was replaced as minister of communications, the bureaucrats did not miss a beat and the reforms continued apace. This would have been unthinkable before 1989.

I saw this change in bureaucratic thinking as early as 1992 when, as investment bankers representing a multinational firm, my colleagues and I were regularly called in to advise the newly formed securities market regulator, the Securities and Exchange Board of India (SEBI), on regulations for securities markets. SEBI not only listened but acted sensibly, taking up those recommendations that would help competition and ensure coverage of financial markets, and rejecting recommendations from domestic and foreign firms with ulterior motives (i.e., protecting their firms' profits at the expense of market development).

For example, the second chairperson of SEBI, G. V. Ramakrishna, tried to convince the Bombay Stock Exchange (BSE) to allow foreign brokers to operate on the BSE. He did this at the behest of indignant foreign brokers whose appeals to the BSE to admit them had gone nowhere. Ramakrishna saw this as essential for breaking the corrupt practices of the BSE. When this failed, he promoted a new stock exchange, the National Stock Exchange (NSE). As we document in Chapter 12, the NSE is a success story in terms of both openness and volumes of trade. Interestingly, both foreign and domestic stockbrokers initially opposed the creation of the NSE: the domestic brokers because it would break their stranglehold on trades and the foreign brokers because they had been conditioned to think that a state-sponsored stock market was an intrinsic contradiction.

One of the rules of foreign investment in Indian markets is that only institutions that are holders of stocks, such as mutual funds, can invest. The government's intent with this rule is to prevent hedge funds and private investors from using the stock markets to make bets on the Indian rupee, which is still not fully convertible at the time of writing. Yet, when some foreign brokers misused their licenses to operate on the NSE by allowing hedge funds and private investors to invest through them, Ramakrishna was remarkably pragmatic. He recognized that the rule was easily broken in many ways. Although SEBI officially was against such practices, in reality, it did nothing to prevent it.

The next chairman of SEBI, D. R. Mehta, significantly built on the reforms of his predecessor and raised SEBI to the level of the best regulators globally. In 1999 and 2000, as a member of a SEBI committee on venture capital reform, I worked closely with Mehta and his colleagues on the reform of venture capital regulations in India. The work was particularly interesting because it was so new to the Indian context.

Venture capital invested in India at the time was less than $30 million a year. Once, in early 2000, when I met with the chief economic adviser to the prime minister, he confessed that he did not know what *venture capital* meant! When I explained it to him, he was intrigued and said that when our team met the prime minister the next day, as planned, I should be sure to introduce the term and explain its meaning carefully! Such cooperation—again, unthinkable prior to 1991—meant that, as a result of our work, the flow of venture capital rose from an average of $30 million a year before 1999 to an average of more than $1 billion a year thereafter.

Even if one accepts my argument that coalition government weakened politicians sufficiently to enable bureaucrats to function, it is hard to know exactly when the bureaucratic attitude shifted from mainly hostile to cooperative. It may have been the accretion of small changes that reached a tipping point; it may have been simply a substantial rise in bureaucrats' salaries introduced by the Congress Party as an election ploy in 1996 (the Congress lost, anyway) that shifted the bureaucrats' thinking away from short-term corrupt practices to long-term strategies for growth.

Despite some people's arguments, it was not a cleansing of political thinking, the ripple effect of which swung the bureaucratic tide. As I document in Chapter 5, politicians have not become less corrupt. If the Congress had its Bofors scandal in the 1980s, the BJP had its Barak missile scandal in 2000.

Neither has there been a gradual change in political ideology at the top. Some have argued that the BJP government pushed harder on reform than the Congress because it is ideologically closer to markets. However, reform has been promoted by every government in power since 1991. It was initiated by the Congress and is supported by even the Marxist government of West Bengal.

Regardless of the actual timing of the change in bureaucratic thinking, its debt to federalism is apparent. As a result, the much-maligned Indian bureaucrat is beginning to play a role that parallels the importance of bureaucracy in Japan. In a political environment characterized by rapid changes in government or, at least, rapid changes of ministers within a government, the bureaucrat is the carrier of institutional memory and offers a steady hand. The words once used to mock Indian bureaucrats, that the British invented bureaucracy while the Indians perfected it, now implies more positive things.

CHAPTER 4

The Diverse Outcomes of Federalism

IN CHAPTER 3, I argued that rising federalism has united politicians and bureaucracy firmly behind reform. In consequence, Indians, for the first time since independence, can buy, sell, save, and invest without fear that their success will lead to new controls by the government. Business leaders of proven integrity such as Ratan Tata, who heads India's largest conglomerate, and software pioneers Narayana Murthy and Azim Premji, are hailed as respected citizens, and their advice is eagerly sought by policy makers. The large body of Indians living overseas, estimated at 20 million and once pilloried for taking the benefits of their state-subsidized Indian education overseas, has an improved status and a voice in policy making.

Certain leading indicators point to noticeable macroeconomic results—the proportion of services to GDP, for example (55 percent, which is relatively high considering the country's state of development), and the growth of private education. A little-noticed but no less important measure is the absence of food-grain crop failures since 1990 due to better agricultural extension services. All these are arguably due to the rising power of states.

The increasing federal character of Indian governance has, of course, several other implications. An apparent drawback of the Indian constitution is that power devolves down from the center to the states and then from the states to the villages and towns. In a truly federal setup, as in the United States, power flows from the lowest to the highest administrative levels. By contrast, in India, for instance, teachers for village schools are recruited and paid for by the district headquarters (a district is an administrative agglomeration of several villages). In the past this led to considerable corruption: District bureaucrats would recruit town-based teachers through their patronage networks. They were aware that the teachers would not show up for work because they did not want to move to the village. When the village government complained, it led to bureaucratic tussles in which the lower-ranked village officials rarely prevailed.

The central government has been looking hard at this issue in recent years, attempting to devolve power down to the villages. A new ministry, the Ministry of Panchayati Raj Institutions (Village Governance Institutions), formed in 2004, is responsible for examining governance at the village levels, although the framework of enhanced village governance came into law in 1993. Its recommendations include greater control of budgets at the village level. Under the recommended system, for instance, village teachers would be recruited and paid for by the village government. It is too early to tell whether this federal system will work, but it appears to be a structural change in the right direction.

FEDERALISM'S PLUSES: THE CASE OF TELECOMMUNICATIONS

A contradiction to the generally positive case for federalism seems to be evident in the electric power sector. Electric power is a state responsibility, and the inability to price electricity correctly or ensure adequate electricity supply appears to be a big failure of the devolution of state power. While trade-union power has been responsible for inefficiencies in supply, the political power of large farmers over local politicians is behind pricing anomalies, particularly the 90 percent subsidization of electricity for rural areas. However, the causes may be deeper than federalism. Certainly, we know that the problem of power shortages and subsidized rural power first appeared in the days of centralism.

By contrast, the growth in telecommunications is viewed as a success of centralism. As discussed in Chapter 1, Indians buy more than six million new cell-phone connections every month—even more than China. It is argued that this is because New Delhi, not the states, controls telecom licensing and price regulation. I shall, however, argue otherwise.

For several decades under centralism, an adequate telecommunications system failed to develop. By 1990, for example, India and China each had six million telephone lines. A decade later, India had 28 million lines while China had 120 million. The Indian government's approach to telecommunications prior to the 1991 reforms is well captured by its official statement, made in 1977, that:

> The primary need of the people is food, water and shelter. Telephone development can wait. In place of doing any good, development of telecommunication infrastructure has tended to intensify the migration of population from rural to the urban areas. There is a need to curb growth of telecom in the urban areas.[1]

In other words, the state was tacitly saying that rural users were migrating to urban areas in order to access telephone services, and that this was something they ought to do something about—not by increasing phones in rural areas but by reducing them in urban areas!

Although it is impossible to prove definitively that regional control of telecommunications would have led to earlier success, the following tale is, I believe, instructive on the importance of federalism: In September 2000, as part of a project to study rural infrastructure, I visited a village, Chandrampet, in the Karimnagar district of Andhra Pradesh, ninety miles from the state capital, Hyderabad. I was surprised to find that, of the approximately 200 homes in the village, none had a telephone. There was not even a public telephone within five miles. But every home had cable TV—a service provided by a village entrepreneur who had a franchise from a large satellite TV firm and who had connected each home by coaxial cable to a central dish antenna.

To the western observer, this relative proliferation of cable TV over telephones would seem very unusual. Americans, for example, typically pay an average of about $50 per month to access cable (or satellite) TV, whereas a phone line for basic services costs only about a third of this. Of course, by now most homes in the United States have both cable TV and a telephone, but given a choice, the telephone is the more essential commodity and is cheaper.

But, in this Indian village, cable TV cost Rs.50 (a little over $1 at 2006 exchange rates) a month for four channels. Even in nearby Hyderabad, a subscription to fifty channels also cost only about $1 per month. The business of cable TV was profitable and flourishing: There were more than 70 million national subscribers in 2000 compared with 30 million phone connections (both landline and cell phone).

Meanwhile, a telephone connection for basic services also cost the user about $1 per month in 2000. The difference with cable TV was that the state-owned telephone company lost money at this price, but the private provider of cable TV made a profit. The implications for villages like Chandrampet were clear: The telephone company rationed the telephone lines in loss-making areas and was particularly slow in making telephones available in rural areas where setup costs were probably 50 percent higher than in urban areas.

It might seem obvious that the cable provider in the village could be onto a profitable opportunity: For a small additional cost for routers and related equipment, he could connect the villagers to each other and to nearby villages over the cable network, providing Internet-based telephony. Because India already had a well-developed fiber-optic backbone network (in this case, accessible within ten miles of Chandrampet), the village could also be easily and cheaply connected nationally and globally and receive voice, data, and Internet services.

The village cable provider faced one big problem: the law. Although cable TV was permitted for the provision of TV signals in a village without a license, using it for providing phone services without a license would have broken the law. The law required a provider of telephony to own a license to provide statewide services. And connecting to the Internet would require him to own a national long-distance license. Both were unaffordable to the village cable provider. Meanwhile, the large state and long-distance licensees—there were only two permitted in each state—had no incentive to franchise Chandrampet's village provider using a technology that would someday compete with their own networks.

A few changes in the rules could make a significant difference. For instance, if a local entrepreneur wished to provide local services, he should have the right to do so and pay fair interconnection fees to the main licensee. Alternatively, the state could do away with the licensee requirement of statewide coverage and allow a provider to operate over any area that he wished to cover. To further cut costs, a provider could be allowed to connect several homes with a single telephone line, rather like the "party line" that was popular in the United States in the 1960s and more recently implemented as the *Ladaphone* project in Mexico. In fact, this is the successful model for cable TV in India, which combines a single satellite dish with cable to many homes.

However, the New Delhi–based regulator dithered over these issues, fearful of upsetting the big licensees. A state-level regulator would perhaps have been more responsive to local needs. The politicians at the states would likely have supported the changes to the rules.

A small Andhra Pradesh–based nongovernment organization (NGO) called the Rural Telecom Foundation (RTF), operating from a rural district in the state (the Ranga Reddy district), showed what could be done with local support. In 2003 it connected fifteen homes within a village with one line, even though, under the rules in force at the time, a line could only be connected to a single home. The village authorities, however, provided the necessary local political cover, while the local member of parliament helped convince the telephone company to "overlook" the event. The MP even inaugurated the pilot project, which consisted of two such lines.

Because the idea of party lines was based on a book I had edited, I was chosen by the RTF to receive the first phone call from the village. As I discovered while chatting with the MP, the advantages were not just lower costs. The homes that had been wired belonged to landless laborers whose main source of income was daily wages during the agricultural season. Earlier, they would queue up in front of the single public phone in the village from 4 A.M. each morning for about three hours on average. Once their turn came, they telephoned all the local landowners (who mostly had private lines in their homes) to ask if their services were needed. After the installation of the lines in their homes, the landowners would call the laborers if their services were needed. This, of course, eliminated the laborers' three-hour wait. Even given their subsistence wage rates of a dollar per day at the time, the saving was well worth the cost of the new connection, which was the equivalent of sixty cents each per month.

What should be clear from the story of Ranga Reddy district's experiment with party lines is that it happened not because of central regulation but because of local support. In the era of centralism, it would have been unthinkable for a local member of parliament to support the project. However, in 2003, his support enabled RTF to do its work, which later made it nationally known.

FEDERALISM'S DISCONTENT: HINDUTVA

In Chapter 3, I argued that the decline of the Congress Party created political "space" for parties with purely regional focuses. Some parties, however, sought to convert regional issues into national issues. The most prominent such subnationalism is the Hindutva movement, or the movement for the politicization of the Hindu faith. The movement began in 1989 with the era of coalition governments, even though it had existed in suppressed forms earlier. Its origins lie in certain urban areas of northern and central India.

Hindutva's political standard-bearer is the Bharatiya Janata Party (BJP), a party formed (under a different name) in 1951 after the dust from Mahatma Gandhi's assassination had settled. Given the inability to find political room for Hindutva in Nehru and his daughter's intrusive regimes, the BJP dabbled with socialism in the early 1980s. In this, it had limited electoral success. In 1989, the BJP moved its religious roots front and center, with an agitation to destroy a 400-year-old mosque and replace it with a Hindu temple, where it claimed a temple had stood earlier. This act, which became known as the *Ayodhya agitation,* gained national prominence and converted this once-regional party into a national party. It helped the BJP nearly double its vote share from 11.5 percent in the 1989 elections to 21 percent in 1991. Since then, the BJP has slowly grown to become the national alternative to the Congress Party, leading the ruling coalitions between 1996 and 2004.

Despite the destruction of the mosque at the disputed site in 1992, the stagnation of its vote at 20 percent in the 1996 elections showed that the BJP's radical strategy was yielding diminishing electoral returns. This led it to switch to a strategy of building an anti-Congress coalition that necessarily included incorporating several moderate parties. This, in turn, required it to soften its radical stance at the center while pursuing a harder approach in the states.

This strategy is ultimately inconsistent. As I document in Chapter 10, it appeared to work in the western state of Gujarat in 2002.

But, the BJP was defeated in national elections in 2004. This has persuaded it to reexamine its Hindutva roots. It has led to an internal tussle within the BJP on its posture toward Hindutva. During this process, which is still incomplete, Hindutva is likely to remain quiescent as a source of national terrorism. Its trajectory within the states over the next few years, however, cannot be predicted with any confidence. The point of my argument is not that Hindutva is no longer a force to be reckoned with, but that coalition governance opened the way for new subnationalisms to suddenly become critical forces. It is still unknown whether the Indian state, and particularly democracy, can deal with it.

FEDERALISM'S OTHER CHALLENGE: KASHMIR

Another subnational concern is the problem of Kashmir, which also affects India's relations with Pakistan. Kashmir is a natural locus for Indo-Pak hostility, given its location as a border state, its Muslim majority, and a history of non-Kashmiri Hindu rule that was considered oppressive by its Muslim subjects.

At the time of partition, facing an armed Muslim insurrection supported by Pakistan, its Hindu Maharaja ceded Kashmir to India on special terms: Kashmir would have its own constitution and governance, except for foreign policy, defense, and communications. It was further stipulated that Kashmir's future status as a permanent part of the Indian Union would be mutually determined by both the Indian and Kashmiri sides.

A war ensued between India and Pakistan over this issue, ending in a cease-fire line brokered by the United Nations. Both sides agreed that a future plebiscite by the Kashmiri people would decide their fate. This undertaking has never been fulfilled by India because it believes that Kashmir would choose to leave India, though not necessarily join Pakistan.

Today, Kashmir is a divided state that reflects the outcome of the 1947 war between India and Pakistan: one-third of its area is controlled by Pakistan, and India controls most of the rest. China also owns a small stake, ceded to it by Pakistan. Both sides of Kashmir have a Muslim majority, exceeding 95 percent. In 1965, India and Pakistan fought a second war over Kashmir.

The state has, since 1947, successively been brought closer to the Indian Union, sometimes by popular will though mostly at Delhi's will. A key breakdown in the process was the rigging of local elections of 1987 by Rajiv Gandhi's Congress Party. This seeded an insurgency that Pakistan quickly supported and that had some early successes. The army crackdown that followed the unrest was brutal and indiscriminate. It destroyed any popular support that might have remained for permanent union with India.

In the ensuing era of coalition governance in New Delhi, there was initially little political will to stop the insurgency. However, by the mid-1990s, Kashmir's pleas to New Delhi finally began to be heard. This was because an important regional party in Kashmir, the National Conference Party, became part of the ruling coalition. Slowly, New Delhi understood what had been obvious in Srinagar (Kashmir's capital city) for several years: that its insistence on integration would continue to make Kashmir a difficult area to govern, even without Pakistan's support for armed insurgency.

In 2002, the first fair elections in fifteen years were permitted in Kashmir by the national government. They brought the People's Democratic Party—led by erstwhile Congress Party member and Kashmiri M. M. Sayeed—to power. New Delhi now recognizes that it needs to behave better toward the Kashmiris, including granting them more control over local matters. New Delhi must (perhaps surreptitiously) surrender its five-decade-long strategy of whittling away at the concept of Kashmiri independence through administrative and legal action.

Unlike the still unresolved problem of Hindutva, Kashmiri subnationalism increasingly shows signs of a resolution. This is an example of how coalition governance initially exacerbated the problem to a point of great danger to the Indian Union. Subsequently, however, the same structure showed that it could deal with the problem. Had centralism continued, the problem would probably still exist.

The Khalistan secession agitation of the 1980s in the prosperous agricultural state of Punjab in northwestern India provides an interesting contrast with Kashmir. As with Kashmir, the secessionist movement had its origin in promises of autonomy given by Mahatma Gandhi and Nehru at the time of independence. Over time, the state was gradually and peacefully integrated into the Indian Union. However, when Indira Gandhi supported a radical Sikh group in order to control local politics, it seeded the violent insurgency that followed.

In the Punjab, the army finally gained the upper hand and the problem was resolved under the aegis of centralism. In Kashmir, decades of centralism failed to resolve the problem, perhaps because of the innate strength of this particular subnationalism.

FEDERALISM AND INDIA'S AMERICA POLICY

From the mid-1960s to 1990, the United States and India ignored each other. From the 1990s on, dramatic changes in India's economic climate have led to an increase in U.S. corporate involvement in India. This has been followed by closer cooperation on geopolitical matters.

The United States first tried to get closer to independent India during the Eisenhower and Kennedy eras but was repeatedly rebuffed. It realized then that, given India's centralized economic and political structure at the time, there was little interest among Indian policy makers for collaboration with the United States. Quite generally, in fact, western democracy had no strategic implications for newly emerging democracies across the globe, including India. Instead, other fellow centralists—and there were plenty in the non-aligned world as well as the USSR—offered more to learn from for India's big problems of underdevelopment and disintegration. The things that U.S. democracy stands for—civic rights such as freedom of speech, and the market economy—were unappreciated in India at the time. And Indian concerns—such as postcolonial national unity and poverty in places where the market economy did not reach—were little understood in the United States.

Even then, the United States might have had an influence on India if it had helped resolve India's external threats. But, after the Indo-China war ended in 1962, the only external threat India was seriously concerned about was Pakistan, particularly over Kashmir. This is where their interests clashed: India's interest in Kashmir was to seek control over its internal politics from New Delhi, but the United States preferred a solution that was satisfactory to India, Pakistan, and the Kashmiris, and it offered to mediate among the various parties.

India's nuclear tests in 1974 further worsened ties during this period. The United States responded by promoting the Nuclear Suppliers Group in order to prevent weapons-grade uranium from reaching India. This had the effect of blocking uranium sales to India, leading India to rely on expensive thorium-based reactors for both energy and weapons development.

The 9/11 terrorist attacks provided an opportunity for a new direction to Indo-American relations. By then, India had experienced the benefits of a decade of economic reforms during which American corporate investment had been significant. Some Indian states, particularly the technology-producing state of Andhra Pradesh, lobbied for an overt pro-American stance. More important, though, was the role of the BJP, which was the national party at the center of the ruling national-regional coalition (The formation of national-regional coalitions was discussed in Chapter 3).

The BJP—which had come to power through the conversion of its original subnationalist platform, Hindutva, into a national cause—was keen to convert America into a supporter of Hindutva. Otherwise, it feared that India's growing economic cooperation with America would always be suspect under BJP rule. It saw 9/11 as a perfect opportunity to do so: America needed friends and was worried that its stance against terror would be viewed as anti-Islamic. A democratic India with a large Muslim minority population and with credibility in the Arab world would be an important ally.

Ironically, therefore, the BJP-led government and the American government came closer for opposite reasons. The BJP was in search for an ally in its quest to legitimize Hindutva, which has strong anti-Muslim overtones. America was in search of an ally that could help it portray a moderate image rather than an anti-Islamic image.

The Indian strategy appears to have worked. In 2002, when India and Pakistan almost went to war over Kashmir, the United States played an important role in resolving the crisis. For the first time, it took a stance that peace between India and Pakistan, its two key allies in the war against terror, was more important than resolving the Kashmir problem.

U.S. interest in resolving India's nuclear fuel problems provides another such situation. India has long sought nuclear fuel for its energy needs but since 1974 was denied it due to U.S. initiatives to block its nuclear weapons program. The reversal of the U.S. stance on Indian access to nuclear fuel, albeit with considerable risk to the United States with regard to nonproliferation, is welcomed by India as a second critical piece of evidence that U.S.-India incentives can be aligned without outside conditions.

Looking ahead, Indian foreign policy is likely to be closely aligned to U.S. initiatives. This is because its interests—economic growth and an internal solution to the Kashmir problem—are in accord with U.S. interests.

A much more passive Indian stance on foreign policy than the prickly approach of the past is, therefore, likely. In its economic condition, India now is where China was in the 1980s or Japan after the Meiji Restoration. Like China and Japan of those times, India too needs to play catch-up for several more years, and it will be reliant on western capital to build the institutions and infrastructure for growth. Therefore, its foreign policy is likely to be much less aggressive than in earlier times.

INDIAN REGIONALISM

What implications does a quiescent foreign policy have for India's regional strategy? India is a large-enough country that its actions have regional implications and occasionally global implications. Recognizing this, and despite occasional talk of an aggressive stance on issues such as energy security and the need to maintain ties that were forged in the era of nonalignment with the third world (and even earlier, as with the Middle East and Central Asia), India will focus internally and will accommodate other dominant forces on external issues.

Evidence on this comes from several sources. For example, following the nuclear tests of 1998, the Indian strategy on deployment and expansion appears to be directed more at border protection from threats by Pakistan and China than an aggressive external posture. India has been willing to accommodate the United States in its war on terror, including its actions against Iraq and Iran, despite overwhelming national disagreement on both stances, in return for U.S. support for India's economic growth.

In short, Indian foreign policy for the region has entered a reactive and accommodative phase. As Lee Kuan Yew (the first prime minister of Singapore) recently said about China, and which appears applicable to India, "I believe the Chinese leadership have learnt: If you compete with America in armaments, you will lose. You will bankrupt yourself. So, avoid it, keep your head down, and smile, for 40 or 50 years."

Relations with Pakistan are likely to remain tense due to the ongoing Kashmir problem. Pakistan's hand has been considerably weakened by the rising representation of Kashmir in New Delhi. The introduction of nuclear weapons in South Asia introduces new uncertainties. Michael Krepon of the nonpartisan Henry L. Stimson Center has argued that the combination of harsh rhetoric, provocative action, and the absence of trust and communication channels (especially in the early stages of nuclearization) invite destabilizing actions and escalation. In the early stages of these programs, the size and disposition of each side's nuclear deterrent tend to be opaque to the other, which can prompt worst-case assessments. Secure second-strike capabilities, in particular, might not exist and are difficult to assess during the early days. One side may believe that the other side is racing ahead in this respect and so may be tempted to use nuclear weapons sooner rather than later.

Finally, behavior might not be rational during moments of intense crisis arising from a miscalculation on the effect of, say, insurgency. Both sides might misread the extent of outside support. For example, India and Pakistan have engaged in brinksmanship—ratcheting up support for insurgency in Kashmir in the case of Pakistan, or coercive diplomacy on the part of India—on the assumption that the United States will intervene to prevent nuclear war anywhere in the globe. If the United States does not intervene as expected, the situation could escalate out of control.

One might hope that at least the possession of nuclear weapons would cause Pakistan to be more cautious about supporting insurgents in Kashmir and both sides to be more cautious about engaging in conventional military operations. The caution with which the United States and the Soviet Union dealt with their confrontation in Europe over many decades supports that inference. But it is no guarantee of quiet on that front.

India's relations with some other neighbors have also been affected by rising federalism and coalition governments. Sri Lanka, in the past, has had difficult relations with India. In Sri Lanka, the neighboring Indian state of Tamil Nadu has regularly supported the Tamil insurgency. Such support has increased in the new environment.

What do these trends tell us about the making of India into the nation-state envisioned by Mahatma Gandhi? Had Gandhi been alive, he would no doubt have been disappointed to see the Congress Party reduced to a minority in parliament. But he might not be too disappointed with the fact that even as regionalism has risen, it has been within the context of a common ambition to create a strong country. Peasant, salaryman, and capitalist are coalescing into a nation. Gandhi would also approvingly note the new focus on rural development and the improvement in bureaucratic quality.

In fact, it might not be too much to argue that the arrival of coalition politics in its regionalized form saved the Indian state.

CHAPTER 5

Corruption

INDIA AFTER INDEPENDENCE IN 1947 became a byword for corruption and its corollary, inefficiency. Javier Salcedo's statement that bureaucracy is the art of making the possible impossible was an oft-quoted description of Indian bureaucracy. The tacit conclusion was that corruption and inefficiency were Indian traits, even if not uniquely so.

This opinion might be changing these days—a tribute to the inexplicable power of high GDP growth in dispelling notions of immutable traits. As this chapter will show, however, what is really happening is the delinking of corruption and inefficiency.

Such widespread corruption in a democracy has been doubly vexing to Indians. They must suffer its consequences while wondering why a democracy that should allow for the imposition of collective will has not been able to impose minimal ethical principles.

The causes are complex. Newly independent India quickly acquired certain strong institutions such as democracy and an independent judiciary. But conditions such as pervasive poverty and the

conflicting interests of the landed and landless made clean governance a challenge. Widespread corruption, however, was most likely
not due to these challenges, at least not initially. Instead, it was an
outcome of the quota system for industrial production introduced
by Nehru. Under this system, a bureaucrat was required to issue the
go-ahead in the form of licenses, permits, and clearances for the
production of most goods and services (the notable exception being
agricultural production). This, in turn, more or less guaranteed that
all goods and services would be in short supply and created the
incentive for widespread corruption in the license-allocation
process.

The bribe paid to the bureaucrat partly filled the gap between
the price of the license and the market price. But only the private
sector—individuals, private businesses, and the like were willing to
bridge the gap with a bribe. The public sector, which competed with
the private sector, was not, of course, going to bribe its own. So, it
started off with a cost advantage over the private sector.

Despite this, the private sector could usually produce goods
more efficiently than the public sector, due to the profit motive. In
consequence, a two-tier economy developed. Every producer was a
quasi monopolist, due to the quota system, but those in the private
sector were more efficient. Consumers purchased the output of the
private sector where possible. Nevertheless, the public sector survived even when it competed with the private sector, as it did in
many fields ranging from steel production to hotel services, due to
short supply and the guaranteed patronage of government business.

Both sectors' output was of poor quality due to the absence of
local competition and so appeared to be woefully short of best
global standards. There was no research or development of new
products, as there was no need. Given the shortage of goods that
such a system created, engineering-related skills such as project
management and product development mattered much less than
turning out a standard, low-end product. If it could be produced, it
could be sold. As such, the incentive for using new technologies

was much less than turning out, quickly, an outdated, but low-cost product.

The more outdated, it seemed, the better. For instance, until the mid-1980s, India's leading automobile producers were the Premier Automobile Company and Hindustan Motors. Between 1964, when Premier Automobiles produced its first car, the Premier 1100, based on the 1937 Fiat 1100, and 1985, when it introduced an equally outdated second model, the 1100 was its only model. During this period, it shared the consumer automobile market about equally with Hindustan Motors' leading model (and its only model until 1978), the Ambassador, based on the 1948 Morris Oxford.

Even as of 2006, the Premier Padmini (the 1100's current name) is still the mainstay of the Mumbai taxicab system, but the more royal-looking Ambassador still leads the Kolkata taxicab market and is even the official government limousine. Although India proponents may validly claim that, at least, India produces cars on its own—unlike, say, Singapore or Indonesia, the distinction of producing a model that was invented prior to World War II offsets that claim a bit. More interesting is that the quality of these two cars is about what it has always been—poor in the sense of low acceleration, need for regular maintenance, uncomfortable ride, high steering ratio, and noise while driving—except for the tinny horn. Yet, they compete with the Hondas and Toyotas now widely available in India because of the low cost of spares and simple requirements for maintenance.

CORRUPTION IN CIVIC LIFE

Because the quality of goods produced by the private sector was better than that of the public sector, it was not long before the private sector began to demand a bribe for the right to buy its products over those of the public sector. This marked the expansion of corruption, beginning with industrialists and bureaucrats in waiting rooms next to ministers' offices, all the way down to transactions involving the common man.

That it was led by the private sector is interesting and probably quite unique. But it was a logical outcome of short supply, price controls, and the better quality of privately produced goods. To get an Ambassador, one paid the dealer a side premium over the list price. The premium on the Premier was higher, which might baffle an outside observer, given the abysmal quality of both.

For those who could not, or would not, pay the extra amount, joining a queue was the necessary consequence. Well into the 1990s, the middle class queued up for everything. There was a two-year wait for a refrigerator, as well as for a motorized scooter. The wait for cars was even longer.

In some cases, such as membership to private sports clubs, availability was so limited that one could grow old waiting. My own application to the Mumbai-based Western India Automobile Association (WIAA) sports club took thirteen years and was approved in 1999. In another case, an applicant to the prestigious Mumbai Willingdon Sports Club found out by sheer accident after twenty years that his application had been approved five years earlier. His club sponsor had died before that, and the club's systems did not permit direct notification. Once he found out, the club was, of course, glad to admit him.

Given the rapacious attitude of the state, it did not stay out of the game for long. There were goods and services that it alone controlled, such as phone connections and electric power. The state-run Tatkal Phone Service, for example, was arranged so that customers paid an "official premium" over and above the "official price" of phone service in order to qualify for early allotment. It almost did not feel like a bribe.

Even up until 1990, for the middle-class people who queued up instead of paying the premium, the wait for a phone connection was over five years! Not wanting to penalize its citizenry to death, however, the state graciously declared that phone lines were heritable assets. This meant that, upon the death of a person, the right to the phone line (including the right to assume the dead person's place in the queue in case the line had not yet come through) was transferable to the next of kin.

In due course, corruption moved from a requirement in fulfilling a transaction for the consumption of private and public goods and services to a normal part of obtaining civic services. Oddly, this was not due to short supply of such services but to the forces of patronage, as a consequence of which public services were overstaffed. For instance, there were too many policemen in the typical urban police force, each grossly underpaid.

So, we bribed them because we could not escape them—there were just too many around. In most western countries, the odds of successfully blowing off a red light are probably over 50 percent. This is because there are not enough police officers to man the traffic signals. In India, the odds are less than 10 percent because there is a traffic cop (sometimes two) at every intersection—ready, willing, overzealous, and remarkably efficient. After all, threatening to ticket motorists is how they earn most of their income!

Of course, the scope of corruption was much wider than this, and, as early as 1970, it had become pervasive. Without the backhander to all types of public servants, urban survival would have been impossible. Some we bribed so we could cheat the service providers: the electrical meter reader, for example, who, in exchange for a bribe would underread the meter, and the telephone man who levied a monthly charge in return for letting us make free long-distance calls. Some we bribed to get us out of trouble, such as the policeman who caught us making a wrong turn. And others we bribed so that they would not hurt us, such as the taxman who was bribed so that he would not harass us (despite knowing that we had paid our taxes fairly). Railway-ticket checker, ration-card issuer, gas-cylinder man, and postman—we had a special, unethical relationship with each.

A government officer posted to a plum position, such as the responsibility to collect *octroi* (a tax imposed on the entry of goods into a city), often paid a bribe to a higher officer to get such a posting. He could collect that back several times over from the share that truckers paid him for undervaluing goods at the octroi checkpoint. Interestingly, such an officer, if single, was prized in the marriage market. If male, prospective in-laws were willing to pay a dowry premium for a groom with a guaranteed income over a run-of-the-mill groom from the private sector! If female, the dowry was often waived.

CORRUPTION'S THIRD FRONT

The corrupt nexus between business and government and the oversupply of underpaid civil servants were not the only sources of corruption. In Chapter 3 I discussed the political corruption that was engendered during Indira Gandhi's and Rajiv Gandhi's regimes. This was caused by the shift from patronage networks to populism as the prime form of electioneering. Under Nehru, the Congress Party obtained its rural votes through supporting landowners—for example, going slow on land reform and exempting agricultural income from taxation.

Mrs. Gandhi tried to break these networks because they were controlled by her opponents in the Congress Party, the so-called Old Guard. She appealed directly to the people through job programs, opening bank branches in rural areas, and so on. Many of these projects were legitimate but many were corrupt.

Rajiv Gandhi continued this pattern. His notorious *loan mela* (loan festival) project must rank among the smelliest examples of corruption ever: The government forced the state-run banking system to disburse small loans between Rs.1,000 and Rs.10,000 (between $100 and $1,000 at the exchange rates of the time)—without collateral or even meaningful identification—to anyone who applied during the loan mela. Consequently, the banking system lost hundreds of millions of dollars. Much of the money was stolen by the wealthy. One such, a Kolkata businessman I knew, Mr. B__, would send a posse of his employees (poorly dressed for the occasion) to the festival site every day during the loan mela. There, by prior arrangements made by Mr. B__, each would collect the maximum sum under a new name and pass the proceeds to Mr. B__.

THE CAUSES OF CORRUPTION

When public-servant corruption was widespread in India, the amounts were never outrageous, even when paid by the wealthy. Everyone understood that a bribe was needed to ensure the public servant a decent livelihood. As such, it was calculated by how much one ought to contribute to the receiver's income, not by one's capability to pay.

This resulted in a strange dignity to the corruption process. Once, as a college-going youth traveling by train within the western state of Maharashtra from Mumbai to Nashik (a four-hour journey), I boarded a train without a reservation, though with a ticket in hand. In those precomputer days, anyone could get a ticket, as there were several trains with standing-room-only compartments. However, boarding a train with reserved seats required separately purchasing a reservation at a nominal cost of five rupees. Because the train I boarded had only reserved seats and was full, a reservation was unavailable for purchase.

I was aware of my transgression, but as the next train was much later, decided to board anyway. When the conductor came around to our cabin, which was intended to seat six persons, he found—to no one's surprise—that there were eight of us sitting there. As he checked each of our tickets in turn, he asked the two of us without reservations to disembark at the next stop. My more experienced fellow transgressor was unperturbed, but I, being new to the game, was deeply upset. I accordingly, quite openly, said, "Why don't you charge us a little premium and allow us to travel?"

To my amazement, the ticket checker, a dignified-looking man probably in his sixties, turned vermilion with rage. He harangued me for a few minutes on my lack of morals and for my assumption that he shared them and said I would definitely have to leave the train come the next stop.

Stung to the quick, I apologized profusely and publicly for my lack of good sense and said I would certainly step down at the next station. When we arrived there about thirty minutes later, I hurried for the exit and disembarked, only to be met by the conductor on the platform. He said, "Now you may give me the reservation cost and an additional five rupees and I will let you get back on the train."

Shocked for the second time in an hour, I paid up and returned to my space in the cubicle. I told my fellow passenger what had happened. He smiled and said that he had paid up some time back, even before the ticket checker had come to check our reservations. It's the standard fee, he said, when I told him how much I had paid. "Then why all the song and dance?" I asked. Came his wise reply, "Can he afford to appear corrupt?"

At one level, it was confusing: all this public display for a paltry amount that he would not give up, an amount that, even in those days, was not enough to buy one a decent meal. But, inside, I also felt ashamed that I had forced a poor man in his sixties to go to absurd lengths to protect his dignity. He knew, I knew, and all the other passengers knew that he took bribes, but it was clear that a lifetime of poor wages was the real culprit.

THE TOLL OF CORRUPTION

The oversupply of public servants might suggest that public service was efficient. For those who paid bribes, it was. For the rest, service was abysmal. Often, this put the public at large at risk. For instance, India is regularly beset by various short-term epidemics typical of a failed health infrastructure. In 2006 alone, epidemics of dengue and chikungunya, both spread by mosquito bites, affected several cities.

In 1994, a serious urban health crisis occurred. A pneumonic plague affected the chronically dirt-ridden city of Surat in the western state of Gujarat and also threatened Mumbai. The newspapers showed sensational pictures of trash piled high in several street corners, with rodents casually sampling the contents in full daylight, while apparently unconcerned trash collectors stood by.

In reality, this had been a feature of several Indian cities for years. Particularly in poorer urban areas, the attitude of the municipal council that was responsible for trash collection was—and, alas, continues to be—cynical to the extreme. If one has no political power, which is typical of those in poor areas, one has no power to get the rubbish collectors to do their job.

Once it led to the plague, however, it threatened the lives of the municipal councilors, not just their constituents. Only then was there an abrupt turnaround. The speed with which the municipal workers in both cities cleaned up was almost unbelievable. Having an overstaffed municipality finally paid off. Mumbai's municipal council also got religion: It placed full-page advertisements in all the newspapers piously advising people not to pick up a dead rat with their hands if they happened to see one. If they did so, they were advised not to mail it in an envelope to the municipality's offices for diagnosis!

The private sector often took advantage of the state's lax standards. In Kolkata, adherence to building codes was abysmal enough so that some buildings were actually leaning! One was the nineteen-story Chatterjee International Center, once Kolkata's tallest building. When I viewed it from a mile away, it looked as though it tilted about eighteen degrees. It stayed like that for several years until it was recently renovated. Another building on Camac Street was eight floors high and had an even greater tilt. Once, walking by, I asked a resident coming out of it if he was afraid of living in the house. He said he had been terrified until quite recently. However, it had finally listed enough that it touched the building next to it and so was now stable!

It might seem as if corruption's toll is solely on the citizen and not on the perpetrator. At most, it is widely felt; the corrupt public servant carries some guilt on his shoulders until he gets rid of it. My encounter with the ticket checker showed, however, that the guilt never quite disappears. In a more direct way, though, public servants are probably the biggest losers of their corrupt practices. Once, visiting a government office that issued ration cards in the mid-1990s (a necessary form of identity at the time), I was struck by the shortage of functioning lightbulbs: for about thirty workers, only two lightbulbs were on. Was the department on a conservation drive, I asked? And, given how dark it was, was it worth it? I was told that, for fear of corrupt officials who might steal them, the government issued lightbulbs at the rate of one per month on a quota system—perhaps unsurprising for a ration-card office. A recent episode of unstable power had exhausted the quota some months ago and new bulbs had been petitioned for. But it would be some months yet before the office could be fully lit again. To date, the office had managed to ensure that at least two lights functioned by collecting a new bulb from a staff member every time an old one burned out.

"Surely you can collect more money than that between you and get a full set of bulbs?" I protested. "Yes," was the reply, "But if we do that and the government finds out, it will delay our allocation." Meanwhile, they needed to repair their chairs as well. When I pointed out that I was sitting on a cane chair and that the cane under me was mostly worn out, leading to a fairly uncomfortable (not to

Kolkata's one-time leaning Chatterjee tower.

mention risky) posture, they showed me that most of them also sat on "torn-cane" models and that visitors did not get the worst ones.

THE END OF QUOTAS, BUT NOT OF CORRUPTION

When quotas were abolished in 1991, the public assumed that corruption, too, would depart. The consequent arrival of planeloads of western businesspersons eager to invest in India was taken as the first positive signal of this as well. But it was to take longer than most had anticipated.

When foreign investors returned to India after 1991, they assumed that in its operating practices India was probably more like Indonesia than any other country in Asia and that like the Suharto family in Indonesia, there was the Gandhi dynasty to be managed. But they also assumed that India was ready to do business. Thus, the type of foreign firm that initially came to produce goods in India was the type used to doing large deals with government and paying the price: the utility companies, the big commodity suppliers and the like, wanting the annuity payments of early access. The *fixers* of New Delhi, long accustomed to fixing bureaucrats for domestic businesspeople, were quick to respond, offering access to the highest levels of decision making for a price.

The foreign businessmen (mostly men, indeed, with a few important exceptions, as we discuss later in this section) found that the system was not ready to receive new foreign firms, especially the midsize and smaller firms that make up the bulk of the American economy. India had opened up enough to make it interesting for domestic enterprise to dream anew. But the institutional structure to allow full foreign ownership in India was not yet there. Many of these foreign businessmen became disappointed and left.

The few successful foreign firms in the 1990s were those large ones that could afford to be carpetbaggers. Certain American investment banks, for example, made lucrative deals to list Indian public-sector giants on the Luxembourg or London stock exchanges. They would make their pitches over a week or so with plenty of glamour and sophistication to policy makers and bureaucrats in Delhi and hope to return with a contract in hand. They mostly succeeded because it involved work that Indian firms could not yet handle. And they succeeded even when they did not see the point of setting up an office in India, given the irregular flow of deals and slim pickings in the domestic market.

This was a game of glitz, certainly, but corruption was also an integral part of it. The American banks provided the glamour; and the Indian bureaucrat, perhaps realizing it was his last time in the spotlight, demanded his price. The Indian public—long accustomed to the lordly and corrupt ways of the bureaucrat—now had the pleasure of seeing him squirming as he tried to polish his "yes, but what's in it for me?" response to someone whose culture he did not understand.

And how were the bureaucrats to respond to the glamorous likes of Enron International chief Rebecca Mark, who, according to her own account, explained her wardrobe style to colleagues in an internal briefing. "Day in and day out," she said, she called on a foreign official who typically spent most of his time with other conservative men, her competitors. "He will not remember most of them," she said, "but he will remember me."[1]

Enron epitomized a regrettable phase in Indian reform. It was remarkable that Enron was successfully portrayed in the Indian media as an electricity giant in the United States, a false image given that it was a midsize trader of oil and gas then (this was the early 1990s). The image buffing, if not worse, helped Enron sign a $2.5 billion deal for setting up a power generation plant just north of Mumbai in Dabhol, Maharashtra. The deal was unfair to Indian consumers and privately opposed even by the private-sector-friendly

World Bank for the lack of transparency in the award process—though the bank lacked the courage to speak openly.

I was peripherally involved in the process. In December 2000, at the invitation of Maharashtra's chief minister, I presented an analysis of the financial impact of the Enron project to the Maharashtra cabinet. It was clear from the financial information available that the project would bankrupt the state electricity board (SEB) by the first quarter of 2001—and I said as much. Indeed, in the second quarter of 2001, the SEB defaulted on payments to the project.

The Dabhol project exposed an unexpected, dark side of western capitalism to Indians long isolated from the West. Western businesses also began to learn that India was quite different from Indonesia. It may be corrupt and opaque like Indonesia, but the press was quite different from other developing countries where they had worked. In those places the press was more or less a nonentity in influencing business outcomes. In the Dabhol case, the press followed Ms. Mark's every move (often breathlessly) and initially took a sympathetic view of the high costs. Once the reason for the high costs was discovered to be unrelated to the cost of inputs, the press turned against Enron. In the process, westerners also discovered through the work of anti-Enron activists like the late P. D. Kaul that civil society in India is a force to be reckoned with.

Another case that exposed the muck on both sides was a fiasco in telecommunications. In 1994, the Indian government asked global firms to join with Indian firms and bid for fixed-line and cellular licenses. An Indian firm, Himachal Futuristic Communications Limited (HFCL), in partnership with Israel's Bezeq and Thailand's Shinawatra Corporation, bid $27 billion—more than five times the combined market value of these firms at the time—for nine fixed-line licenses. This was possible only because the bid terms had been deliberately and corruptly set, allowing even small participants entry so that they could resell the licenses to more credible providers down the line for a large profit.

Of course, the winning bidders were unable to achieve financial closure, and their bid collapsed. Ultimately, the telecom minister who managed the bid process was found with Rs.11 million ($300,000) in cash at home and was prosecuted for corruption. The company that allegedly bribed him was HFCL.

Surprisingly, even more credible firms—both domestic firms such as the Birla Group, and their foreign partners such as AT&T, grossly overbid, as they later discovered. For the market was still too small to justify the sums bid. The domestic partners then used the law to shield both themselves and their foreign partners by citing delays on the part of government. The government fought back in the courts and would have won—except that it would probably have bankrupted at least some large Indian business houses of long-standing and close ties to political parties. It was not until a new government came to power in New Delhi in 1998 that the issue was resolved—through the government's capitulation.

However, the end of quotas gradually ended corruption in accessing goods and services. The government shifted to governance by regulation rather than by quota. The domestic private sector, which had introduced corruption to the general public in the 1950s, led the way out by increasing output. By the year 2000, the rules and regulations had become sufficiently sensible that it finally made sense for foreign firms to set up shop in India.

WHY CORRUPTION REMAINS A PROBLEM

There are three sources of corruption. One of these, the extraction of illegal payments to compensate for scarce goods and services, disappeared with the end of quotas and the consequent increase in economic efficiency. Two problems remain from the old days: the continued presence of underpaid and oversupplied public servants, for whom corruption is the only recourse, and corruption for the purpose of vote gathering.

A recent court case neatly captures both these causes of corruption. In December 2006, the Delhi High Court overturned the lower court's verdict acquitting Manu Sharma, the son of a prominent politician, Venod Sharma, of killing bartender Jessica Lall in the presence of several witnesses. The defense did all it could to prevent a fair trial: At the retrial, it emerged that the defense's actions included bribing and threatening witnesses. The police, by their own admission, shielded the accused and sought to derail the case.

More than thirty eyewitnesses initially filed testimony, but later retracted and turned hostile toward the prosecution. One witness, a prominent Delhi socialite, whose testimony remained unchanged, was the owner of the restaurant where Jessica was murdered. That made a key difference to the outcome. Venod Sharma was later exposed in a sting operation by *Tehelka*, the famous investigative journal, as having organized the payment of millions of rupees to some of the witnesses. The only comment that the erstwhile Delhi police commissioner made on the final verdict was that the judgment seemed to be motivated by a judge with an agenda, but that it showed that the police could at least, on occasion, be critical of themselves!

The speed with which the retrial was held and a verdict delivered (the original verdict was delivered in February 2006, although the murder occurred in April 1999) was unprecedented and seems to have been a direct outcome of the public uproar that followed the initial verdict. It is, of course, too early to tell if this was an isolated occurrence or a forerunner of positive change. A cautionary note was sounded by the erstwhile solicitor general, Harish Salve, who responded to a TV reporter's question on the verdict with "Jessica Lall's case is only one of hundreds such that never get reported because less prominent people are involved." It is unlikely that anyone from the police or those who paid illegal bribes on behalf of the defense will ever be prosecuted.

Meanwhile, a new source of corruption has presented itself, or rather, a new variant of the old quota system. In India's booming economy, the goods in short supply are now land and civic infra-structure. Corruption is a factor in determining who gets to build what, how much, and where. In most cases, building permits are given liberally in return for a bribe, with no consideration of additional infrastructure needs such as roads and water. Sadly, it is the poor, who lack adequate infrastructure to begin with, who suffer the most.

The United Nations Human Development Report for 2006 notes that in a run-down area of Mumbai, Dharavi (a slum that houses two million of Mumbai's population), "It is estimated that there is 1 toilet for every 1,440 people. In the rainy season, streets, lacking drainage, become channels for filthy water carrying human excrement. . . . In a typical case, 15 families share one tap that works for two hours a day."[2]

Yet, cities like Mumbai and Delhi record one cell phone per person. In other words, a majority of Dharavi's residents probably have one cell phone in the family while sharing a toilet with over a thousand others. Even in the spiffy Churchgate district of Mumbai, where apartment prices exceed 10,000 rupees per square foot, water is supplied for two hours a day, usually in the evenings at around 8 P.M. Residents keep large tanks in bathrooms and kitchens to store the water for use during the rest of the day; but some items such as washing machines and dishwashers can only be used with the water at full pressure. So a maid is sure to be home at 8 P.M. to operate these essential appliances.

As these cases illustrate, the problems caused by corruption are reducing in some ways. The Jessica Lall case shows this, as does the success of companies in removing supply shortages. One might also expect less corruption in civic life as an outcome of the improvement in the wages of public servants and a reduction in their numbers; but it will take several years to feel the full impact of these. Nonetheless, as long as the population remains so poor, it is unlikely that political corruption will disappear entirely.

In the slums of Mumbai there is one toilet for every 1,440 people.

Meanwhile, a new type of corruption in the form of policies that ignore the rights of the poor and underprivileged in favor of the rich is becoming evident. In a growing economy, the incentives for such institutional corruption are higher because higher bribes are more affordable than when the economic pie is small. Mustering the collective will to tackle this form of corruption remains a challenge for India in the twenty-first century.

CHAPTER **6**

The English Language and India's Future: Mental Workers or Metal Bashers?

IT WAS DECEMBER 2006, and I was about to launch into a talk on India's knowledge economy and how it should be financed. The setting was the plush Grand Hyatt Hotel near the Mumbai airport, and the event was the commencement of the annual conference of The Indus Entrepreneurs (TiE), a Silicon Valley–headquartered organization of South Asian professionals. The audience of about 1,000 mostly young professionals looked eager, or so I optimistically assumed.

Eager, in turn, to show off my Hindi (despite living overseas) along with my technical knowledge, I said, *"Gyan arthavyavastha mein kamgaron ko takniki ya professional shikshan ka darkar hei jabki paramparik arthavyavastha mein log kaam karte huwe sikhte hein."* ("In a knowledge economy, workers need a technical or professional education whereas, in a traditional econ-omy, they learn on the job.") A thousand pairs of keen eyes suddenly turned blank. I went on: *"Seva kshetra mein ek khasiyat hei: utni hi kushalta chahiye jitni seva mein hei; jabki karkhane mein, aam mazdoor machine chala kar kushal saamaan bana sakte hei."* ("Services are unique in one respect from other sectors: The provider needs to be as skilled as the service provided, whereas in manufacturing, an unskilled laborer can produce skilled goods by using machines.") The blank eyes now turned desperate. At this point, I switched over to English. The audience tittered, relieved that it was all in good humor and that I was finally moving into a language they understood.

Later, several audience members who stopped to chat with me on their way out asked why I had spoken those few words in "unin-telligible Hindi." I told them I was testing their intellectual distance from India's heartland rather than geographical distance—from large cities like Lucknow or Varanasi in the central Indian province of Uttar Pradesh, where the audience would have had no difficulty in understanding my words. I had chosen to speak a Sanskritized form of Hindi, one rarely understood in Mumbai, which is the capital of the state of Maharashtra—where Hindi is subject to multifarious other influences, including Bollywood's Hindustani, Marathi (the na-tive language of Maharashtra), and the local slum-dweller's patois, Tapori.

NEEDED: AN ENGLISH-SPEAKING COUNTRY?

India is a multilingual country in two senses of the word. First, many Indians speak more than one language, although only one will typi-cally be spoken fluently (most city dwellers are fluent in two). Sec-ond, there is no single language that most Indians speak. This sometimes causes despair among the culturally sensitive at the Min-istry of Education. But in reality, it is just one dimension of India's little-understood educational situation.

The first dimension is the quality of English: whether it is good enough and whether it is spoken widely enough. This is not only about whether India can continue to grow as a global provider for services such as call centers and software development. There is something far more important at stake: Once a critical mass (even if it is a minority) of the country agrees that sophisticated concepts will be communicated only in English, English will likely become India's language of development. If that happens, one would argue that a better standard of English should be taught as part of the general curriculum throughout the country.

India may be moving in this direction. Already, as part of its colonial heritage, India has several million English speakers. An exact number is not known, and the number who are fluent in English is probably below 50 million, but the origins are known. In the 1830s, the archimperialist Thomas Macaulay, a member of the Governor General's Council, convinced the state to drop local languages from state secondary schools and teach only in English.

Macaulay and the council's aim was not to spread English to the masses. Rather, he argued:

> It is impossible for us, with our limited means, to attempt to educate the body of the people. . . . We must at present do our best to form a class who may be interpreters between us and the millions whom we govern; a class of persons, Indian in blood and color, but English in taste, in opinions, in morals, and in intellect. To that class we may leave it to refine the vernacular dialects of the country, to enrich those dialects with terms of science borrowed from the western nomenclature, and to render them by degrees fit vehicles for conveying knowledge to the great mass of the population.[1]

Macaulay, despised by the nationalists who led India's freedom struggle (which included many, like Nehru and Muslim League leader Muhammad Ali Jinnah, who were dependent on English for communicating their ideas of independence), assumed that the masses would not learn English, thus requiring an elite to mediate the transfer of western concepts into the vernacular.

There are more choices available than this limited one conceived by Macaulay. First, we may consider whether enough of the elite already think of the issues of the day in English. If so, a critical mass may have been reached and it therefore makes sense that the rest of the country should learn English. If this is not done, the divide between the elite and the rest, so evident in India today, will continue to grow and leave the poor behind.

It turns out that Macaulay was prescient in his hope for the role of English in India. Not only is English widely spoken, but it is the language of the elite in science, commerce, and a host of other important fields. English is the language through which their sophisticated concepts are conveyed. The people in my audience at the TiE convention were part of the elite and behaved exactly as Macaulay had hoped they would: They thought and communicated their most sophisticated ideas in English. Worse, their Hindi was so "enriched" by English that even if they comprehended my grammar when I spoke those few sentences in Hindi, they did not understand my concepts. I had used three terms of science borrowed from the western nomenclature for my first sentence: *knowledge economy, professional,* and *traditional economy.* Of these, my audience had only understood the second—*professional*—when I said it in Hindi. Alas, that was only because it was the one term I did not translate into Hindi! (Readers unfamiliar with Hindi may have noted the word *professional* among all the unfamiliar foreign words in the first sentence of my transliterated speech.)

I concluded that the business elite of India has not yet taken, and will not be able to take, the second step recommended by Macaulay, that of enriching the vernacular dialects "with terms of science borrowed from the western nomenclature and to render them by degrees fit vehicles for conveying knowledge to the great mass of the population."

Is an extreme solution, an all-Hindi-speaking population, adequate for India's economic growth? Many countries, such as China, have done perfectly well with a nearly monolingual population. No one accuses the Chinese of suffering from speaking only Mandarin (over 53 percent of the population do so), even if many Chinese policy makers think that they would do even better if the Chinese knew more English.

India, however, will have more difficulty in progressing economically if it is monolingual in a native tongue. This is because its development strategy includes a focus on services. This is unlike China's manufacturing-focused strategy. Language matters far more for services than for manufacturing. English is the platform on which the world's most sophisticated economic ideas are expressed. India's unusual turn toward services rather than manufacturing will, therefore, be unsustainable without "Macaulay's children."

Even if there is no guarantee that services will continue to dominate the Indian economy, services will still be important. This means that the workforce will need language skills that will be useful as it shifts from low-end jobs such as working in a corner shop or bashing metal in factories to high-end services such as doing mental work in the information technology sector. Although the language of the corner shop and the factory floor need not be English, that of higher-end services will have to be.

The other extreme, an all-English population, might succeed except that English is not currently portable across these tasks—even within a city, let alone an entire nation. An English-only educational strategy is as ill-suited to running a corner shop as a Hindi-only education is to a career in information technology. So, we are up against a challenge: The corner shop is as much an essential feature of the economy as the software shop and will employ many times more people than software shops for decades to come. Generations yet unborn will earn their living in corner shops.

From a purely commercial viewpoint, then, there is something to be said in favor of the widespread teaching of English, while, during the transition to English, other tongues must be learned. But is there more than the transition problem that makes other languages necessary? If there is to be a common language, then that language must serve not only the scientific and business classes but the political, cultural, and social classes throughout the country as well. English, however, obviously cannot be the language for transmitting all sophisticated concepts. This has already been proved. For example, various expressions of Indian culture, such as classical music, are based on local languages.

One could envision an alternative to an English-only situation in which English-language training is accelerated while retaining the vernacular. In other words, Indians should be bilingual in English and another language. For convenience, I term this process *English bilingualism.* If it works, it would be an unusual, though not unique, success. There are some highly educated, rich countries in which the most advanced concepts in science and the humanities are discussed in multiple languages by the same groups of people. Some countries in Western Europe, such as Switzerland, come to mind. Then why not India, albeit with a somewhat more specialized division of language? English would be the language for science and business, while the vernacular would be the language of humanities and culture.

That might seem far-fetched to outsiders. The costs of implementing English teaching across the country might seem to be too high to even contemplate such a strategy. In reality, however, it is already happening. As the case of the Varanasi taxi driver discussed in Chapter 1 shows, despite the absence of state policy for implementing English bilingualism, parents all over the country are already implementing this of their own accord if they can.

I experienced this firsthand as early as 1986, long before India was a software success, when I helped with a survey of rural areas of southern Saurashtra (a region in the western state of Gujarat). The survey asked parents of secondary school students what subjects they thought would be useful for their children. We thought that their answers would be on job-oriented subjects, such as farming and blue-collar trades such as equipment maintenance. Because computers were relatively new then to rural India, we wondered whether computer education would make the list. To our surprise, English topped the list—followed by computer education!

The state is yet to respond to this need. Because parents will not wait, the children are taught the local language in school and are taught English after school by private tutors. This is an unnecessarily costly method of becoming English bilingual, and it does not serve the real purpose of parents—that their children learn sophisticated scientific concepts in English. Instead, the children learn science and commerce in the vernacular using texts and teaching methods that are not up-to-date. This keeps them behind the country's elite. In their private English classes, they are taught by tutors unfamiliar with idiomatic English and whose proficiency lags even that of the concepts the students are learning in the vernacular. Thus, the students learn an English that they cannot internalize and whose quality remains poor. Under such a policy, the metal bashers and corner-shop workers will have difficulty becoming mental workers.

THE SEEPING-IN OF ENGLISH

Even so, it is a big change from the past. Slowly, as a result, India will be a country where bilingual fluency—in a native tongue and English—will become a reality.

I sought to assess the importance and quality of English in late 2006, when I swung through parts of Allahabad and Varanasi, two towns in the poor region of eastern Uttar Pradesh. Uttar Pradesh is India's most populous state and is located in the country's heartland. I had been invited to speak at meetings organized by universities and chambers of commerce on the subject of the evolving services economy. At each stop, my presentation, delivered in Hindi (the same Sanskritized Hindi that the Mumbai audience had failed to follow), discussed how the knowledge economy was evolving, the role of services, and India's place in this. Midway through each presentation, I would have explained the importance of services and how India was beginning to make its mark in services that were often quite sophisticated, such as software. I would then pause and ask my audience (in Hindi): "Well, do you think a company like Google could be invented in India?"

First, to my surprise, I noted that every single member in every audience I spoke to knew about Google. They all used it daily.

Second, the conversation at that point always slipped seamlessly into English. This was because the audience needed to use terms such as *innovation*, *search engine*, and the aforementioned *professional*. The pure Hindi equivalents of these are so arcane that their use would be the equivalent of raising the dead. They could, of course, have used the colloquial Hindi equivalents, which are, perhaps unsurprisingly, *innovation*, *search engine*, and *professional*. This makes it somewhat pointless to state in Hindi that, say, "Google's search engine is based on an innovation that required technical and professional skills" when all the words with ideas embedded in them, with the exception of the word *skills* would sound exactly as they did in English. Hence, it is easier at that point to speak in English.

Third, I observed that people did not mind speaking English. This surprised me: I had thought that those in smaller towns with limited English would be particularly protective of their native tongue. The reality was quite the opposite. This was perhaps because of their comfort with who they were—an identity missing in the more rootless large cities. There was no sense of missing out on the excitement of the big cities, a feeling one often comes across in small towns in America. In fact, most people expected to live in these small towns through their lives and were happy to do so. As the vice chancellor of Allahabad University said to me: "We may be a forgotten town in the new India, but that is fine. We've produced three of India's prime ministers, and will produce more."

This also disproved statements some politicians have made about the cultural loss faced by the masses because they are forced to learn English. Interestingly, it is in India's bigger cities that such false ideas are bred by India's most aggressively nationalistic politicians—a generally ugly breed in themselves—who are obviously as out of touch as I am with small-town India.

Despite their comfort with English, they were happy that I, an outsider, had taken the trouble to speak in their tongue. As the dean of Banaras Hindu University put it in response to my surprise at his students' very high standards of Hindi and comfort with English, "They may speak to you in English, for that is an aspiration. But they think in Hindi, for that is their culture."

Last, but not least, the audiences generally thought that inventing a firm like Google in India was only a few years away. This surprised me, and I generally took it to be a form of chauvinism—for which I was unprepared, given the thoughtfulness of their other reactions. I would try to provoke my audience by pointing out that whereas India's most successful IT firm, Tata Consultancy Services (TCS), had taken thirty-two years to get to where it was today, it still had lower revenues than eight-year-old Google (in fact, only marginally more than Google's profits!). But the audiences would have none of it. They would give me examples of innovative local startups that they knew of, especially in the telecom field, in which Indian local markets are deep and offer great learning opportunities. Even the faculty at the universities I spoke at often pointed out that when I spoke about the lack of world-class innovation in India, I was looking at the past. They suggested I study the training that their students currently received. I would then understand how aware they were of the latest trends, thanks in part to the Internet. Yet, when I asked for the evidence of their work, they could not provide it and I could not see it. I was to ponder this puzzle for months before I got my answer.

CHAPTER 7

Walking on Water, or Getting into an IIT

AS I HAVE NOTED IN CHAPTER 6, in the absence of a more English-friendly state policy, English is seeping into education, though from outside the school system. But it is a slow process. In the meantime, the sophisticated services face difficulties recruiting enough English-speaking professionals to match the large capacity of telecommunications infrastructure the country has built up to provide such services. One sees this most obviously in the exported services such as information technology and call centers. Since 1999, during my annual visits to Indian software and IT service companies, I have noted that recruiters speak worryingly of rising wages and the shortage of good talent. They are right to worry. On average, since then, wages have increased by up to 12 percent a year. For example, in 2002, my records show that a fresh graduate from Delhi University, one of the country's premier universities, could join a call center at a salary of Rs.8,000 ($175) a month in Delhi. As of 2006, the comparable wage rate is $220. Likewise, the wage in a software firm for a fresh engineer with an undergraduate degree was $450 per month as of December 2006; four years ago, it was $300.

The story is actually worse than a 12 percent rise in wages. Because of the high-growth environment that India is seeing these days, demand is growing faster than capacity. In 2002, the wage of Rs.15,000 would enable hiring top engineering graduates. Since then, the software industry has grown at 40 percent a year. Today, Rs.20,000 buys only average quality. This has happened even though average educational standards are rising regularly.

The apparent paradox is readily explained: In 2002, only the best engineers were in demand; now demand has increased so much that even the graduate at the bottom of the class can get an engineering job. Earlier, the engineer at the bottom of his class would be forced to take a low-end commercial job. Now, software firms will hire him—but, because of the uncompromising nature of the work, firms often provide in-house training. Often, this is not just software training but training in idiomatic English, particularly American English, and other communication skills, including basic grammar.

The situation is worsened by attrition. Attrition rates of 20 percent per year are common, although the average is about 12 percent in the IT services industry. A call-center company I visited in 2006 told me its attrition rate was 7.5 percent. I was impressed—until my host clarified that this was a monthly rate!

Even where the supply is high, a new phenomenon has appeared: Top Indian talent has become as globally tradable as Chinese television sets. Although this is not an entirely new phenomenon, the dimensions have changed. Until the late 1980s, the best engineers and management graduates went overseas for Ph.D.'s. In large part, this was because it was an easy migration strategy. Now they get offers from the world's best engineering firms, consulting firms, and investment banks, luring them away from Indian shores. The losers, apart from Indian firms, are the American universities, which are no longer an attractive destination. In response, firms operating from India are making some hard decisions about paying near global-standard wages for their best talent.

Even so, the stories one reads in the press of a severe shortage in the software and call-center export shops due to a shortage of English-speaking, skilled workers overstate the problem. First, there is at least a fivefold pay gap between American and Indian wages. A temporary call-center worker in the United States costs the employer upward of $20 an hour, once all costs are taken into account, including equipment and space. By contrast, the raw cost of a recruit in India in 2006 averaged about $1.50 an hour, and the all-in cost was about $3. If wages in India continue their 12 percent rise while U.S. wages rise at 2 percent and the exchange rate holds, the gap will close in about twenty years. Of course, this may be an unrealistic projection, since both supply and demand parameters can change. But it indicates that sending work to India to save on labor costs (the labor arbitrage story) is valid.

Second, the reality is that certain industries like call centers are growing at 40 percent a year and, yet, wages are rising by 12 percent. In other words, through a combination of higher productivity and an increasing supply of educated graduates, the industry is managing quite well. In other, more traditional industries, the rise in wages is similar, but the growth rate of these industries has been about 15 percent a year, well in excess of the rise in wage rates.

Fortunately, too, the erstwhile India premium is now an India discount. Even until recently, getting the best premium talent to work in India required paying a premium to developed discount nation wages because India was considered a hardship post with limited growth opportunities. When reform began in the early 1990s, not many believed it was sustainable and did not want to risk their careers. During my tenure in investment banking in the early 1990s, for example, the senior management was paid a premium of about 30 percent over comparable U.S. wages to work in India. The situation today is the reverse: Senior management will now accept wages of 30 percent below the comparable U.S. wage to work in India.

One reason for the wage discount is that an India experience is a valuable calling card—in fields as diverse as finance and diplomacy. For example, the American embassy now has one of its largest staffs in India (though still somewhat smaller than China), and experience in India is considered a long-term career asset by diplomats in its consular corps.

Another is that working conditions have improved along with the excitement of working in a high-growth economy. Consequently, many Indians living overseas are willing to return to India for lower wages. And, finally, the cultural advantages and aspects of living in one's region of origin have become more important.

THE QUALITY OF TECHNICAL WORK

Resolving the problem of teaching English will help, but it will not resolve a fundamental problem: Education needs content beyond what is currently provided. This is the second dimension of the problem of education in India. And it is not due to a shortage of funds. For example, in both India and China, public expenditure on education is about 13 percent of total government spending. Yet, China appears to have gathered a better harvest. For example, according to a World Bank survey in 1998, India had 0.3 scientists and technicians per thousand people, ranking forty-second of sixty-two countries, well below China at 1.3 (twenty-fifth) and Ireland at 2.0 (twentieth).[1]

There are other indications of quality problems, and many causes. First, acquiring advanced skills is acknowledged to be no easy or short-term task. It is not by accident that even the relatively advanced new economies of Asia—Singapore, Taiwan, Hong Kong, and Korea—may have caught up with the West in manufacturing but have failed to create branded products (Korea's Samsung, perhaps, excluded). In services such as banking, software, retailing, telecommunications, logistics, and insurance, there are no global brand names from Asia, not even from Japan.

For decades, there was a quality shortfall even in India's most advanced field, information technology. Evidence from patent registrations and from analyses by the Ministry of Human Resource Development suggests a lack of advanced IT skills in India. As recently as 2001, a government report stated the following:

> Obsolescence of facilities and infrastructure are experienced in many institutions. . . . The IT infrastructure and the use of IT in technical institutions is woefully inadequate. . . . The barest minimum laboratory facilities are available in many of the institutions and very little research activity is undertaken. . . . Engineering institutes have not succeeded in developing strong linkages with industry. . . . The curriculum offered is outdated and does not meet the needs of the labor market.[2]

Further, the interaction between university and industry was minimal. There were few academia-industry research partnerships, as well as few consultancy assignments for faculty from industry. There was also very little independent research. Until recently, faculty members—even at the prestigious Indian Institutes of Technology (IIT)—were not expected to do research. As of 2001, the average number of citations over a five-year period for a faculty member at the IIT was less than three. By comparison, at MIT the average is 45, and at Stanford University it is 52. India produces about 300 master's degree graduates and 25 Ph.D.'s in computer sciences each year, while the United States produces 10,000 and 800, respectively.

Like many Asian countries, India set up a research system independent of the university system hoping to isolate the former from the latter's stodginess. For many decades, research was underfunded and unproductive. Of late, there have been improvements, even if there is still a long way to go. For example, the Council of

Scientific and Industrial Research, the premier independent institution that employed over 13,000 researchers in 2003, filed almost 500 U.S. patents that year. By contrast, the University of California system, with a fraction of that number of science researchers, earns about 400 patents a year.

One problem that hurts India today is that higher education has always been a policy priority over primary or secondary education. (In Nehruvian times, the problem was seen as a solution and then became entrenched.) China spends about two-thirds of its education budget per capita on primary and secondary education. In India, until 1990, the corresponding ratio was one-third, although it is currently close to the Chinese percentage. As the southern state of Kerala has shown, greater spending on primary and secondary education (Kerala spends nearly twice as much as other Indian states, on average) pays off in terms of development: Kerala has the country's best human development indicators, such as on female health and child nutrition, and has emerged as one of India's high-growth states in recent years.

But spending on higher education is poorly managed, even at the prestigious IITs and the Indian Institutes of Management (IIMs). The origins of the IITs go back to the 1950s, when the first of these were set up, beginning with Kharagpur in eastern India. Nehru's vision of an Indian industrial powerhouse would require engineers (although Nehru envisioned them as crafting manufactured goods rather than designing software). The Massachusetts Institute of Technology was the declared model on which the IITs were to be based. They were established with help from the best engineering universities around the world, including the United States, the erstwhile Soviet Union, and Germany.

For several decades there were just five IITs, whose elite product found employment in modestly paid engineering jobs and contributed nothing of significance to the economy. This was because the demand was as modest as the supply, a consequence of the era of the industrial quotas that limited output. Not surprisingly, a large number of the best graduates went abroad (as late as 1986, for instance, 59 percent of the IITs' fresh graduates left India to study abroad, mostly in the United States).[3]

The remainder usually joined the public sector rather than the private sector. There was no difference in pay between joining the best private-sector firms such as Tata Engineering and the best public-sector firms such as Bharat Electronics. The public sector had, however, several advantages, such as lifetime employment. It also had the advantages of legacy: housing, comfortable work, and steady, though small, raises in pay. Indeed, the middle class of India was created around the public sector. The public sector also offered better growth opportunities, as, unlike the private sector, it was less constrained by licenses and quotas.

In India's short-supply economy, the initial demand for management education was also built around the production function: inventory control, production-systems and supply-chain management, and cost control were the management functions in demand by Indian companies. Those best suited to be trained in the production function were, quite naturally, engineers. The Indian Institutes of Management, founded in the 1960s with support from Harvard University (at Ahmedabad) and MIT (at Calcutta), typically recruited newly minted IIT graduates, usually without any work experience, and taught them production management skills. The two IIMs produced only 300 MBAs a year. Like the fresh engineering graduate, the IIM product also entered heavy industry.

Those who were not engineers had much weaker job prospects. I am an example. I entered IIM Calcutta in 1974 with an undergraduate degree in economics and found that the job-worthy courses were built around production management, in which I had little interest and even less competence. My interest instead was in economics-related management courses such as financial management. But, although the portfolio-management and capital asset pricing theories of Nobel Prize winners William Sharpe and Harry Markowitz had become standard curricula in western MBA courses by then (as

I was to find out later), there was no course on the subject at IIM Calcutta.

Instead, IIM Calcutta's business economics and finance department was dominated by a number of eminent left-wing economists who were willing to train us in the Marxist view of economic history and other courses of equal use in finding a job. Perforce, I ended up taking the left-wing economists' classes. Luckily, I found that several universities in the United States were willing to overlook what Indian employers would not. One of them, fortunately, was even willing to pay for my doctoral studies, so that is what I did next.

Interestingly, when I visited IIM Calcutta in 1982 after completing my doctorate in finance at Northwestern University, the capital asset pricing model was still unknown at IIMC. The logic was simple: There was still no demand for financial managers in the Indian economy.

Since those days, the quality of education at the elite institutions has undoubtedly improved. There are many reasons for this, as we will discuss later in this chapter. Unfortunately, an improvement in the standards of governance is not one of them. Until that happens, it is likely that the ability to constantly improve standards will largely be through imitation, as currently happens. The best-run institutions of India observe the syllabi, libraries, and other infrastructure of the best American universities. They aspire to as close a copy as they can afford. But the governance remains what it has always been, creating a mismatch and leading to poor imitation. India's need—to catch up quickly and then march in its own unique direction that the world will look up to—is not going to happen under this approach.

For the moment, though, higher education, especially technical education, serves its purpose of finding a job. The students of India recognize this and compete fiercely for admission to the best universities. For instance, it is common for a student to complete high school and then spend a year preparing for the common entrance examinations to the IITs. Because of the difference in costs, many of the best Indian students choose not to go to equally prestigious overseas universities if they get into an IIT. The acceptance rate is less than 2 percent, which is lower than rates even at the best American universities. I know of an applicant who applied to the IITs and, as a backup, applied to Yale University! He (and his parents) were upset when he was turned down at the IITs. He is now doing well at Yale.

IMPROVING GOVERNANCE IN HIGHER EDUCATION

Improving the management of higher education requires the state to play a role more sensitive and less intrusive than its current role, best described as one size fits all. In the United States, a wide range of state roles has been observed, from regulating fees and costs (a *regulator state* similar to the current role of the state in the Indian higher-education system) to deferring to institutional values and providing money to higher education without taking an active role in defining or ensuring that priorities are met (an *advocacy state*). In between, a *steering state* focuses on policy outcomes and tries to structure the market to realize those outcomes.

Obviously, the role of the state is constrained by the dependence of that educational institution on the state for resources and on the charter of the institution. In general, private institutions will be different from state institutions. They will be less reliant on the state for money and, in consequence, more independent in the design of their structures of governance. Within U.S. state universities, the role of the state tends to focus more on advocacy for upper-tier institutions, whereas lower-tier institutions are usually more tightly regulated in order to improve access to less-privileged populations.

For instance, in California, the role of the state in managing, say, San Jose State University is like that of a regulator and may even be considered intrusive. The state plays an active role in determining salaries and fees in order to relate costs to affordability. It also plays a role in setting admission requirements and assessing infrastructure, such as campus space and library facilities. Faculty must fulfill high teaching requirements, and research is less important than teaching.

The outcome is generally considered to be positive: For instance, more engineers in Silicon Valley are graduates from San Jose State University than from any other university.

In the great public universities, such as the University of California at Berkeley, the state plays a steering role, though in a limited way: It sets fees and costs in order to shape the market but otherwise does not interfere with administration once policy has been set and basic strategies agreed to.

And, finally, in private universities such as Stanford University, the state supports its goals by funding research and student scholarships but does not otherwise interfere in setting policies. In this case, the state plays the role of an advocate of the university's priorities.

In India, the state has, as we have noted, traditionally played a heavy-handed, regulatory role, implemented by layers of bureaucracy leavened with corruption. Faculty, by and large, are not accountable for their performance in the classroom, and students even less so. Young, idealistic faculty often get discouraged by the combination of boorish administrators, entrenched faculty, and apathetic students. The best leave—usually for western shores.

Some things have certainly changed in recent times. For instance, even in some poorer states, at universities such as the state-run Devi Ahilyabai University in the state of Madhya Pradesh, faculty have access to the same electronic journals and databases as the faculty at Stanford University. The situation is undoubtedly as good at the larger Indian universities. This means that the state is finally paying attention to the infrastructure, including the "soft" facilities like electronic journals, whose absence has hitherto been the bane of the system.

But too little has changed, I believe, to conclude that a change in governance in the universities is leading the change in quality. For instance, the role of the college principal or university vice chancellor (equivalent to a university president in the United States) remains bureaucratic rather than strategic. The state insists on this for fear of corruption down the line. For example, the principal is usually required to approve even petty expenditures; I observed, in late 2006, one such person busy signing a sheaf of approvals in triplicate. I asked him why he did this. He said that he was still awaiting state approval to hire a provost to help out!

On a visit to my alma mater, the Indian Institute of Management, Calcutta, I discovered that the institute's director (equivalent to the principal) spends the bulk of his time on internal administration and very little on helping market the institute's image or on fund-raising. In an American university, this would be unacceptable.

The heads of all the dozen-odd higher-education institutions I visited in 2006 were always busy with managing faculty recruitment. When I asked why one would expect an efficient outcome if the principal/director had to personally interview every prospective faculty appointment when he had no particular expertise to make an assessment, the answer was the same as when I asked why the head must also approve petty expenses: The state insists on it because of the fear of corruption down the line.

The fear of corruption arises not because of a lack of controls down the line (there is, if anything, too much control) but because of an expectation of bad behavior. Perhaps we believe the lies fed to us by the Orientalists, those western scholars of the eighteenth and nineteenth centuries with prejudiced views of eastern behavior. For instance, one of them, George Trevelyan, once wrote, "Respect for the obligations of blood-relationship is so strong in the Hindoo mind, that jobbery and nepotism flourish in Oriental society to an extent which would seem inconceivably audacious to the colder imagination of a western public servant."[4] So, as a result, the college principal must scrutinize petty expenses and faculty appointments because, if not, an underling will siphon off the cash and the recruit will teach poorly (and bring his relatives in).

The most direct evidence on the quality of governance is its effect on students' academic intensity. When I was giving a public lecture in Allahabad University in October 2006, bombs (yes, bombs, not firecrackers) were going off as a result of student demonstrations in the distance (though, thankfully, not in protest against my talk). The event was so routine that only outsiders like myself commented on it. When I remarked after my talk that there had been some unusually loud firecrackers going off nearby, my listener laughed and said that these were actually small bombs going off in the distance and that an average of a dozen such explosions a day were routine.

Even in the more sophisticated environment of IIM, Calcutta, I found that my audience of budding MBAs was still out of date. Part of my talk dealt with how the knowledge economy relied on transnational networks. I queried them (as I had not queried their counterparts in the smaller towns) on certain fundamentals of social network theory and on Stanford professor Mark Granovetter's important work on weak and strong ties. Although this had been part of MBA curriculum in strategy and organization behavior for at least a decade in the best U.S. universities, the IIM students had not heard of it.

In Chapter 8, I note the common complaint among the cutting-edge IT firms operating in India: that rote learning still takes a heavy toll on the creativity and project management skills of the Indian student. This is a problem inherited by the student from her days in grade and high school, and the higher-education system has done nothing to alter it. Instead, it nurtures it through static and uninnovative curricula. If anything, the new generation is rapidly giving up studies in the humanities and social sciences in favor of engineering, medicine, law, and other practical fields. This does not bode well for the nurturing of their creative spark.

Therefore, there seem to be other reasons for a general improvement in teaching standards. One is the increasing global exposure of the faculty. The best faculty members at the public universities regularly get lucrative assignments overseas in the Middle and Far East. These are usually temporary, but their salaries will typically be at least five times their earnings in India (which, as of 2006, were capped at a little over $1,000 per month). This keeps the faculty members up-to-date and is a strong incentive to maintain their competence in between such assignments when they return to their home base.

Private universities, once condemned in India for their easy-money attitude, are a new and increasingly important feature of the education landscape. Since being allowed to offer higher education in the 1990s, they have mushroomed. They, too, have played a role in improving the quality of education. They are typically run as for-profit organizations, although many are run by nonprofit trusts as well. Initially, most were poorly equipped and staffed, and they offered degrees of questionable quality. The market has since efficiently sorted out these quick-buck types from the more serious ones. The best are beginning to approach at least the regional public universities of India in quality. The poorly paid public university faculty is an easy source of recruitment. The private universities have cherry-picked the best, as they are easily able to afford at least twice the wage.

Of course, this puts further pressures on the public universities, many of which are seeing their best staff members leave in large numbers. Earlier, even the most mediocre state-run university had the best faculty because there was nowhere else for them to teach. Now, there is healthy competition for faculty—the public sector's lure of permanency being offset in many minds by a shorter tenure of higher wages and low bureaucracy in the private sector.

Private firms are another driver of improved quality. The bigger ones—including several multinationals—finance university scholarship. Currently, this occurs mostly in information technology and includes such innovative firms as IBM and Microsoft. Texas Instruments alone claims research collaborations with more than 400 colleges in India.

EDUCATION AND FREEDOM

Perhaps the most definitive sign of a change in India's education system became visible to me in Indore, a town in India's Hindi heartland, to which I traveled in late 2006. I visited a startup there that produced downloadable applications for cell phones. I was particularly intrigued by its religious software, for want of a better term. It allowed the user to download video clips of prayers of all the major Indian religions.

Its quality was so good that I asked to meet the developers—a compact team of one woman and three men. None of them spoke the Queen's English or even a close substitute. But their English was certainly good enough for the fairly sophisticated work they did. In other words, the gap between the Silicon Valley engineer's standard of English and theirs was substantially greater than the quality of output each was capable of producing.

The Indore engineers whom I met had all been locally educated. They were all trained in Java 2ME, the industry standard language for mobile applications. Because they catered to the Indian market, they were abreast of customer needs. For example, they offered prayers for both genders because the worship is sometimes different for men and women. The firm was doing so well that it had planned to double its staff to fifty-six persons in twelve months. The promoter also knew his market well. When I asked him why he had chosen to develop software for worship, I expected him to say that he had found a need and filled it. He did say this, but added, with a twinkle in his eye, that he chose religious software in part because those who downloaded such software tended to refrain from the sinful act of using pirated versions!

A month later I was in Bangalore, and it appeared to be a world unconnected to Indore. Instead, it was better connected to Silicon Valley, judging by its sleek office buildings, sophisticated backup power systems, and engineers who had worked in the United States and understood its sophisticated markets. The work done here was also innovative.

What, I asked myself, linked the software worker in Indore to his Bangalore counterpart? English, certainly, even if they differed in the sophistication of its use. But if, as I have argued, sophisticated concepts in commerce and technology can only be delivered in English, how was it that the engineers of Indore, with their modest English, could do so well? Kanwal Rekhi, an icon among Indian engineers in Silicon Valley and an astute observer of trends in the subcontinent, says that "once you have the fiber and you know what the market is, there are people who can do this work (software development) everywhere in India."[5]

I came to a different conclusion than that fiber-optic cables had collapsed the economic distance between Bangalore and Indore. I concluded, instead, that the linkage between the two engineers lies in freedom. Nobel Prize–winners Amartya Sen and Jean Dreze have eloquently argued that conventional measures of growth, such as technical progress, are just instruments. They note, "[These instruments] have to be appraised . . . in terms of their actual effectiveness in enriching the lives and liberties of people. . . . We have to see what these goods and services do to the actual opportunities and freedoms of people."[6]

For India's workers, whether in Bangalore or Indore, the freedom to participate in the country's growth is the main change that has happened. This has had a wonderful impact on their incentive to train themselves and upgrade the quality of their lives. It was such a powerful incentive that even the state's regressive role in the quality of education had been offset. Of course, with more sensible state policy, much more could have been achieved.

Thus, I realized, finally, what the audiences of small-town India were really telling me in response to my question on whether a Google can come up in India. Unlike in the past, the Indian workforce wants to be educated. In one way or the other, through the private and the public sector, through the Internet and on the job, it is doing just that.

CHAPTER 8

India and the IT Industry

INDIA HAS BEEN EXTREMELY SUCCESSFUL at providing services to the world, from developing software to manning call centers. There have been many theories as to why, but there is no single answer.

For example, knowledge of the English language is often noted as a key Indian (and Irish and Israeli) advantage; the size of the workforce is another, but the success of Ireland and Israel, which employ only about 30,000 engineers, each belies this. The Philippines' 20,000 software engineers speak English in the American style and work in an environment with better and cheaper telecommunications, roads, and electricity. Yet they are well behind India in the quality of the software they develop. Even in simple call-center work—where American English may be considered as an overriding advantage—the Philippines lags behind India.

Infrastructure is another negative for India relative to the other countries named. In addition, China, keen to catch up with India in software, offers government support and superior infrastructure at a lower cost. It has stronger connections to technology and venture capital companies via the diaspora. There are more than twice as many engineers of mainland-Chinese origin in Silicon Valley than of Indian origin, for instance.

China even produces a better quality of software engineer than India, if one goes by the patent record. Even so, innovative companies like Yahoo! and Adobe are shifting their highest-quality work from all over the world, including China, to India.

Indian government policy has, generally, been unhelpful. In the 1970s, when India began exporting software, policy was statist and protectionist. The state seemed to actively hinder private enterprise in software. It imposed high tariffs on the imports of hardware and software and discouraged foreign companies from operating in India.

But if we consider another key talent that is needed, entrepreneurship, perhaps we shall emerge from the quicksand of unsatisfactory explanations. Indian industry has created a class of determined and innovative entrepreneurs—even if they were not the most technically up-to-date in all fields. That is because after independence entrepreneurship had to be highly productive in order to offset the effects of hostile government policy, crumbling infrastructure, and expensive capital.

BODY SHOPPING AND THE MIND OF THE INDIAN PROGRAMMER

With no significant domestic market and no exposure to world markets, it was impossible for India to conceive of a new software product like the Microsoft operating system. Hence, Indian software began as a custom service—that is, software programs were written to specifications provided by their customers.

To the retail user reliant on mass-produced packaged software like Windows, this might seem like an expensive way to produce software. And it is. Despite this, the global custom-made software industry as of 2007 is worth about $400 billion a year, about twice the size as the packaged-software industry. The reason is that large companies in retail, banking, insurance, telecommunications, and others who view their offerings as proprietary regard the software that is behind these offerings as a competitive tool. For example, a large bank such as Citigroup that offers its customers online banking wants to make its service better than the competition. For this, it needs to customize the service in ways that distinguish it from others. This almost always requires writing software that is specially tailored to the service. It costs more, but it is willing to pay the price.

I hasten to add that India did not invent the writing of custom software. The business was invented by companies like GE trying to capitalize on IBM's decision in 1969 to separate the selling of hardware from software. IBM did this by specifying open standards for its hardware. An independent software provider could use these standards to develop software that would work on IBM's machines.

After IBM made that fateful decision, the software world was never the same. Earlier software firms survived in an IBM-dominated world by providing simple services such as computer maintenance and time-sharing. After 1969, they could also provide software for operating the computer and for specific industry applications that IBM's software engineers might not have written well. A large independent software vendor (ISV) industry quickly developed. By 1974, when India began exporting software, the ISV business was already well developed in the West, particularly in the United States.

At that time, the large mainframe manufacturers, such as IBM and Burroughs, were established in India. Burroughs had a joint venture with TCS, a division of India's largest industrial group, Tatas Industries. As S. Ramadorai, the CEO of TCS told me, "Burroughs soon noticed that our engineers did an excellent job of installing and maintaining Burroughs's products in India. So they asked us if we would send a few of our best engineers to the U.S. to do the same for Burroughs's clients in America." Thus began the business of software exports. TCS sent programmers to the United States to install the systems of Burroughs. The industry's term for the business was *body-shopping*. It was an odd term because the best minds, not the best bodies, of the country were being sent overseas.

The Indian software industry thus began by recruiting for western companies. It sought talent that could mimic western programmers using the same production techniques. The difference is that costs were lower than the West's owing to India's low labor costs and its large labor pool. This approach, termed *labor arbitrage*, had already succeeded in East Asia a decade earlier, though in manufacturing. It was to be replicated with even greater success by China—again in manufacturing—a few years later.

However, there were some differences between China's mass-based manufacturing and Indian software exports. The first difference was that, for the first two decades, software exports from India were not exports of written code. Instead they were exports of people to clients' sites in the United States and other places to write code.

Second, the technology exported to China was, for the first two decades, simpler than what was used in the West. The output that emerged from Chinese factories was of second-tier quality. By contrast, Indian programmers, from the very beginning, worked side by side with western programmers in the same work environment and used the same equipment. They were held to the same benchmarks of productivity as their western counterparts.

Still, it was more expensive than writing the code on Indian shores. There were many reasons why this more expensive method of writing software came to be. First, the usual heads-I-win-tails-you-lose game played by India's statist government resulted in the government, as always, winning.

India's largest installed base of computers was of IBM machines in the early days. In 1973, the government, concerned that foreign companies were using India as a dumping ground for obsolete technology, decreed first that IBM and other multinationals could only operate in India under special conditions. Essentially, they had to sell a majority stake (at least 60 percent) in their Indian operations to domestic interests, either through a private placement or through a public listing. IBM, fearing a loss of control over its intellectual property, chose to leave India in 1978. After IBM left town, the government then announced that it alone, through a state-owned subsidiary, would be allowed to maintain and supply software to IBM's machines in India.

Because IBM was the largest provider of mainframes in India, this prohibition meant that it was not possible for domestic private firms to get any significant local business and, more important, to learn about computing on IBM's machines.

Second, the government imposed such high tariffs on imported hardware and software (135 percent on hardware and 100 percent on software) that it became unviable for a software vendor to buy a computer in India. The government also discouraged hardware imports, arguing that the existing base of computers was adequate for the country's computing needs. Not until 1979 did India's largest software house, TCS, finally obtain permission to import a mainframe. That was five years after it began to export software engineers; even then, according to CEO S. Ramadorai, the high tariff meant that TCS essentially bet the firm on this single action.

Third, the cost of telecommunications was prohibitively high. The government did not think it important for people to own phones, as I have noted in Chapter 4. So, the state made it unduly expensive to connect India with the outside world by modem to download software and work collaboratively across the oceans.

It was, therefore, cheaper to send programmers overseas where their clients could allocate them work, involve them in teams, and write code. In the 1970s, many programmers from the best Indian institutions such as the IITs were paid a thousand rupees a month as their starting salary, or the equivalent of $150. This was less than a fifth of equivalent U.S. programmers. The programmers typically went overseas for no more than six months at a time (in order to stay within visa guidelines). They returned for a few weeks before being sent overseas again. Once their contracts with their Indian employers ended, many of them emigrated permanently to the United States, often to work for their erstwhile firm's clients.

THE BEGINNINGS OF A DOMESTIC SOFTWARE INDUSTRY

Although exporting the programmer rather than the program was a clever way for Indian firms to circumvent high operating costs at home, there was a drawback. It limited learning at home.

By contrast, many American software vendors began in the same way as the Indian software firms, sending their programmers to work on clients' computers. Over time, the programmers began to work offsite from their employers' offices. Some vendors took on whole projects and began developing them in their own offices. Thus, they transitioned from body-shopping firms to project management.

In India, the high costs of hardware and software prevented the transition from body-shopping to project management. This forced the Indian software firms to be little other than recruiting firms on behalf of western clients. This continued until the early 1990s. The industry thus remained tiny at a time when the global software-exports business was beginning to boom. It is a sad epitaph to the truly heroic efforts of Indian software entrepreneurs that, thanks to the state's hostility, not a single software product of any significance was produced in India during this period, either by a domestic or a multinational firm. The services provided by Indian software firms—

mostly system maintenance and small coding projects—occupied the bottom rung of the value chain.

Even the multinational presence was tiny until the mid-1990s. Some multinationals, notably Hewlett-Packard and Texas Instruments (TI), had begun developing software in India in the 1980s. They set up software operations in Bangalore on the basis of promises from the Indian government of a new, more open India. However, they found that the promises given in Delhi were unredeemable in Bangalore. The low labor costs of India were insufficient to offset other high costs and the difficulties of doing business in bureaucratic India.

For instance, initially, the state government of Karnataka (Bangalore is the capital city of the state of Karnataka) was suspicious of TI's motives. Even after New Delhi gave permission for TI India to use a state-owned satellite to transmit data to its Dallas offices, a bureaucrat was still sent every day to TI's Bangalore offices to monitor the use of the satellite. Every evening when TI's India operations completed its daily work and before its work was transmitted to Dallas for engineers there to continue the work (TI's version of the 24/7 model), the bureaucrat would show up. Sitting in front of a printer, he would scrutinize the lines of code that emerged to see if TI was contravening the law. However, after three years, he stopped coming. Perhaps his supervisor decided that the strain of reading undecipherable code made the job too demanding!

Technology came to India's rescue in the 1990s. The workstation and the Unix operating system were introduced at the start of the 1980s. Unix, and its programming language, C, quickly became the industry standard. This allowed a software writer to write code for any computer while sitting at his workstation. The low costs of the workstation relative to the mainframe made the software writer "hardware independent," and the widespread adoption of Unix/C required him to know just the one language.

Just as it revolutionized the software business in the United States, Unix revolutionized the Indian software industry. Software firms now could afford to buy workstations in India, even with the high tariffs, and do the work in India. Slowly, the business of software firms shifted from exporting programmers to exporting software—and the costs came tumbling down.

THE RISE OF BANGALORE

The shift to doing work in India created a need for real estate. Suddenly, Mumbai was no longer as attractive a place to do business. As the country's commercial and industrial center, real estate in Mumbai was costly. Still, Mumbai had become the software industry's center due to its access to capital.

The talent for the software industry was, however, largely located in the south. This was a legacy of the previous century when local patrons created a large technical-education industry focused initially on health and engineering vocations. Of the south's desirable locations, Bangalore, with its relatively mild climate, history of industrial activity, low trade-union presence, and cosmopolitan culture, stood out and became the natural locus for this industry. Interestingly, this was a replay of a situation fifty years earlier, when the British colonial government had chosen Bangalore to locate its aerospace and telecom industries for many of the same reasons— although distance from potential war zones to the east and north was also an important reason.

The shift of work from sending programmers overseas to doing it in India coincided with the financial reforms of 1991. Over the next decade, the state introduced a new mind-set in its policy makers and bureaucrats. Control was replaced by information disclosure. Regulation and the policy mind-set changed to a procompetition and promarket stance.

For the IT industry, the new policies were welcome. With the shift of work to India, it now needed capital to buy real estate and to build large campuses. Obtaining such financing from the capital markets would have been impossible prior to 1991. The rules for obtaining risk capital, which were set by the stodgy office of the Delhi-based Controller for Capital Issues, were working-capital-based. In other words, only working capital could be raised through equity markets, whereas money for fixed assets such as land had to be borrowed from a state-run long-term lender.

However, after 1991, a new regulator based in Mumbai, the Securities and Exchange Board of India (SEBI), was formed. SEBI's rules merely required adequate disclosure. It did not require that certain sources of funds be matched with particular uses. The highly profitable IT firms promptly began to plan public issues of equity capital.

One of the first was Infosys, the country's second-largest software exporter. Even so, Infosys's IPO initially faced public resistance. The reason was that the public was uneducated about the prospects of a business that could grow without a plant and machinery. Whereas, Infosys's IPO stated that the funds to be raised would be used for building a campus and to provide housing for its employees in Bangalore.

I recall this well because I was very much "John Q. Public" on this matter, despite heading the largest foreign investment bank at the time. I recall wondering why the market would provide risk capital to support a housing and office-building project in a tepid real estate market such as Bangalore. It sounded a bit like supporting a public-works project with low returns.

Luckily, the brilliant head of research at our firm came through with such a strong recommendation that I was overruled. We purchased a large chunk of Infosys stock from its investment bankers, and this helped the issue succeed. It turned out to be the best investment our hundred-year-old firm had ever made!

LARGE FIRMS MOVE UP THE VALUE CHAIN

The shifting of software development to India was to have a profound impact on the industry. Apart from saving on travel costs, learning about project management now became possible. Equally important, economies of scale were now possible for the first time. Earlier, the programmers sent overseas were billed on the time spent. Now, firms could offer fixed-price contracts and benefit from economies of scale. They could also write software tools to automate repetitive code. Further, earlier they had to send only top-class programmers overseas, since each could be given any work and would have to perform well. Now, they could use lower-quality programmers for the simpler work and retain their aces for complex work. Not surprisingly, the profits of IT firms began to soar as they shifted work to Bangalore. The decline of telecommunications costs that came after the Internet revolution and changes in Indian telecommunications policy (documented in Chapter 3) further increased their profits.

Since then, the changes in the work in the Indian service companies typify the evolution of the entire Indian services ecosystem. The evolution of the established companies has been stunning in terms of size, breadth of offerings, and depth in verticals. The other change is in the number of new companies that are entering the market with specific skills in high-value-added activities. The new companies are important in increasing the spectrum of activities being offered, and these companies are entering the market with specific domain expertise or skills that are not easily imitable.

Classifying the large Indian software-services providers is increasingly imprecise, because these companies are evolving to include other engineering services and business-process service provisions. The common thread here is that all engineering services are about using software—be it in integrated circuit design, the engineering of products, or providing back-office services.

The last five years have seen a quantum jump in the ability of the major Indian software-services companies to undertake large, complicated projects. Only a decade ago, Indian companies were largely confined to low-level coding and programming. More recently, Indian companies have proven capable of undertaking bigger projects and portions of the software-services value chain that are higher-value-added.

The first dimension of undertaking larger projects is having sufficient numbers of employees. At the end of fiscal year 1999 (March 2000), the largest Indian service provider, TCS, had 17,000 employees, and Infosys and Wipro, the next largest, had approximately 7,000 each. By March of 2006, TCS had 63,000, Wipro had 54,000, and Infosys had 45,000. As of September 2006, TCS had 78,000, Infosys had increased to 66,000, and Wipro had 61,000—plus all three companies had ambitious hiring plans. Though still smaller than IBM, with its global employment of approximately 330,000 (of which approximately 140,000 are in IBM Global Services), or Accenture, with 140,000 employees, the Indian service companies are increasingly able to undertake even the very largest outsourcing contracts.

The Indian companies are ultimately interested in capturing the highest-end work such as R&D services and system integration. There are already indications that some of the service companies are having success particularly in the "D" portion of R&D. For example, in my interviews with Wipro, India's third-largest software firm and one increasingly active in the semiconductor chip-design field, I learned that only three years ago its work was largely confined to the lower-value-added steps of verification and physical design. In the last three years, overseas customers have contracted with it to provide the higher-value-added areas of digital and analog design—and even the architecture of the chip.

The Indian vendor benefits because it can receive improved rates for the project *and* it allows its Indian employees to develop new capabilities. This, of course, satisfies their desire to improve their skills, thereby aiding retention. When one considers that all of these service companies are striving for the same goal, namely moving up value-added ladders in their product areas, the second dimension of changes may be appreciated. Wipro, for example, has become the world's largest vendor of for-profit contract R&D, employing 14,000 employees to do such work. In 2005, the firm filed 58 invention disclosures on behalf of its clients.

Finally, the large Indian companies are broadening their business bases by offering ever more services. For example, in 2006 TCS announced that it had contracted with Boeing to work closely with its customers to design the interiors of new aircraft Boeing had purchased. This contract for $30 million to $70 million led to TCS establishing a laboratory in Chennai for the design of aircraft interiors. Though just an example, it is illustrative of the ability of these companies to broaden their business bases and presumably to increase their value addition.

The Indian companies are remarkable in that they have developed superb process skills. To prove itself, Indian industry had to adopt various global standards for process excellence, whether they were the Capability Maturity Model (CMM) standards for software process maturity, which placed enormous emphasis on creating standardized documentation, or various International Organization for Standardization (ISO) standards. In the business-process area, the influence of the Six Sigma program pioneered by Motorola and made famous by GE is pervasive.

These programs were crucial for Indian vendors that carefully examined and standardized their service-production processes. Just as important, they constantly experimented with methodologies for improving them. They created metrics for measuring efficiency and quality. There is an uncanny resemblance to the way in which the Japanese adopted the Deming/Juran Total Quality Control (QC) ethic after World War II. It is unknown what the QC practice and ethic is at U.S. competitors such as IBM Global Services, Accenture, and EDS, but it is clear that customers will not tolerate quality deficiencies if the Indian vendors can deliver certifiably better quality.

The large Indian companies have, as a consequence of their improved quality of work, become desirable employers. TCS's S. Ramadorai believes that the Indian operations of some global service companies are not yet doing their highest levels of value-added work in India. This is perhaps due to issues of managerial control. Because the Indian service providers do not suffer from this difficulty, he believes they are more desirable employers.

In the beginning of this chapter, I posed the question as to whether the quality of domestic entrepreneurship might explain India's superior performance in the technology industry. Judging a nation's entrepreneurial propensities is difficult at best. The Global Entrepreneurship Monitor of 2002 gave India a high ranking—second among the thirty-seven countries (both rich and poor) that it surveyed.

I have tried to demonstrate that Indian entrepreneurship was primarily responsible for creating its software industry. However, as long as it was hamstrung by the state, the industry remained small and, relative to the world's best performers, not innovative. It took the industry's large companies, such as TCS, Infosys, and Wipro, another decade after the 1991 reforms to consolidate the simpler advantages from the state getting out of the way—scaling up, acquiring a solid financial footing, and so on. Since 2000, the domestic software industry has evolved even more rapidly than before, acquiring scale, depth, and scope at an unprecedented rate.

Many countries, having established a domestic industry, have seen that industry slip away when the barriers to foreign investment were dismantled. Since the mid-1990s, India's domestic software companies have faced a similar situation. The competitive threat comes not just from multinationals but from returnees. The impact on the industry as a whole and on the domestic companies is a fascinating subject whose final outcomes are unknown at this time. We turn to this topic in Chapter 9.

CHAPTER 9

The Overseas Indian and the Multinational Firm in IT

A MOST INTERESTING DEVELOPMENT for the IT industry has been the recent role of the returnee nonresident Indians (NRIs) and multinational IT firms in the Indian IT industry. Professor Martin Kenney of the University of California, Davis, and I have been jointly studying this evolution.[1] From a trickle in the early part of this century in response to the downturn in western economies, the flow of NRIs has rapidly increased as India's success has enabled them to do well in India. The lure for the NRIs is strong. As one of them put it to us, "Where else in the world can I work in an environment where growth rates of 30 percent a year are the norm?" Although their number is unavailable and is probably not very large as a percentage of the workforce, their impact has been significant.

The first discussions of NRIs, whether seen positively or negatively, were couched in terms of a brain drain. The criticism was severe because the NRIs had used their subsidized Indian education to do well overseas with no return for their mother country. Of course, what critics failed to state was that, had such persons stayed home, most would have been unproductive and frustrated like those who stayed behind, as documented in Chapter 5.

The leading Indian software services firms, such as TCS, Infosys, Wipro, HCL, and Satyam, were not established by NRIs, though several of the founders had received degrees in the United States. A few of the early multinational corporations (MNCs), such as Hewlett-Packard, had NRIs in prominent positions, but the population was generally too small to wield significant influence. This suggests that in the early phase the NRIs had only a limited effect on business. They were, however, becoming important as examples of what Indians could do abroad when unfettered by Indian bureaucracy.

I have already noted that several of the early employees of Indian software firms ended up overseas working for the same firms that they were contracted out to by their Indian employers. There is no evidence that any returned home to establish startups. This boded poorly for the domestic software industry. As academics Siwek and Furchgott-Roth noted in 1993:

> For 1986 to '87, 58.5 percent of IIT graduates in computer science and engineering migrated. . . . [The result of this they believed would be] that certain programming activities will continue to leave the U.S. to some extent [of course, at that time the vast majority of Indian programmers were dispatched abroad and worked on the customer's premises]. These activities are more likely to emphasize maintenance rather than basic software design and development.[2]

Even in the late 1990s, scholars evaluating the movement of highly qualified personnel from India to foreign nations saw this as a net loss for India. However, during the dot-com bubble at the end of the 1990s, certain scholars revised the assessment of brain drain, which many had viewed as a negative. They began to see it as a positive brain *gain*, precipitated by overseas nationals who transferred skills they had learned abroad to their homeland.

The true significance of the NRIs is recent and can be roughly dated from the collapse of the Internet bubble, but even more important, it dates from the *growth* of opportunities in India. From my interviews with managers (often NRIs) of cutting-edge technology firms in India, including branches of such innovative multinationals as Adobe and Yahoo!, it appears that NRIs are valued for their familiarity with U.S. management styles, and Silicon Valley's in particular. These are rapidly replacing the hierarchical Indian management style. As the founder of an IT startup in Bangalore said, "The returning NRIs brought with them the sense of execution ethics and accountability that prevails in the U.S. marketplace."[3]

In our interviews with MNC managers and startup executives, we learned it was this execution ethic and deep understanding of how to organize high-performance product-oriented firms that has turbocharged the movement to higher-end work. Within the MNCs and also the Indian startups intent on selling to the global market, NRI managers are particularly important because they have developed world-class management skills abroad. The ability to attract them to India by paying near-U.S. salaries (approximately 60 percent of U.S. salaries for high-level managers) means that seasoned global-class managers are available to manage MNC operations and startups aiming to penetrate the global market.

The availability of global-class managerial talent means that these new operations will not stall for lack of domestic talent trained to take on a global role. In our Indian interviews, we met a number of managers who had career paths that included U.S. education and successful careers at U.S. high-technology firms and startups. They were either returning to India permanently or, at a minimum, returning for extended periods. Their role can be conceptualized as roughly analogous to battle-tested veterans guiding an army consisting almost entirely of highly trained and motivated officers and noncommissioned officers. The returned NRIs appear to be performing exactly this function in India. Over time, some of these raw recruits will also become experienced leaders, creating a pool of home-grown leaders to work alongside the NRIs.

Internationally experienced Indian managers play an important role at the interface between the Indian subsidiary and the MNC headquarters. Over the past five years they have been vital in jump-starting the growth of MNCs, particularly Silicon Valley subsidiaries. The value of these professionals cannot be overestimated. They are vital in convincing headquarters that their Indian subsidiaries can take more and more responsibility for higher-value-added projects. They perform a similar role as key liaisons in binational startups. As Venkat Panchapakesan, manager of Yahoo! India's operations, noted in an interview we did with him in late 2006,

> Prior to 2003, we focused on product extension work. But, around 2002 and 2003, we noticed that we could recruit engineers return-ing to India after significant work experience in the U.S. Their availability allowed us to shift from product extension work to tak-ing on components of a project in its entirety.

Hence, with the returnee NRI have come much more sophisti-cated management practices that are helping break down a key bar-rier to services offshoring, the "face-to-face problem." It is widely known that most services resist remote production because of the need for face-to-face interaction between the provider and the con-sumer. This is obvious in some consumer services, such as having one's hair cut. But it becomes a serious issue when firms wish to undertake innovative work through offshoring.

Until recently it was impossible for multinational teams to coor-dinate closely with one another. However, the returnee NRI is dem-onstrating that coordination is much easier if the cultural benchmarks are the same. It is not actually a technological problem or a time-zone problem but different approaches to solving a problem that have caused coordination to be such a headache.

Google, Yahoo!, and other highly innovative firms in Silicon Val-ley now rely on Indian teams heavily staffed with returnee NRIs at the managerial level to produce the same level of innovative work that is expected of its Silicon Valley offices. In Yahoo!'s case, 80 percent of its Bangalore managers are returnee NRIs. Google is so confident of its India recruitment that it gives new hires a choice of working anywhere in the world that Google has operations, including its Silicon Valley headquarters.

NEW BUSINESS MODELS

The innovative business models being pioneered in India by Yahoo! and others are a part of a larger group of business models that are being explored. Each of these has advantages and drawbacks. The most commonly discussed model is the follow-the-sun (FTS) model, which takes advantage of the time differentials between the United States and India. Effectively using the FTS model is not as simple as it may sound. Initially, many believed that one site would work on the problem and then simply upload it to be worked on at the other site. When everything was working smoothly the model seemed flawless. However, when there were problems with the other team's work that required discussion, everything stopped until the team on the other side of the world explained the problems. If there were numerous difficulties, soon each team would blame the other, and the project might be so impeded that the FTS model was actually slower and more expensive than simply doing the entire project in the high-cost environment.

The FTS solution to this problem was to partition the work. For example, the coding would be done in the United States and testing would be done overnight in India. Or, in data entry or even data-mining applications, the data are processed in India after the end of the U.S. working day and are then ready for use in the United States the next morning. This way there is a clear partition in the work, and responsibilities are well-known. In some cases, the Indian employees are doing low-end routine work, such as data entry or software testing and debugging. But, in other cases, such as the data-mining area, the work can be quite sophisticated. So, the FTS model can offer significant savings in time and costs.

A variant on the FTS model is the division of labor model (DOL). In DOL, a project is broken into various components that are largely modular, meaning that work on the components can proceed with only limited interaction between the two (or more) groups. Often, when the melding of these parallel efforts occurs in chip design for example, it may be necessary to bring everyone together at one location for extended periods of time for fine-tuning and problem solving. Another challenge posed by this approach is that certain functions such as quality assurance may occur at each location. But undoing the redundant efforts by reverting to a single location that houses the common function may cause considerable delays.

A model that is increasingly being adopted by technology firms is what might be termed a total responsibility model (TR). The TR model transfers the entire responsibility for a business unit or functional activity to India. Initially, this is often for a smaller peripheral project, and almost always, at least initially, the responsible manager is an NRI who has had experience in Silicon Valley or in other overseas locations. Often, the NRI is hired overseas and is transferred to India. These persons have the credibility, contacts, and execution ethic of the home-country firm or, at least, embody the ethos and have the ability to execute in ways that headquarters expects.

For many firms this has become the dominant model for organizing the liaison between the U.S. and Indian operations. Moreover, significant responsibility is being transferred. For example, Adobe India has full-product responsibility for PageMaker and FrameMaker. At Broadcom, total responsibility for developing ASIC designs for certain products is vested in the Indian operation. At Yahoo! the India Development Center (IDC) is the global center of excellence for data mining and thus has primary responsibility for this function.

Yahoo! India's experience in reaching its present stage of work is instructive of the time, effort, and commitment required. In 2003,

Yahoo! established its IDC and hired 150 engineers. By December 2006 it had grown to nearly 1,000 employees. But what is more interesting is how its work has evolved. Initially, the IDC operated entirely as a back office for Yahoo! Palo Alto. In general, the work transferred to India was low-value-added and mundane. The result was unacceptably high rates of attrition that were sapping the cost savings. To address this problem, in 2004 Yahoo! moved first-level project management to India, a step that gave the IDC more ownership but created conflicts with Palo Alto–based managers. The solution to this was to move complete responsibility for major activities such as data mining to India. Now the Indian functional manager reported directly to an executive in Palo Alto. With the increasing success of the Indian operation, functional responsibility not only for data mining, but also for mobile applications and podcasting was moved to the IDC.

SAP has another sophisticated model that builds large software programs and has multiple development centers around the world. You could call it the matrix model, in which each product is developed in two centers, not one. In this model, product managers necessarily work in more than one location; they are forced to see SAP as a whole—something more than just their local center.

The idea was that managers could be burdened with complexity, and the higher one went in the managerial hierarchy, the more complexity there would be. Finally, for the individual programmer, his or her immediate supervisor must be local. Preferably, two levels of supervisors were local. The objective of this was to give the programmers immediate feedback and supervision. The matrix model appears to be quite complex but is a method for overcoming localism; it forces interaction and cooperation across the firm's global development centers.

These models for managing the Indian operations may not be that different from those developed by MNCs to manage other mental labor abroad. However, there is one enormous difference between the operations in India and other nations: scale. Indian operations are very often the largest that these MNCs have outside their home nations. Just their size means that properly managing them has direct implications for the firms' success. Ineffective or incompetent integration with the global operations will be extremely costly. By their sheer size, improving operations and extracting more value from the Indian operation may be the most important international business-management challenge that these firms face.

THE ROLE OF STARTUPS

The first sparks of truly unusual innovation are beginning to be observed. The startups are leading the way. A data-mining firm called Marketics Technologies provides an instructive example. In the United States, the data-mining industry for consumer products is highly fragmented, with small, specialized firms usually staffed by highly credentialed researchers. Marketics has approached data mining using a Smithian division of labor model: The more routine work such as data preparation and preliminary analysis is done by the less credentialed employees, while the most sophisticated parts of the work are handled by the most highly trained employees. In March 2007, Marketics was acquired by a large BPO firm, WNS, for $65 million.

Although firms such as Marketics are far smaller in terms of employment (as of November 2006, Marketics employed 400 individuals) than the more general firms, they are growing very rapidly, and it seems safe to say that more firms will emerge as Indian entrepreneurs discover new niches in which part of a service-production process permits offshoring and offshore outsourcing.

Even in simpler work, innovation is visible. In the spirit of South-South collaboration, I offer an example from Pakistan rather than India. A firm called TRG based in Lahore, Pakistan, offers small

American offices a virtual receptionist. I witnessed one such at work in early 2005. Musarrat, aka Margaret, was receptionist to a six-person office in Washington, D.C. Equipped with a TV screen that enabled her to see visitors, she welcomed them to the office, letting them in through a door that she could control from Lahore. As they entered, they realized that they were speaking to someone on a screen, producing a most-bemused look. Margaret would direct them to the kitchen in case they should want water or coffee, meanwhile informing the staff member whom the visitor had come to see that the guest had arrived. She routinely ordered supplies and fulfilled all the normal requests made of a typical receptionist. While I observed, a staff member called and asked her to order a pizza for him; another asked her to order a cab. Since she had the Washington, D.C., yellow pages with her (a hard copy!), this was easy for her to do.

Margaret, paid $300 a month by her employer, can do the work of several such receptionists. Her employer estimates that she could do up to six, although at the time of my observation, she was managing fewer. With the cost of equipment and bandwidth at less than $5,000 a month for six offices, she could replace six receptionists, each earning $3,000 a month.

Another firm, Tutor Vista, based in Bangalore, offers a simple solution to the problem of K–12 tutoring: The student gets a private tutor over the Web, available 24/7. The tutor (who works from home) is provided with the schoolbooks of the student. Tutor and student communicate over the Web through voice, e-mail, and instant messaging. The tutor covers all subjects: In case there are areas in which the tutor lacks knowledge (foreign languages, for example), Tutor Vista will fill the gap through another tutor with the appropriate knowledge. Customers pay $100 per month. Tutor Vista's CEO told me that by late 2006, the firm was adding twenty students a day and has a drop-out rate below 5 percent.

TRG, Tutor Vista, and Marketics operate in cities with large labor pools and relatively sophisticated infrastructure. The system

Tutoring American schoolchildren over the Internet.

is now spreading even to smaller towns with relatively primitive infrastructure but in which the quality of labor and its low costs compensate. I observed a New York bank's servers being maintained from a cramped twenty-two-person office in Indore. Indore is a poor city in India's heartland, several hundred miles from any of India's software hubs. Due to frequent power outages during the daytime, the office relies primarily on automotive batteries connected with an inverter during these times. Yet, its CEO assures me that the system has never failed.

On the contrary, he thinks that he has a unique small-town advantage of even cheaper labor than in the big cities of India. He pays his engineers the equivalent of $300 a month, or about a third below comparable big-city wages; rent and other costs are about two-thirds below big-city costs. He cites scalability as another advantage. Indore has a population of two million and several good engineering schools, thus providing a large pool of talent. When I met him in late 2006, he was busy planning to double his workforce, to be funded out of the profits of his business, thereby proving his point.

As Marketics, TRG, and Tutor Vista show, innovation is happening. There is a profusion of startups in India. The quality of innovation they display and the technologies they use are much more variable than in Silicon Valley for the simple reason that the Indian environment can still absorb lower-end technologies.

Nevertheless, the highest-end in innovation is also visible. Many of the most innovative startups have operations in multiple locations, especially in Silicon Valley. In some cases, this was because the initial establishment of an Indian operation was undertaken by a Silicon Valley firm for reasons of cost saving. Over time, this relationship shows signs of change.

Ketera Technologies, a Silicon Valley–based firm that develops enterprise software, opened its own Indian operations in Bangalore in 2004 after two years of experimenting with vendors. Its former

Silicon Valley–based vice president of engineering, Raj Shah, noted in 2005 that, given the speed with which it was possible to transfer sophisticated work to India, he expected that "only customer-facing roles will need to stay in the U.S." As he then remarked, "I do not see the need for my role in the U.S. as currently described in a year's time!"[4]

Raj was off the mark on timing. About six months after making that remark, in December 2005, he told me that his role in Ketera was over as the work had been transferred to Bangalore. As he put it, "I began to miss the hallway and coffee station side chats that had generated many of our innovative ideas. Then I saw, on a visit to Bangalore, that the informal chats were happening, but they were happening in Bangalore. That is when I realized that my role would soon be over." Raj went on to join Google in Silicon Valley. Part of his initial mandate was to grow its India Engineering. He now coordinates engineering resources for all worldwide centers for Google.

The exact division of labor in Silicon Valley varies by firm. In some cases, the division is between lower- and higher-value-added work, but this makes it difficult to retain the best Indian engineers because they share the universal engineer's motivation to be involved in interesting cutting-edge products. So one of the key issues faced by these firms is how to partition the projects so as to motivate the Indian engineers or, alternatively, which projects to assign to the Indian team. Each of these requires a leap of faith by the U.S. headquarters staff.

Firms such as Ketera challenge the traditional belief that the Indian subsidiary does lower-value-added work than is done in Silicon Valley. One observes almost every conceivable combination in practice. For example, Insilica, a fabless chip firm, has approximately fifteen employees at its Silicon Valley headquarters. These include the C-level executives (all of whom are NRIs); marketing, sales, and operations; the functional heads of imaging and the system-on-a-chip (SOC) groups; and a couple of engineers to support program management for customers. The rest of the firm is located abroad. Such firms are part of a growing tendency for Silicon Valley startups to establish an Indian subsidiary very early in their life cycles or even to have an Indian operation as an integral part of their business plans.

Other startups, from their inception, have essentially all of their engineering and product development in India. For example, the business model for Arada Systems, a startup aiming to provide software solutions around IEEE 802.11 Wi-Fi solutions to the telecommunications, industrial, outdoor, and automotive markets is to have all of the development done in India—and to continually increase the size of the Indian team—while maintaining a small staff in the United States.

There are an increasing number of startups that use growing Indian markets to establish their products prior to advancing into global markets. One apparently successful example of this interesting strategy is Tejas Networks, which designs telecommunications optical switches (actual manufacturing is handled by a contract assembler). Established in May 2000 in Bangalore, it has grown to 300 employees, with 85 percent of its revenue coming from India (the expectation is to grow by 100 employees next year and to double revenues). Except for the chairman, based in Boston, all of the founders (all are returnee NRIs) are in India, and the firm does not yet have a sales office in the United States. However, Tejas plans to grow its foreign sales dramatically in the next few years and make a stock offering on the Indian market. The rapid growth in the Indian telecommunications market (the wireless market in particular) offers Indian firms an opportunity to reach significant scale prior to entering the international market.

One assumption regarding these startups that aim at the global market is that their operations are divided between India and the United States, usually Silicon Valley. I met two firms, Telsima and Insilica, that had operations in Europe. Telsima, a startup established in 2004 to develop WiMAX-based broadband wireless-access software for data-intensive and mobility applications, has its main development center in Bangalore but also employs thirty-five persons in Trzin-Ljubljana, Slovenia, where it purchased a firm with personnel who had sophisticated radio-frequency experience. Insilica purchased a Flextronics semiconductor-design group located in Slovenia that does system-on-a-chip development (an integration of all the components of a computer) and is now integrated with the Silicon Valley and Indian operations. Another similar example was Athena Semiconductors, which was recently purchased by Broadcom. Athena was headquartered in Fremont, California, with a forty-engineer design team in Bangalore, India, and another twenty-three engineers in Athens, Greece. In these firms, the Silicon Valley headquarters continues to be responsible for overall coordination; however, the Indian operations also interact directly with the European branches. The point here is that there are cases in which the Indian operations are key links in a global knowledge network. Of course, working in such environments leads to important learning on the part of the Indian managers.

Still, as I noted, working in the same office can be important for managing certain cutting-edge uncertainties. Broadcom, a leading fabless semiconductor firm, credits its 200-member India team with more than 100 U.S. patents in less than three years. India has done so well for Broadcom that it is one of only three locations that Broadcom permits to initiate new projects (the others are San Jose and Irvine in California); it does not extend this authority even to highly educated locations such as Singapore and Israel, where it has operations. Yet, when it comes to taping out the chip, the final stage before it is manufactured, Broadcom finds that it must bring its engineers face-to-face. The complexities of managing the uncertainties of the logic circuit with the physical layout are just too high to manage through remote communication at that stage.

Finally, there are the startups for the Indian market. This is roughly analogous to the many successful Chinese startups that have listed on the U.S. and other markets. There are a variety of business models here, a number of which are simple translations from the United States, such as travel, auction, and job-listing sites.

Although not very original, these can be good investments for venture capitalists. There are also startups serving the burgeoning local cell phone market through offering applications, such as ring-tone downloads. As was the case with China, the rapid increase in wealth is creating a massive and relatively underserved market with enormous pent-up demand for services. This is also creating a large underserved market that does not speak English, or, in certain areas, even Hindi and other local languages. Here there are opportunities for voice recognition/translation software. For local and international venture capitalists, this offers numerous investment opportunities that require small capital investments.

For venture capitalists, India has traditionally not been as attractive for its local market as for cost savings in serving global markets. These are still significant. According to the CEO of Tejas Networks, building an equivalent telecommunications equipment firm in Silicon Valley would have cost between $100 million and $150 million, whereas Tejas will have cost between $30 and $50 million. In another case, a software/ASIC design firm with fifty engineers in Bangalore pays an average of $40,000 per year per engineer. Compare that to an average salary of $180,000 in Silicon Valley. That is an annual burn rate of $2 million versus $9 million. When comparing the Indian engineers to Silicon Valley engineers, many believed the Silicon Valley team was superior but not sufficiently superior to justify the cost differential, especially when factoring in the NRI advantage.

The role of U.S. venture capital in the startups is, therefore, becoming significant. Although the interaction between the venture capitalist overseas and the Indian teams is not as frequent as would happen were they in the same location—typical interactions are limited to quarterly board meetings—the venture capitalists have been able to help find markets, key consultants, and acquisitions in other countries. In this, they go far beyond the domestic venture-capital firms, whose role for the global-class startups continues to be relatively minor.

CREATING THE ECOSYSTEM FOR
THE INDIAN IT INDUSTRY

Economic ecosystems exist and have existed in many nations. My particular interest here was to show the interaction between two different but interrelated ecosystems, the first for offshore services provision and the second for entrepreneurship. The entrepreneurial ecosystem of interest is what the Global Entrepreneurship Monitor, a nonprofit organization that produces publications on entrepreneurship, terms *high-opportunity entrepreneurship*, to distinguish it from small-scale startups often in the informal retail, agricultural, or manufacturing sectors that have little chance of growing to be significant firms. The two ecosystems discussed here do intersect, as services offshoring provides a space in which the entrepreneurial ecosystem can grow.

There is an ecosystem for entrepreneurship emerging in India, especially in Bangalore and a few other cities such as the New Delhi National Capital Region, Chennai, Hyderabad, and Mumbai. The critical factors in this entrepreneurial ecosystem are NRIs who have returned either to manage startups or to join established MNC firms, particularly Intel, Cisco, Broadcom, Yahoo!, Google, and others with entrepreneurial roots in Silicon Valley. These returnees have contacts in the United States who can be used to mobilize resources.

There are many ways these contacts might operate. For example, their contacts in Silicon Valley might develop a business concept based on low-cost Indian engineering and then contact the returnees to establish and manage the Indian operation. The returnee is responsible for organizing and recruiting for the offshore delivery operation. In this case, the returnee would be a critical member of the startup team. Of course, the NRIs often have important managerial positions in the U.S. subsidiaries in India. Such positions provide important insight into new business opportunities, so they would be well suited to leaving to establish their own firms. They could then build their sales and marketing teams in the United

States (the Israeli model). The NRIs are particularly well suited to establishing global-class operations in India.

The MNC subsidiaries also are promoting Indians to positions of responsibility in which they learn global-class management and R&D skills that could later be used to start new firms. In the case of Israel, the MNCs were important training grounds for managers. As I have shown, increasingly sophisticated work is being undertaken in the Indian subsidiaries, and this is particularly significant in cases where the management of entire business units or products has been delegated to the Indian subsidiary. Thus, a cadre of Indian managers who have the capability of establishing and managing a startup is also being established. So the first requisite for creating an entrepreneurial ecosystem already exists: high-quality entrepreneurs and a labor market replete with skilled managers.

The ecosystem for service provision is much larger than the one for entrepreneurship, as it encompasses the large, established Indian firms; the MNCs; and the entrepreneurial startups. It also includes the central government through the medium of the Software and Technology Parks of India (STPI); the lobbying arm of the industry, NASSCOM; university and research institutions; and a plethora of facilitating organizations such as real estate developers, lawyers, talent search organizations, training agencies, and facilities management firms—all of whom ease the establishment and operation of global service provision. Though the main reason for this ecosystem's existence is to supply existing firms, new startups can also draw from it. The rapidly expanding entrepreneurial ecosystem certainly benefited and, perhaps, would not have been possible with the service-provision ecosystem that predated it.

Until recently, there were few global-class venture capitalists deeply knowledgeable about technology markets operating in India. This is rapidly changing, as major Silicon Valley venture capital firms have established Indian operations. In addition, there are an increasing number of domestic venture capital firms, although these

A software exporter's power source—car batteries—in Indore, Madhya Pradesh.

have yet to become important actors. Moreover, the Indian government is relaxing the various regulations that inhibit venture capital firms. There seems little doubt that if Indian entrepreneurs can create firms that have successful exits, either through listing on global or Indian markets or merger and acquisition, there will be more investment.

The role of Indian universities (discussed in greater detail in Chapter 7) in the development of this ecosystem is mixed. There can be no doubt that the typical Indian university graduate makes an excellent worker, and the graduates from the elite universities and Indian institutes are as good as any in the world. In terms of research, the elite Indian institutions are improving, but they are not yet on a par with tier-one U.S. universities in terms of publications. All of the top institutions have established incubators and/or science & technology parks, which do have some startups. However, thus far there have not been any global-class startups established by Indian professors or students. Whether this will change in the short-term is doubtful. At this point, the most important contribution of the Indian higher-education system to the entrepreneurial ecosystem is a high-quality graduate who can be hired by industry or accepted at the best foreign universities for advanced education.

A system in which there is a rise of 32 percent per annum in the workforce could strain itself trying to grab up all the best engineers. India is facing such a strain. Attrition appears to average 12 percent annually, and salaries rose by 15 percent in the past year. The salary gap between the fresh engineer in India, who earns about $5,000 a year on average, and his counterpart in a developed nation is still substantial, but the gap narrows to less than 2:1 at senior levels.

Despite a generally rising quality of output from the engineering schools, due in part to increased private provision, the average quality of engineer appears to have fallen. This is because demand has increased more than supply, forcing firms to dip deeper down in the talent scale in order to obtain the numbers they need. IBM India, for example, sorts through 60,000 resumes a month, interviews

10,000, and recruits 1,000. Infosys reports that it receives 1.2 million job applications a year.

Firms operating in India are managing these issues in various ways. Many larger firms have in-house training systems. The large firms further rely on their reputation as good employers offering growth and interesting work. Others orient graduates toward their particular requirements. Texas Instruments India, for example, has partnered with more than 400 Indian college campuses, supplying digital-signal processing kits and other course material.

Indian universities and research institutes have done an excellent job of providing a well-qualified workforce capable of creating value in the global economy after significant, but not exorbitant, post-education training. Firms operating in India must compete with western universities luring their brightest young people abroad for further education. The question for India is where to invest its limited dollars—K to 12, or higher education? In Chapter 7, I argued that the historical neglect of K–12 education had cost India dearly. There is also a strong argument for India making a concerted effort to improve its postgraduate educational system. Such an effort would require a significant investment in the research capabilities of its universities. But it may be quite difficult, given the shockingly low professorial salaries in public and private universities, which is already sending some of the best professors to private industry. For a nation entering the global economy on the basis of its citizens' ability to provide mental work, investment in improving the educational system at all levels is and will continue to be of critical importance.

In addition to the ecosystem to support entrepreneurship, India has developed an ecosystem that supports long-distance service provision. In an uncanny resemblance to China's development into the global factory, India may be becoming the global office—and the term *office* is used in the expansive definition—that is, nonphysical work in all its dimensions. Today, office work is predicated on computers linked to a network—much of such work is divided into its constituent parts and can be undertaken remotely. The implications of this statement are enormous, as office work is the largest portion of the overall employment in developed nations.

The multinational service providers in India are diverse in terms of industry segment, business model, and size. For example, even while many financial-service firms use Indian service providers, they are also establishing Indian subsidiaries. For example, JPMorgan Chase plans to have 9,000 employees in India by the end of 2007, Bank of America employs 1,500 employees in two different Indian cities, Deutsche Bank has plans to increase the size of its Indian operations to 2,000 by the end of 2007, and Credit Suisse announced that it was establishing a subsidiary with 1,500 persons in India. In the case of Deutsche Bank, part of its Indian operation will be research staff. Goldman Sachs and Morgan Stanley, the elite investment banks, already have significant research employment in India. In effect, the world's largest banks now find it necessary to have an Indian subsidiary. The side effect of the establishment of operations by so many banks is the development of an ecosystem replete with a labor force experienced at handling financial back-office functions.

There already have been some successful exits on the Indian markets, such as Sasken, a fabless-semiconductor contract-services firm, and a few on the U.S. exchanges such as Exl, which is a BPO firm. Mergers and acquisitions have also led to successful exits. For example, IBM acquired the BPO startup Daksh in 2004 for $160 million and an older Indian IT infrastructure-maintenance firm, Network Solutions, for an undisclosed price; EDS acquired the BPO startup Mphasis for $380 million; and R. R. Donnelly purchased the high-end BPO firm Office Tiger for $250 million. There have been successful exits, and there are likely to be many more as the Indian economy grows and some of the recent startups such as Tejas Networks mature. The previous successes and the large number of recent startups suggest that an entrepreneurial ecosystem is being established in India, particularly in Bangalore.

GLOBALIZATION OF THE INDIAN IT INDUSTRY

The ability to transfer IT-enabled work to anywhere in the world that has the appropriate infrastructure makes India iconic but not unique. Other nations, including the Philippines, Mexico, Hungary, Poland, and China, to name only the most prominent, are also destinations for this IT-enabled work. Having said this, India is clearly the center for this offshoring and has the richest and most sophisticated ecosystem to support the transfer of this work. What is happening is that relatively sophisticated global divisions of labor are being developed through which combinations of offshore and nearshore service support can be given. Sophisticated telecommunications networks allow real-time intercontinental synchronization, enabling the establishment of global networks for service provision.

Another development is that the Indian operations of the MNC firms are receiving global mandates for the provision of certain services or products. For example, Bangalore is the headquarters for Hewlett-Packard GlobalSoft, a globally focused software-development and IT-services company offering third-party services. HP is also considering divesting its BPO business, HP Global eBusiness Operations, also headquartered in India with around 6,000 employees providing financial and other services. For many MNCs, India is the first developing nation to receive global product mandates. SAP Labs India, which employs more than 3,000 persons, is now the largest SAP laboratory outside of Germany and is developing itself as a global center of excellence for certain functions. Adobe India, as noted, now has global responsibility for PageMaker and FrameMaker software.

NEW CHALLENGES FOR THE IT INDUSTRY

The Indian software industry today faces the opposite of the problem it faced when it first began. In the 1970s, hostile government policies forced the domestically funded Indian firms to export their best programmers overseas. Today, with government off its back, the industry relies on returnee NRIs for its sophisticated workforce practices and for the foreign capital that will fund them.

In the larger scheme of things, this is a satisfactory situation only as long as India plays catch-up with the West. The returnee NRIs can help in this process but cannot, almost by definition, exceed their own background. Doing better than the West is only possible if India develops its own innovative ecosystem based on domestically trained engineers and capital.

This may be some years away, for several reasons. First, even catch-up takes time, especially if the target is moving as rapidly as the software sector. Second, it needs the quality of the workforce to improve at a pace greater than that of the West. This requires the quality of university governance and the level of universities' interaction with industry to be well ahead of its current level. At the moment, the level of interaction between universities and industry is low. For instance, I estimate that over 90 percent of the final, fourth-year engineering projects of the typical computer science undergraduate student are done within the university environment, not in a corporate laboratory, as is more typical in the West.

The current state of Indian entrepreneurship in the IT industry has evolved considerably from its recruiting-firm character of the early days. First, though understanding the entrepreneurial environment is difficult because of its complexity, many new firms with a wide variety of missions are being formed. Second, with venture capital and other professional services now available, an ecosystem for supporting entrepreneurship is being built—although there remain serious gaps in university-industry interaction. Third, the availability of returning NRIs from high-level management positions, often in U.S. startups, is providing Indian startups and the Indian subsidiaries of U.S. startups seasoned professional managers. Fourth, it is possible to build near-global-class or global-class startups in India. Fifth, there is every reason to expect a continuing and accelerating pace of startup formation; it is possible that in the next two years there will be some attractive exits either through public listing or M&A. If these exits occur, they will have a powerful, positive effect on the pace of startup formation. The ecosystem for entrepreneurial startups is rapidly maturing, and this should increase the rate of startup formation and the willingness of venture capitalists to invest.

As India develops its IT talents, one is led to wonder if all communication will soon be virtual simply because it is cheaper and it works. Paul Maglio, a cognitive scientist at the IBM Almaden Research Center in California, who researches this question, is doubtful. As he points out, at the cutting edge of innovation, the ability to communicate is more and not less important; and face-to-face communication is usually a must.

By contrast, Ayan Mukherji, a senior vice president of engineering at India's third-largest software company, Wipro, argues that the discipline induced by remote communications has had a powerful effect on the quality of work. No longer, he argues, can an engineer working with a colleague get by with unclear communication. The absence of tacit understanding enabled by face-to-face communication forces the engineer to communicate his requirements explicitly and clearly, an outcome that in fact leads to much better outcomes than before. As Ayan puts it, "Remote communication, especially across time zones, prevents carelessness."[5]

Both Paul and Ayan have a point. Communicating over the wires improves the quality of what can be communicated and even increases the limits of what can be communicated between people who do not know one another well. But a limit, as I noted for Broadcom, is still likely to exist.

One should not overemphasize the success factors, of course, no matter how significant they are in improving India's capabilities to execute high-value-added work. While the achievements of the last few years are stunning because of the change in the quality of work, there are still obstacles to doing more of the highest-quality work in India. The absence of detailed market knowledge and inter-action with the most sophisticated customers in the world handicaps the ability of Indian engineers to work in many areas.

As the manager of a large MNC noted in a statement that was repeatedly echoed in several firms that I visited in late 2006, "It is easy to do cutting-edge work in India and to manage large projects. The difficulty is in launching products from India, especially the last stage between putting it all together and going live. There is also a gap in capability in conceptualizing projects from India."[6]

A final dimension is that it takes time to build sophisticated capabilities in-house. As the case of Yahoo! shows, it takes two to three years before high-end work can be done in-house. I have found this to be typical across several firms. This is probably due to a combination of building the firm's work ethic in a new environment, concerns about lack of control, the changing maturity of Indian en-gineers and, last but not least, refining the business model.

The initial motivation when a firm enters India is to access lower-cost labor. This motivation is unlikely to change completely as long as India is a cost-effective environment. As a result, the Indian subsidiary is likely to undertake much mundane service work that the MNC's home-country employees find repetitive and uninterest-ing. But efforts are ongoing to also transfer higher-value-added work to the Indian subsidiaries that are showing not only the ability, but the desire to undertake higher-level work.

This model is understandable from two perspectives: First, U.S. employees are often willing and even eager to shift such work to India. Second, for management, the risks are low. If the low-level work is of acceptable quality, then managers will feel more comfort-able shifting higher-level tasks that require more discretion and capabilities. Not surprisingly, the Indian managers and employees soon find the original work uninteresting, and attrition rates can be challenging. Whether an operation whose sole activity is mundane can be sustainable is unclear. A serious turnover issue may arise if the most capable Indian personnel are unsatisfied with their work. Nonetheless, there can be no doubt that such work still occupies a preponderance of the work done in India. And for many MNCs this allocation of global responsibilities is likely to remain.

BANGALORE'S OPPORTUNITIES AND CHALLENGES

Bangalore is the chosen destination for all the major technology firms. Yet, today's visitor to Bangalore might be somewhat disappointed at the signs of success. This is perhaps not unlike the metamorphosis of Silicon Valley from an agricultural area to a less attractive spread of warehouse-type offices and laboratories— though Bangalore's development is accompanied by pollution and bad city planning.

The garden city, as Bangalore was known, is choking on its success, with automobile fumes, power and water cuts, a shortage of roads, hotter days, and fewer gardens in sight, as the available space gets converted to apartments and housing. Some of these mimic the best American housing complexes, with fenced-in security and clubs with swimming pools, tennis courts, and fitness equipment. But many more are left outside the fence than inside it, so there are worries of a digital and ethnic divide. The most educated persons of Bangalore are not the natives (Kannadigas) who claim the city as their own but instead are from nearby Tamil Nadu, Andhra Pradesh, and other regions.

This divide suddenly and tellingly became visible when the legendary Kannadiga actor Raj Kumar died peacefully of natural causes at the age of 77 in April 2006. Raj Kumar had played the action hero in more than 200 Kannada films in his career. Fans rioted several times over the next few days in expressions of anguish at his death and when they felt they were denied a proper view of his body. But

The Asian miracle: coping with pollution and crowded roads.

many observers felt that people were also rioting at Bangalore's prosperity, in which—as construction workers, maids, and chauffeurs—they could not share. As Atiq Raza, the brains behind AMD's microprocessor chip who now runs an engineering software house out of Silicon Valley with offices in Bangalore, put it to me in early 2007, "We are paying 15 percent higher every year to retain the engineers we hire while the salary we pay our company chauffeurs has not changed. It is still Rs.3,500 a month (about $80)."

Bangalore epitomizes the challenges of the new India. There is excitement at the global implications of what is being built, even as there are doubts about who within the country will benefit and who will be left out. From a business viewpoint as well, the future is difficult to predict. But if the past is prologue, the Indian ecosystem for services provision and for entrepreneurship looks very promising indeed. There can be no doubt that India is challenging the traditional view that it is not possible to do highly sophisticated work there and deliver it remotely. In this way, India is debunking the concept of a global division of labor based on stages of development. India is pioneering a new model of development based on mental labor rather than physical labor.

THE IMPORTANCE OF MULTINATIONALS

At the end of the Chapter 8, I raised a question of some importance to Indian policymakers and domestic firms. Does the rise of the MNC in the Indian IT industry since the mid-1990s pose a long-term threat? At the moment, there is enough growth for all. The question is what will happen in the long-term.

There is little doubt that the MNCs plan to make India an integral part of their operations. The decision to create an IT offshore unit in India is no longer a policy decision but a strategic one regarding timing and business model. Firms such as IBM, HP, and Accenture each have more than 10,000 people in Bangalore. Some, such as IBM, expect to have 100,000 by 2010 and to spend $6 billion by then on developing outsourcing from India. As one drives through Bangalore—always at a snail's pace, owing to its crowded roads— there is ample time to see the many buildings with "famous" names like IBM, Dell, HP, and Accenture plastered on top—no doubt a recruiting tool in the hot IT market that is Bangalore.

The multinationals have helped the Indian software industry break out of its low-end work of writing code to client specifications. Some, such as the Fortune 100 company Cisco, have publicly stated that they are committed to seeing 20 percent of their top management emerge from their India operations and for India to be the second-largest center of innovation after their American headquarters. Cisco has even designated Bangalore as its second global headquarters after Santa Clara, California.

New fields, such as contract R&D for automobiles, have emerged. Software product development and contract R&D made up over a quarter of the IT industry's revenue in 2006. This is undoubtedly linked to the rising presence of MNCs.

Most Global 500 firms (and many smaller companies) now have a direct presence in India through subsidiaries; others maintain a presence through work that is outsourced to an Indian services vendor or a developed-nation service vendor that delivers at least part of its service from India. The largest of these firms, such as Citicorp, have multiple Indian operations that can include contracts with Indian outsourcers both in IT and business-processing outsourcing (BPO), and contracts with MNC outsourcers like IBM and Accenture that have an Indian component in the delivery model and have one or more Indian offshore subsidiaries.

The MNC subsidiaries can be divided into two groups: First, subsidiaries whose sole role is to work for the parent, e.g., Yahoo!, Google, Cisco, General Motors, HSBC, Citicorp, etc. Second are subsidiaries of IBM, Accenture, HP, EDS, Convergys, and others that provide outsourced services. Of course, many of these MNCs are also transferring their internal work such as human resources and finance to their Indian subsidiaries. Both MNC groups are experiencing growth in size, spectrum of activities, and the quality of work they are undertaking.

The MNCs are interesting because, as we have discussed, they are pioneers in understanding how to do high-value-added work in India and in implementing the business models that make this possible.

The lessons for the future of leadership of the Indian IT industry are probably more widely applicable than just to India. The Indian experience shows that it takes several decades for a high-technology industry to grow via domestic entrepreneurship. Allowing MNCs at the earliest stages will no doubt jump-start the process and raise value addition more quickly than if only domestic companies are allowed to operate. However, this benefit may be at the cost of industry leadership. The recent rapid growth of MNCs and Silicon Valley–headquartered startups suggests that the IT industry's leadership will increasingly have to be shared between the domestic companies that founded the industry and the newcomers from abroad.

CHAPTER 10

Faith and Tolerance

ARRIVING IN AHMEDABAD, the western state of Gujarat's largest city, on a December morning in 2006, my thoughts were on the sectarian riots that had rocked the city nearly five years earlier. From my window seat on one of India's newest airlines, SpiceJet, Ahmedabad looked like any other Indian city as seen from an airport: a mixture of greenery and tin shacks. The greenery belongs to the airport and is closed off from the outside world by high walls. Outside these walls, the burgeoning migrant population rules the roost from its tin shacks. There is no space for roads or trees in between these shacks, and hardly any for the people themselves.

In March 2002, riots maimed the 400,000-strong Muslim community of the city, which made up over 10 percent of its population. Within a month, 1,000 Muslims were killed and 200,000 permanently lost their homes in an intense pogrom unleashed by Gujarat's chief minister, Narendra Modi. Because of this terrible event, Modi is incredibly popular. A friend of mine from Ahmedabad expressed a commonly held belief that "if Narendra Modi puts his dog up for election, the dog will win by a landslide."

I was curious to see how that ill-fated city had fared since the riots. My earlier visits to Ahmedabad had revealed a city increasingly divided by religion since the mid-1980s. The Muslim population has been ghettoized through a systematic, state-sponsored, violent effort to stamp out any signs of economic resurgence. In response, foreign investors and many domestic ones as well stayed away.

Then–prime minister Atal Behari Vajpayee, whose Bharatiya Janata Party ruled in Gujarat, was reluctant to visit those hit by the riot. He stayed away from Ahmedabad for weeks after the riots were over. Even when he finally visited the city and had made a public statement, it incited passions rather than calmed them. Rather than ask for peace, he, like his party colleague Modi, argued that the riots were a justified, even restrained, retribution for the burning of Hindus in a train elsewhere in Gujarat. Later, it emerged in an official report of the federal government that the burnings had been staged by Modi's government in order to start the riots.

Even so, the riots were not an uncontrollable, anguished response to this staged event, as made out by the state government. The president of India at the time, K. R. Narayanan, was constitutionally barred from speaking publicly (under Indian law, the president may only speak publicly with the permission of the prime minister and the cabinet). He was later to say that "the Gujarat riots were the result of a conspiracy between the BJP governments in the state and at the Centre, which also led to the army not being given powers to stem the violence."[1] Narayanan said he wrote several letters to Vajpayee during the riots, asking him to deploy the army and quell the violence. Instead—perhaps to catch the post-9/11 neoconservative mood in the developed world to which he thought Indians should subscribe—Vajpayee was later to state, "Wherever Muslims live, they don't like to live in co-existence with others . . . instead of propagating their ideas in a peaceful manner, they want to spread their faith by resorting to terror and threats."[2]

A local BJP legislator from Ahmedabad, Maya Kodnani, captured the moral stoop of her party when she told a fact-finding team,

"There was nothing the state could do to stop the violence. There was a natural hatred and anger in the heart of every Hindu and we could not control it."[3] Several witnesses later alleged that Kodnani had been with the mobs on the very first day of the riots. Kodnani denied the allegation, but it was later confirmed by cell phone records obtained by the *Indian Express* newspaper. The records placed her in the thick of the riot-torn area, conversing with individuals who were later indicted for inciting and leading the riots.

A Muslim who lived through the riots, traumatized but physically unharmed, wrote about the relief camps set up by the state government. They all lacked basic amenities, such as water taps and electricity, and no food or living supplies were provided. The NGOs took over the state's job, focusing on providing food and water. "Over 100,000 Muslims are in the camp," he wrote in early March:

> The divide [between Hindus and Muslims in Ahmedabad] is very clear: On the one hand, you have people enjoying normal life— going to work, schools, parks, restaurants, socializing; on the other hand, the Muslims, including people like us, are afraid to venture out of the house. There are reports of VHP [Vishwa Hindu Parishad—a BJP-affiliate] activists collecting details of Muslim children from various schools, which is a nightmare for us.

He further wrote:

> The other day, I came face to face with VHP activists after attending a NHRC [National Human Rights Commission] meeting [with a group of Muslims]. They surrounded [our group] and began threatening and abusing us, even pulling the beards of some of the group . . . and giving us the ultimatum that either "leave the country or live on our conditions." This happened in the presence of the media and the police, who just stood by and watched.[4]

Women in particular were targeted. Indeed, the riots seemed to be characterized by sexual assaults. Harsh Mander, an experienced officer of the Indian Administrative Service, who visited the riot-hit areas on a fact-finding mission ten days after the riots began, wrote,

"I have never known a riot which has used the sexual subjugation of women so widely as an instrument of violence. . . . There are reports everywhere of gang-rape of young girls and women, often in the presence of their families, followed by their murder by burning alive."[5]

A six-member fact-finding team of women (among whom were two Muslim women) who visited the city a month after the riots reported the following:

> [We were] shaken and numbed by the scale and brutality of the
> violence that is still continuing in Gujarat. Despite reading news
> reports, we were unprepared for what we saw and heard; for fear
> in the eyes and anguish in the words of ordinary women whose
> basic human right to live a life of dignity has been snatched away
> from them. . . . Among the women surviving in relief camps are
> many who have suffered the most bestial forms of sexual vio-
> lence—including rape, gang rape, mass rape, stripping, insertion
> of objects into their body, stripping, molestations. A *majority* [my
> emphasis] of rape victims have been burnt alive. There is evidence
> of state and police complicity in perpetuating crimes against
> women. No effort was made to protect women.[6]

Instead, the police usually stood quietly by until the mob had finished its work and then urged them to burn the victims completely so as to leave no evidence.

THE BURDEN OF CIVIC RESPONSIBILITY

The report also indicts the press, noting that parts of the media stimulated the violence in various ways, ranging from false reporting to silence about the carnage:

> Sections of the Gujarati vernacular press played a dangerous and
> criminal role in promoting the violence, particularly in provoking

sexual violence against women. . . . On February 28th [the day the violence began], *Sandesh*, a leading Gujarati daily, in addition to reporting the Godhra tragedy in provocative language, ran a story on page 1 saying the following: "10–15 Hindu women were dragged away by a fanatic mob from the railway compartment." The same story was repeated on page 16 with the heading "Mob dragged away 8–10 women into the slums." The story was entirely false. The police denied the incident, and other newspapers, including the *Times of India*, could not find confirmation of this news. A day later, on March 1, 2002 Sandesh carried a follow-up to this false story on page 16. . . . [Some days later], *Sandesh* did publish a small retraction . . . but the damage had been done.[7]

Most disheartening of all, it seems clear that while the riots were planned and executed by the state in conjunction with hired gangs, most locals were passively guilty of doing nothing. One could argue that, in a more civilized society in which the police do their jobs, the locals ought not to have to respond. After all, stopping a rioting mob in India is fairly simple. Thanks to tough gun-control laws, rioting mobs in India use sticks, crowbars, and gasoline, apart from the sexual tools that the fact-finding team wrote so dispiritedly about. These laws are so tough that even those in danger of being killed by a mob are not allowed to obtain licenses to own firearms.

As police reports have repeatedly noted, stopping a riot is as simple as an armed policeman challenging a rioter to cross the threshold of unacceptable behavior that will result in him being shot. The presence of just one policeman bearing a firearm is known to be effective against an unarmed mob of dozens. This is why then-president Narayanan was so keen to get the army in action to quell the Gujarat riots: Past experience had shown that an independent force could do so almost immediately.

There is much, however, that the common man could have done but did not do through public action. For instance, the Mumbai riots of 1993 showed the possibilities and power of cooperation. As in Ahmedabad, the police generally ignored the rioters or abetted them, provided they were Hindus. In response, citizens created *Mohalla Ekta Committees* (Locality Unity Committees) that, in many areas, ensured that Hindus and Muslims would immediately respond to reports of rioting and calm their constituencies. Other groups created networks of fifty or more persons (primarily, influential Hindus) connected by the phone. If any one of a network received a call from a Muslim family under attack from the rioters, they would inform each other and descend, en masse, to the scene in a few minutes to face the rioters. Having lived in Mumbai at the time of the riots, I was aware of several such confrontations leading to the rioters backing off when faced with these groups. Yet, in Ahmedabad, the common man lost his sense of civic duty or, at least, tolerance of other religions.

PLURALISM AND TOLERANCE

Ahmedabad that winter morning in 2006 when I visited had the signs of a city on the move. The roads were wider and cleaner than before. The cell phone towers, India's signature of progress, were everywhere. The airport still had a small-town feel, but that appeared likely to change soon, judging by the construction going on in the terminal area. Indeed, the thriving middle-class feel to Ahmedabad was evident as my host and I drove on the Ahmedabad-Gandhinagar highway to the institute of management, where I was to deliver a speech on entrepreneurship to about 200 MBA students.

Even more than its erstwhile nineteenth-century rival to the south, Mumbai—itself a debtor to the enterprise of Gujarati migrants in its early days—Ahmedabad felt like what Indian cities should look like at the current stage of the country's development. Where Mumbai shocks with its extravagant high rises perched amid slums conveying (correctly) the impression of a symbiotic relationship between the haves and the have-nots, Ahmedabad appears to have greater equality—smaller apartments but fewer slums. Similarly, the salaries that high-end professionals earn in Mumbai are

View from a luxury hotel.

benchmarked against the West. For example, the CFO of a large company operating from Mumbai would commonly earn at least $100,000 a year. In Ahmedabad, she would be more likely to earn $10,000.

Like most Indians, Ahmedabad's inhabitants are religious. Indians worship primarily at home. Their external forms of worship in temples, churches, and mosques, though more visible in recent years—especially as ways of displaying identity—remain a minor part of the time spent in prayer.

To many Indians, the Western concept of God is of a being far removed from one's own being. The high ceilings of the church and the raised icon of Christ at the altar seem to convey both majesty and distance. The Eastern religions are different, including the Eastern (and earlier) version of Christianity. God is close at hand and to be worshipped, often absorbed, in all His manifestations—the shrine of a saint that one may touch; an icon of clay so tiny that one can, and does, hold Him in one's hand; and the enlightened human beings through whom one may come closer to Him.

One consequence of such a close, personal relationship between man and God is the belief that destinies, both worldly and spiritual, are different across individuals. Even worshippers of the same faith are expected to have differing beliefs because of their different personal experiences in worship. Hence arises the need to be respectful of someone else's beliefs—one is expected to learn from them and, perhaps, even practice them if they appeal. To Indians, tolerance is a consequence of a common belief that each person will have a spiritual path that is unique but offers learning opportunities for all.

This may sound very subtle but is real enough in its impact. The *rakaabi* believer was a common and respected worshipper in the Calcutta of my childhood. *Rakaabi* is a local word meaning "a plate onto which one fills one's food." The rakaabi believer sampled all faiths, filling his (spiritual) plate with the aspects that suited him best. Mostly, he would find something of value in each faith. For

A flock of crows checking out Mumbai's Bombay Gymkhana Club, where the elite also flock.

instance, in Calcutta, the city of my birth, it was common for Muslim business families to begin their financial year on Diwali, the Hindu festival that celebrates the triumph of good over evil. Christmas was traditionally called *Bara Din* or "big day," a status not given to any other faith and celebrated by thousands of non-Christians with attendance at Mass. The foremost exponents of the esoteric Hindu rite of *tantra* in Calcutta were Muslims. So where did this tolerance go?

THE SOURCES OF SECTARIAN CONFLICT

Even up to the 1970s, Ahmedabad (named after a Muslim sultan of the fifteenth century, Ahmed Shah) would have been considered an unlikely site of sectarian riots. Apart from its citizens' reputation for focusing more on business than on social division—a trait that made it India's industrial leader by the time of independence from Britain—it was a leader in public action around the independence movement. Since the 1980s, it has, however, been a regular site of Hindu-Muslim conflict. Was Ahmedabad a microcosm of things to come in the rest of India? And if so, why?

It is common to blame the caste system for many problems, including those between Hindus and Muslims. The Hindu caste system has indeed been the source of great discrimination (and violence) against weaker castes and outcasts. It, therefore, challenges the tolerance that arises from the personalization of religion just discussed. Although the date of origin of the caste system is not exactly known, it was certainly well established by the early nineteenth century. The caste system identifies the Brahmins as the highest caste responsible for priestly and scholarly activity, thus taking responsibility for spiritual and intellectual governance. The Brahmins share governance with the Kshatriya (warrior) caste, which took responsibility for temporal governance; the other castes were below them in importance of work done, such as trading, farming, and processing goods and services. The lower castes are named differently in different regions of the country.

The status of those outside the caste system, such as untouchables (Dalits) and tribals, is disputed. Some have argued that they are not Hindus (although many, if not most, would think of themselves as Hindus) because they are outside the caste system. The Dalits and tribals make up about a quarter of the population, the lower castes about half the population, and Brahmins and other religions the rest. Muslims are the largest minority faith, making up about 13 percent of the country's population.

The caste system remains intact in modern times, though the lower castes would gladly give it up. It exists, therefore, because of resistance to change from the upper castes. Although often explicated as a sensible division of labor in earlier times and of little modern relevance, the fact is that upper-caste Hindus have not surrendered their caste identities in modern times. They maintain them in temple rites, caste-compatible marriages, and caste-based voting. This shows that the adherence to the caste system must be explained by deeper roots. Some have argued that the higher castes were alien conquerors, others that skin color was a factor, and that the higher castes still have an internal sense of superiority on one or more of these accounts. Others of the high castes, perhaps a little more enlightened, have argued that the existence of the caste system represents a past that they wish had not happened even as its sheer and overwhelming presence forces them to live with it in the present.

Examples of a culture vitiated by the caste system indeed exist, although it is not obvious that this applies only to Hindus or more generally to a nation beset by oppressive colonial rule for generations. A noticeable though minor impact is the obsession with fair skin colors. This shows up in matrimonial advertisements and the overwhelming commercial success of a facial cream called Fair & Lovely that is meant to "unlock the secret of glowing fair skin . . . (and) unveil your natural radiant fairness in just six weeks." On its

Web site, the company making the product (Hindustan Unilever Limited, a subsidiary of the global firm Unilever) used to call its product "the miracle worker," which was "proven to deliver one to three shades of change."[8] Protests from women's rights groups forced it to change its advertising. Its Web site now merely notes: "A woman's passion for beauty is universal and catering to this strong need is Fair & Lovely. Based on a revolutionary breakthrough in skin lightening technology, Fair & Lovely was launched in 1978."[9]

Some scholars argue that the origins of Hindu-Muslim rivalry, too, lie in the caste system. The argument is that many Muslims converted from Hinduism to escape the strictures of their low-caste birth (only partly true). The current rivalry is simply a version of intercaste rivalry made more deadly by the Muslims' renegadism. The argument is used to explain why Hindu-Muslim conflicts are usually between Muslims and upper-caste Hindus (although, as communal riots in Gujarat and Maharashtra have demonstrated in recent years, this is not always the case) and why caste conflicts often segue into Hindu-Muslim violence.

Others argue that the roots of the conflict are ancient ones. The origin of Hindu aversion to Muslims is often asserted by Hindutva activists to have old roots, going back to the year 1026. This was the year that the Muslim Mahmud of Ghazni laid waste to the Somnath temple, one of Hinduism's holiest temples, during one of his periodic summer raids from his home base of Afghanistan. Mahmud's motives are disputed by historians, because a leading general of his army was a Hindu. At least he appears to have had pillage as a motive (possibly secondary if not primary) for his raids, as evidenced by their frequency and by the fact that he also raided and destroyed Muslim establishments in the Multan (now part of Pakistani Punjab).

Proponents of Hindutva aver that all Hindus have felt an aversion to Muslims since then. The aversion increased when the Mughal emperor Babur built a mosque in 1528 on a site allegedly consecrated to the Hindu god Ram, another disputed event. These two events concretize, in the minds of Hindutva protagonists, the sense of oppression that they feel on behalf of their ancient co-religionists who, despite constituting a majority of the population, were subject to several centuries of Muslim rule.

A third possible cause is the economic decline of the Muslims. It was during British rule that Hindu-Muslim antagonism became increasingly evident, and there appears to be a link between the Raj's differential treatment of Hindus and Muslims and the rise of communal rivalry. What is known is that, relative to the Hindus, the Muslims declined economically during British rule. Some have argued that this was because, in their minds, Muslims collectively felt so much anguish and resentment at the loss of their status as the ruling elite when Mughal rule ended that they mostly retreated into a shell. They switched over from secular education to studying only the Quran and, thus, declined. Interestingly, this argument is usually made by Hindutva proponents, who use the same argument to explain Hindus' lack of protest to Muslim rule in earlier times.

However, in an age of poor communication and in the absence of nationalistic or other impulses to create a common Muslim ethos, this conclusion must be dismissed as being as far-fetched as the notion that Hindus, collectively since 1026, have kept the embers of revenge for the destruction of Somnath temple alive in their hearts.

Instead, the more straightforward explanation for Hindu-Muslim rivalry is that the British chose to discriminate against Muslims. The reason for this is also straightforward: as conquerors of the Mughal empire, the Raj, like any good Orientalist, assumed that Islam was the ruler's primary identity and that the conquest of India required retribution against Muslims. A century later, both Hindus and Muslims originated a mutiny in 1857—the most serious challenge to British colonial rule. Again, the British blamed the Muslims because the mutineers were under the command of the last Mughal, Bahadur Shah Zafar. Once they took direct charge of India from the East India Company in 1858, the British continued to discriminate against the Muslims for government employment, hoping that a decline in their economic status would reduce the chances of a second mutiny.

By 1871, a British writer, William Hunter, examining the state of Muslims in Bengal, found the following:

> Now all sorts of employment, high or low, great or small are being gradually snatched away from the Mohammedans [Muslims], and given to other races, particularly Hindus . . . The proportion of the [Muslim] race, which a century ago had the monopoly of Government, has now fallen to less than one twenty-third of the whole administrative body. This, too, in the gazetted appointments, where the distribution of patronage is closely watched. In the less conspicuous office establishments in the Presidency Town, the exclusion of Mussalmans is even more complete. In one extensive Department the other day it was discovered that there was not a single employee who could read the Mussalman dialect; and in fact, there is now scarcely a Government office of Calcutta in which a Muhammedan can hope for any post above the rank of porter, messenger, filler of ink-pots and mender of pens.[10]

Thus, by the early twentieth century, from being the most educated and elite group during Mughal rule, the Muslims of India had been, to quote Hunter, "reduced to bahistee [water-carriers], woodcutters, peons or pen menders in offices."[11] By the time of partition in 1947, even a sympathetic writer like Urvashi Butalia was, perhaps unconscious of the class distinction implicit in her writing, to state that the exchange of population (Hindus going to India, Muslims to Pakistan) had the following impact:

> [In India], the departure of barbers, weavers, tailors, goldsmiths, and others en masse to Pakistan, crippled certain aspects of life, particularly in Delhi. In Pakistan, the departure of accounts clerks, bankers, lawyers and teachers dealt a similar blow, *albeit at a different level* [my italics], to life there.[12]

This was a far cry from the status of the Muslims in earlier times. In 1844, William Sleeman, a colonial official, wrote about the madrasas (Muslim-run schools providing both secular and religious education) in Delhi:

> Perhaps there are few communities in the world among whom education is more generally diffused than among Mohammadans in India. He who holds an office worth twenty rupees a month commonly gives his sons an education equal to that of a prime minister. They learn, through the medium of Arabic and Persian languages, what young men in our colleges learn through those of Greek and Latin—that is, grammar, rhetoric and logic. After his seven years of study, the young Mohammadan binds his turban upon a head almost as well filled with the things which appertain to these branches of knowledge as a young man raw from Oxford—he will talk as fluently about Socrates and Aristotle, Plato and Hippocrates, Galen and Avicenna (alias Sokrat, Aristotalis, Aflatun, Bokrat, Jalinus, and Sena); and, what is much to his advantage in India, the languages in which he has learnt what he knows are those which he most requires through life.[13]

The Raj did not just discriminate against Muslims for jobs but also used the tools of the educational system. Arguing (successfully) to the Viceroy's Council that the printing of Arabic and Sanskrit books be stopped and that all students in state schools from the sixth year of schooling onward would only learn English, Lord Macaulay was to say in 1835:

> I am quite ready to take the Oriental learning at the valuation of the Orientalists themselves. I have never found one among them who could deny that a single shelf of a good European library was worth the whole native literature of India and Arabia. The intrinsic superiority of the Western literature is, indeed, fully admitted by those members of the Committee who support the Oriental plan of education. It is, I believe, no exaggeration to say, that all the historical information which has been collected from all the books written in the Sanscrit language is less valuable than what may be

found in the most paltry abridgments used at preparatory schools in England. In every branch of physical or moral philosophy, the relative position of the two nations is nearly the same.[14]

However, despite their reduced economic and social status, the relative social and economic decline of the Muslims was not the source of Hindu-Muslim friction during British rule. Prior to the independence movement, religious differences were encountered and contained within the social structure of the village and efforts to manage its negative outcomes were the province of the social reformer. Change was painfully slow, even though some areas, such as in Maharashtra, saw significant change in the caste system over the nineteenth century.

RELIGION AND POLITICS DURING THE INDEPENDENCE MOVEMENT

The trouble with the Indian form of religious tolerance, which had served India well over the centuries, was that it was relatively easily captured by politicians. The problems began when the Indian state was being conceptualized in the independence movement. The Western-educated Nehru preached the importance of secularism as a core component of Indian nationalism. This, to him, meant the Western concept of separation of church from state, protected by the law.

But it did not take immediate root because it could not overcome the daily learnings at home at the foot of the deity or at the prayer mat. Several leaders of the freedom struggle evaluated their participation in religious terms. This was obvious for leading theocrats. It was also true for some democracy-minded Congress leaders who viewed the nationalist uprising as part of their righteous duty as Hindus.

Gandhi initially supported Nehru's view of secularism. Like Nehru, he argued that India constituted, in geography and ethnicity, a nation and, therefore, had the right to create a state with sovereign rights. But he soon discovered that this very Western concept of nationalism quickly aroused a host of hitherto dormant religion-based subnationalisms as well.

This led him to change his views on secularism. Perhaps it was because he was deeply religious and could understand things in a way that the self-described atheist, Nehru, could not. Gandhi realized that the Congress Party would need some definition of secularism if it was to bring disparate groups together, but it could not be the Nehruvian definition. So, Gandhi arrived at his version after experimenting with different approaches.

The secularism that Gandhi preached was that the state needed to include religion—but should include all religions equally. Nehru, of course, never agreed with this principle and thought that it made Gandhi focus too much on religion as the primary identity of the Congress Party's members. Nehru would have rather had them develop a common identity based on pride of territory.

Gandhi thought that he had settled the issue early on in the independence struggle with his vision of secularism. Indeed, during the earliest stages of the independence struggle, a religion-based view of nationalism was far from being on anyone's mind. However, secularism was soon to be challenged—not by Hindu-Muslim rivalry but by the older problem within Hinduism, that of untouchability.

The political groupings around untouchables and lower castes, whose political power is currently beginning to convulse the political systems of India, began organizing themselves within the framework of the Congress Party's overall goals for nationhood during the independence struggle. Thus, while still a member of the Congress in 1927, the untouchables' leader B. R. Ambedkar convened a gathering of 10,000 delegates who condemned the British for banning the recruitment of untouchables into the army.

Initially, the Congress rejected the admissibility of such movements within the party. Proposals for the first constitution for a free India drafted by the Congress Party in 1928 (the Nehru Report, drafted by Jawaharlal Nehru's father, Motilal) made no special provisions for underprivileged groups (despite internal lobbying by Ambedkar's group).

The untouchables' group in the Congress Party first publicly opposed this. When it was unable to obtain a response from the Congress leadership, Ambedkar directly approached the colonial government. At the time, the colonial government was readying for elections based on separate electorates for different religious groups. Ambedkar was able to convince the colonial government that untouchables should elect their own leaders.

This precipitated a crisis in the Congress Party. Gandhi, after first showing support for Ambedkar's position, decided (apparently under pressure from his wealthy, upper-caste supporters) that this was unacceptable and began a fast in protest in September 1932. After negotiations with Gandhi and considerable public pressure occasioned by the prospect of Gandhi's likely imminent death, Ambedkar finally came to an agreement with the Congress Party whereby, instead of separate electorates of untouchables, seats would be reserved within the legislative councils for untouchables. This system continues to this day. Ambedkar, however, never quite bought into the agreement and continued to agitate for more protection for untouchables.

The agreement with Ambedkar was public proof that the Congress was willing to accommodate rather than quell subnationalisms by giving them political space within the party. The genie was out of the bottle: Subnationalisms based on religion now began their long road to becoming an integral part of Indian politics.

Ambedkar, for instance, would go on to encourage untouchables to convert out of Hinduism to a religion that treated them with equality. He himself became a Buddhist toward the end of his life. He also created a new political party for untouchables that would be successful against the Congress in the reserved seats in pre-independence elections. Although Ambedkar would later once more make his peace with the Congress when India became independent and would go on to draft independent India's first constitution, which officially abolished untouchability, he remained bitter about the untouchables' status until his death in 1956. Ambedkar's successors have helped achieve his visions, though. Today, they have achieved the goal of ruling India's largest state, Uttar Pradesh. The untouchables are a political force to be reckoned with.

The role of Muslims within the Congress also changed as an outcome of the acceptance of religion-based subnationalisms. Initially, the combination of discrimination and economic decline under the British, experienced by the population at large, led to the Muslim population's general support for Gandhi's nationalist project. But the Congress's willingness to accommodate active subgroups ultimately led to the creation of a Muslim group within the Congress. This group would later, under Muhammad Ali Jinnah, join the Muslim League to further its aspirations for autonomy and greater power for Muslims. Ultimately, this led to the creation of the country of Pakistan.

Nehru did have one chance to impose his secularist views on the Indian people and reverse this apparently dangerous trend. Thanks largely to him, the constituent assembly formed to create independent India's first constitution adopted laws that banned the use of religion as a political instrument. For instance, it is illegal for an Indian politician to campaign or otherwise make public statements on the basis of favoring or disfavoring one religious group over another.

SECTARIAN CONFLICT AND POLITICS IN MODERN TIMES

Though Nehru won the constitutional battle, his successors lost the war on the ground. The laws are not enforced (recall Vajpayee's statement about the riots being justified to get a sense of the actual respect for this law). Early on, the government was persuaded to use state funding to support religious places of worship from independence onward, thus creating a political constituency for the involvement of the state in religion. Since then, secularism India-style has come to mean the Gandhian version of equivalent support by the state for the worldly expressions of the different religions.

The form that Pakistan took was also to have a significant effect on Hindu-Muslim relations in India after independence. Initially, Jinnah did not ask for an independent Pakistan. Indeed, when he rallied his supporters around the now-famous two-nation theory, his political ambitions did not run to the creation of an independent Muslim state. He was merely asserting what would be considered, in modern terms, a subnationalism—a view echoed by that arch Hindutva nationalist Veer Savarkar, who foreshadowed Jinnah when he wrote in 1925 that the Hindu and Muslims were "two antagonistic nations, living side by side in India."[15] When Jinnah and the Muslim League asserted that Muslims, too, composed a nation, they wanted autonomy for Muslim-majority states within a grand Indian confederation. They hoped for a contiguous stretch of land across north India linking Punjab and Sindh in the west to Bengal in the east, a land that would accommodate all the subcontinent's Muslims over a period of time.

With independence, what Jinnah got was, as he described it, a "mutilated, truncated, moth-eaten" Pakistani state consisting of two entities separated by a thousand miles. It had enough ethnic heterogeneity within it to form multiple nations. This destroyed any chance of a gradual migration of Muslims from their current homelands all over the subcontinent. As we have documented in Chapter 2, partition was a short, bloody event from which neither India nor Pakistan has since fully recovered. Nonetheless, Pakistan, which received a much greater proportionate infusion of people into its newly independent territory, has been worse affected by the problems of nationalism.

At independence, then, the mass of Muslims in what was independent India did not migrate to Pakistan. Most chose not to go and many could not, given the logistics involved. Those in north India found themselves considerably weakened by partition: The Muslim League leaders whom they had voted for were now in Pakistan, as were most of those who had been the business and social elite of the Muslim community in north India.

Thus, with independence, Muslims of north India lost their social capital—their ability to tap into a network that offered them education, jobs, and other opportunities for development. It is important to stress the north Indian aspect in order to understand the current state of the Muslims in India. The Muslims in the south did not see the same migration of the elite and were able to maintain their economic status versus the general population. Therefore, it should come as no surprise that Hindu-Muslim conflict is a north Indian problem.

The lack of social capital was particularly harmful due to Nehru's political style, which was based on power being concentrated in Delhi and flowing out to the rest of the country through a patronage system based on elites. Nehru's approach can be explained by the fact that he was too preoccupied with his project of state-building based on a large public sector and centralized politics to pay attention to sectarian or any other issues that he considered divisive. This can be seen in his approach to the linguistic division of states: It was only when the language issue took a violent turn in the 1950s that he responded by creating states based on language.

The elites that Nehru relied on, such as the large landowners in rural and urban areas, had grown accustomed to favoring those segments of the population to which they were connected. The connection could be contractual, such as an agreement with itinerant laborers, or by some other tie, such as family or religious community. Under Nehru's statist system, with the migration of the Muslim elite, the Muslim masses thus lost their sources of patronage with nothing from the state to replace it.

Over the next several decades, the economic status of Muslims thus continued to decline relative to the Hindu population. Nevertheless, Nehru's charisma and secular outlook on the one hand and his general intolerance of civil society organizations (especially those based on faith) on the other, which he considered divisive, kept the new state free of communal unrest during his tenure.

This was to change with Indira Gandhi. In Chapter 3, we documented her populist style. Like Nehru, Mrs. Gandhi was centralist. Unlike him, she was a populist politician who disfavored institutions such as internal democracy within the Congress Party or an independent polity, preferring to go directly to the people at election time, while interfering with the Congress's (and every other party's) internal affairs otherwise.

As the Congress Party inevitably decayed under such conditions, the elite patronage system began to be captured by other parties. The Hindu-leaning BJP and the Communist Party were the only parties hardy enough to survive Mrs. Gandhi's onslaught on their freedom of functioning. The Communist Party was, however, not comfortable with elite patronage, for obvious ideological reasons. It preferred to occupy the political space vacated by the Congress through building up its cadres of urban volunteers who helped build the party in both urban and rural areas.

The BJP was very comfortable with elite patronage, as its ideology favored private enterprise. As this network shifted increasingly to its side, its vote share started, of course, to rise. A new element of violent confrontation with Muslims made its appearance. More germane to Muslims, especially those in urban areas, was that sources of livelihood were further restricted.

Many industrial houses, for instance, could openly refuse to hire Muslims without fear of legal retribution—and many still do not. I was surprised, when I visited the two-wheeler manufacturing unit of one of India's prominent and long-established business houses in the early 1990s, to find that the unit had an open policy of not employing Muslims. The spokesman for the unit indicated this quite openly, arguing that, because they did not employ women either, I should not view it as religious discrimination!

Under Rajiv Gandhi, the populist tendencies increased. Taking a page from his mother's book, Rajiv began to use religion for political advantage. We have documented his role in the murder of 3,000 Sikhs in 1984, as well as in later riots that killed large numbers of Muslims. From his pedestal, it perhaps appeared as a form of harmless blood letting: Those killed did not have the political power to retaliate, and his prestige among some segments of the Hindu population increased.

With each riot, Muslims moved further into their rotting ghettoes for safety. It became a vicious circle, as they were reluctant to move out of the ghetto for livelihood, thus creating a small, poor, nearly self-sufficient economy within the ghetto. Of course, in consequence, livelihoods suffered, as did the quality of education, because the increasingly Hinduized state was unwilling to provide good teachers or make special efforts to improve economic opportunity. Even in a dynamic city such as Mumbai, a visit to the ghettoes of Muslim population (and there are several dozen such) reveals the city's dark side: A reluctance to venture out has created conditions of poverty and ignorance ripe for exploitation both by outsiders and unscrupulous insiders.

This can sometimes lead to contested outcomes that are bad for Muslims, as well as for Hindu-Muslim relations. For example, in personal law, whereas Hindus are governed by a uniform civil code that has been accepted through the democratic process, some Muslim groups initially objected to governance by such a code. They argued that their religion required different rules. This argument was accepted by the state under the Gandhian principle of secularism. So, although the original framers of India's constitution argued in favor of a uniform civil code, they did not insert it as a constitutional requirement on the grounds that different social and religious groups would become ready for such uniformity at different points in time.

Some interesting outcomes occur in consequence. For example, Muslim men in Pakistan are governed by a uniform civil code on marriage that restricts them to monogamy. Muslim men in India, held back from social reform, are not similarly restricted. Their situation is not unique and has little to do with faith. A number of tribal groups that practice polygamy in India were not forced to comply with monogamy laws via the loophole of precedent practice.

For the Congress Party in the postindependence era, the impact of Gandhian secularism has been dramatic. The party's efforts to remain inclusive have led it to incorporate factions with their own religious "isms." Accommodating these factions leads the Congress to pursue often contradictory policies, sometimes appeasing the forces of religious radicalism and sometimes opposing them.

Its approach with untouchables and Muslims is an example; the Congress initially sought to accommodate rather than reject lower-caste groupings. Later, when the Congress under Mrs. Gandhi was to move away from its institutional moorings and drift toward a personal populism, these caste groupings became increasingly unstable within the Congress. Often, they sought out other nationalist parties that would accept them, or formed their own national parties, or turned to newly formed regional parties with which they had common cause—with adverse implications for civic harmony.

In summary, although it could be argued that the absolutist Nehruvian approach might have led to considerable civic strife anyway, the equidistant Gandhian approach has certainly been a troubling approach to manage. With the exception of the Communist Party, all political parties have tried to develop religious constituencies overtly, despite its illegality. Violent conflicts among them on the basis of religion have been common in the recent past. They have sought to involve the masses in their deadly struggle for political supremacy, an effort that has severely weakened the country.

TOLERANCE IN PRACTICE

Meanwhile, the citizens of India press along, sometimes affected by the politicians' intrusions and sometimes hanging on to their roots. During a visit to the southern state of Kerala in 2000, I stayed overnight at a popular beach resort, Kovalam. Early in the morning, walking on the beach, I saw a shrine to a sufi (Muslim) saint. I went in, paid my respects, and came out. The shrine keeper was standing outside and, as the worshipful at that hour were scant, was amenable to a chat.

The sufi saint, he told me, had lived in the area several years ago and, on his death, had been buried at the beach. Subsequently, fishermen found that if they prayed at the shrine, their safety seemed to be better ensured when they went out on the open seas. Over time, the shrine had become a site of respect and prayer for fishermen of all faiths in the area. I was familiar with this phenomenon of sufi shrines becoming sites for multifaith worship on the basis of such extranatural events. It is common in many parts of India, particularly in the western state of Rajasthan. William Dalrymple has noted its occurrence throughout the domain of the Eastern Orthodox church in the Middle East. It is probably one of the origins of conversion to Islam in India as well.

As I departed, the keeper and I introduced ourselves formally, at which point I learned that his name was Ashok. Surprised, I asked him if he was a Hindu, which he averred. A Hindu keeper, isn't that unusual? I persisted. Ashok, in turn, asked me which part of the country I was from. I replied that I was from Calcutta and was about to postscript that with "from east India." Before I could do so, however, Ashok looked amusedly at me and said, "You northerners are all alike, you will not understand. This god protects all of us and not just Muslims. So, why can I not be the keeper of the shrine?" Aside from possibly quibbling about his "northerner" syllogism (which was excusable from the viewpoint of a resident of Kerala) I found that there was little I could debate with in that point of view.

PROSPECTS FOR SECTARIAN HARMONY

Lord Acton, writing in the days of nationalism's birth in 1862, argued that nationalism, though "more absurd and more criminal than the theory of socialism," was a necessary step in the evolution of human society. This is because it was the only force strong enough to replace the "two greater evils" of his time: "the absolute monarchy and the revolution."[16] For Gandhi, the great evil of his time was monarchy's analogue, colonialism. What he did not expect was that both during his time and to the present day, nationalism could transmute itself from its initial goal, as historian Eric Hobsbawm described nationalism's changing face in the twentieth century, from being "a milder substitute for social revolution" into "the matrix of fascism."[17]

It seems odd that after so much political maneuvering and affirmative action, the untouchables, lower castes, and Muslims remain oppressed, particularly in north India. The government has tried since independence to tackle this problem but lacks the collective will to enforce its own laws. For instance, it has reserved jobs for untouchables and tribals. But, in one form or another, these quotas are rarely met. The reality is the continued exclusion of these groups from the economic and social mainstream, including access to government jobs, education, and a role in the nation's governance. Some groups have benefited: Ironically, once reservation became constitutionally sanctioned, the groups most able to benefit have been in areas where lower castes have traditionally been well educated and politically organized, as in the southern state of Tamil

Nadu. These are, of course, the groups relatively least in need of reservation.

As author Christophe Jaffrelot has argued, India after independence became a system that is a political democracy without being a social democracy. Migration to the urban areas, often driven by caste or faith-based discrimination in the villages where it originated, does not usually help, although the caste problem or religious problem is often not described as such. Instead, it is described as a problem of class or income differentials.[18]

An example is the status of the urban slum dweller. In Mumbai, for example, slum dwellers make up over a third of the city's population. Yet, many have no political power because they are recent migrants who live illegally on land that they have no right to occupy. The state rarely grants them voting rights. Unable to organize themselves, the slums are regularly reviled by the press as hotbeds of gangsterism. The destruction of their miserable tenements made of tin and cardboard by the police, under pressure from their next-door high-rise neighbors, is regularly applauded by the middle class.

This is sheer hypocrisy, of course. The reality is that without the slums, the middle classes would not find janitors, electricians, and other low-end service providers, nor the many small-scale manufactured goods such as apparel that are produced in the slums.

It also hides a sectarian problem. As has been documented for Mumbai and is probably true in other urban areas, the two largest groups of occupants of slums are the untouchables and the Muslims.

With the end of single-party rule in 1989 and the arrival of the new era of coalitions in which a national party (the Congress, BJP or, in some states, the Communists) creates an opportunistic though stable coalition with regional parties (see Chapter 3), the political power of Muslims and lower castes has changed. Many of the regional parties formed since 1989 are lower-caste-based. They oppose the Muslims' traditional *bête noire* and the upper castes for

A Mumbai slum with a view.

Another Mumbai slum.

the same reasons of economic and social discrimination. Thus, they offer Muslims greater political leverage than a more inclusive party like the Congress, in which they must compete with more powerful groups. The negative aspect of such coalitions for Muslims is that the regional parties are largely led by populists who do not allow their parties' internal affairs to run democratically or otherwise be institutionalized. Plus, many are run corruptly. Once the founding leadership of such parties loses the capacity to attract its constituents, the parties are unlikely to survive.

Nevertheless, Muslims have been coalescing politically with lower-caste-based parties because they have limited choices. In most states, political leadership has degenerated to the point of almost complete control of some tier of the caste system. This is not to say that the upper castes have the upper hand. On the contrary, in states where their share of the population is relatively low, as in, say, the southern states of Tamil Nadu and Andhra Pradesh, it is nearly impossible for a Brahmin to become chief minister. Only Tamil Nadu has had Jayaram Jayalalitha, a Brahmin, as chief minister, but her appeal arises from her personal relationship with her mentor, the late M. G. Ramachandran, who was a lower-caste leader.

Perhaps the most adverse consequence for the nation of sectarian conflict is the politicization of faith. It means that the primary identity of a politician is his faith. In consequence, it means that faith, more than merit, determines who will lead. Gandhi's perhaps unwilling sacrifice of his initial ideal of a civic nationalism for the sake of the greater good of independence means that civic nationalism has disappeared from the states; no more so than is his state of birth, Gujarat, where a Muslim is about as likely to become the state's chief minister as the perpetrators of the 2002 Ahmedabad riots are to being brought to justice—that is, zero.

However despicable the politicization of religion, it is here to stay, and all religions and sects within religions have learned to play the game. "Cast your vote" now means, in most states, "vote your caste." In the short-term, this can have dangerous implications.

When a religious group (or subgroup) comes into power, it recognizes the increasing fragility of its rule. Very quickly, it seeks to cement its rule through dramatic acts, as Narendra Modi did in Gujarat. Less noticeably, a wave of "ization" of bureaucracy follows—Hinduization, Yadavization (a lower-caste grouping prevalent in northern states), and so on. This is followed by the "ization" of political governance, if possible.

In some cases, this is of minor import and even amusing. For example, the number of verses in the Hindu religious text, the Upanishads, is 108, giving this number a mystical significance. When the Hindutva-leaning BJP-led government formulated its Information Technology Action Plan in 1998 that would "transform India into a global software power by 2008," it contained 108 recommendations. At that time, due to an emerging research interest of mine, I had read and commented on earlier drafts, which contained considerably fewer than 108 recommendations. As I read the final version, it seemed to me that various sections had been added that were superfluous or were simply not serious recommendations. For instance, recommendation 23, "IT Software and IT Services companies, being constituents of the knowledge industry, shall be exempted from inspection by Inspectors like those for Factory, Boiler, Excise, Labour, Pollution/Environment etc." did not make sense. Neither did the final recommendation, number 108 of the plan, which was not a plan but an instruction for implementation, as it stated, "All necessary instructions, notifications and amendments to procedures/Law shall be issued by the respective Ministries/Departments within three months."[19]

I was later told by an official in the Ministry of Information Technology that the number of recommendations was explicitly increased under orders from higher-ups from fewer than seventy to match the number of verses in the Upanishads!

In another case, a state-approved text for second-grade students in Uttar Pradesh refers to a Hindu mythological hero departing to heaven in an airplane in a factual tone. But, education is probably the most serious area of contention, an example being the large-scale revision of school texts under M. M. Joshi, the erstwhile BJP minister for human resources, to restrict tales of national heroes to Hindus.

Because the laws for tackling discrimination already exist, the real problem, as I have noted, is a lack of political will. It appears that success in removing religious discrimination requires the determined action of civil society. The latter, in turn, requires organization, finance, and other skills. So far, this capability has been generally lacking in Indian society. In its absence, the laws will simply not be enforced.

For example, in 2006, the movie *Fanaa*, a patriotic film about Indian Kashmir, was released in Indian theaters. A commercially successful movie, its release in Gujarat was, however, effectively prevented by politicians from the state's ruling BJP. The film's main actor, Amir Khan, had made a statement that villagers displaced by a dam project that primarily benefited Gujarat needed to be re-housed. In response, there were calls for the banning of his film by local media and government officials of the ruling BJP. Although the courts clarified that the release of *Fanaa* in theaters in Gujarat was legal, no government official in Gujarat was willing to accept the legal sanction. It quickly became clear that the ban was not because of Khan's statement on dams but because he is a Muslim. In other words, the Gujarat government did not accept Khan's right to make a statement about government behavior, simply because he is a Muslim. There was nothing New Delhi, which at the time was ruled by a Congress-led government that opposes the BJP nationally, was willing to do either.

In the absence of political will, it is no surprise that the police, too, follow the do-nothing orders of their supervisors—the chance of their being held to account is, again, zero, in parallel with their political masters. Over time, this attitude must filter further down and, sometimes, its limits can make for a chilling tale. I remember a friend of mine from Ahmedabad, Sanat, describing an incident during the sectarian Hindu-Muslim riots of 1984. A neighbor of his, a successful architect, was the only Muslim in a walled-in complex of twenty-six homes in the posh Navrangpura district of Ahmedabad. When the riots began, the architect felt relatively secure. Alas, his walled-in world proved to be no security at all. The mobs came to his home using address lists provided to them by the municipal authorities. As they beat down his door, he escaped from the back to Sanat's house. Sanat bravely risked the mob's wrath by protecting the architect while they burned down the architect's house, though not before they plundered it. Sanat tried to reduce the pillage by going into the architect's house to see if he could retrieve any valuables. To his shock, he found the neighborhood convenience *lari-wala*, the guy who sold petty convenience items on a small pushcart and who had served the architect many times, decamping with the architect's TV set. "Why are you doing this?" he asked, only to be given a cold stare of the underprivileged getting a small chance to get even. The architect later left Ahmedabad, as did Sanat, both disgusted by their experience of the riots.

That winter morning in 2006, as I went through my day of presentations at the management school in Ahmedabad, I was received with affection by both faculty and students. It was only as the day wore to an end that I got the answer to my inner query. During the question and answer session that followed my lecture, a student asked if distance mattered any more in an environment where technology enabled remote communication. I responded, in a lighter vein, that it also could protect people's culture. A (Muslim) woman in a veil might have a difficult time communicating with the Jack Straws of this world face-to-face because of his cultural inhibitions, but tucked away in a call center somewhere in the East—Bangladesh, India, or even East Anglia—her right to communicate while wearing a veil was protected because the recipient of the call would not know that she wore one.

Instead of the titter that I expected this kind of joke to receive, there was stunned silence, and, after a long pause, someone asked another question on a different topic. I realized then that I had raised a taboo topic simply by mentioning a Muslim in my talk. By ghettoizing its Muslims, Ahmedabad's Hindus hoped to displace them from popular consciousness. Otherwise, the sin that they had been silent accomplices to in 2002 would be unbearable. If, for a while, Muslims were not mentioned in middle-class society, they could perhaps mentally conclude that the Muslims were there by choice and lack of capability.

I have heard the same statements made by some whites about blacks in American cities. As the immortal Ali of Tarquin Hall's excellent novel *Salaam Brick Lane* might say, "The ghetto is a voluntary place to be in, innit?"[20] Ahmedabad wanted to become a confident, prosperous, middle-class city by hiding inconvenient truths about its treatment of its Muslim population.

Ahmedabad's Muslims seem to have bought into the fiction. When the BJP launched its national election campaign in Gujarat in March 2004, twenty Muslims were on hand to garland Maya Kodnani, the legislator who is alleged to have participated in the 2002 riots by leading a mob that killed eighty-five people in a matter of minutes. Schoolteacher Nazir Khan Pathan, whose Sun Flower Primary School was burnt by rioters in 2002, was one of those who garlanded her. He captured the capitulation of the Muslims of Gujarat when he said, "When you live in the river you don't earn enmity from the crocodile. We don't want to move from this locality where our forefathers lived."[21]

The Hindu voters of Kodnani's legislative district obviously agreed, electing Kodnani with 75 percent of the votes, rewarding this apparently hands-on instigator even more than the prime organizer of the riots, Narendra Modi, whose share of the vote in his own constituency, was marginally lower. So have the police, which dropped its investigation of Kodnani's role in the riots citing a lack of evidence. In fact, no one to date has been convicted in the Ahmedabad riots.

In Chapter 4, I wrote that the regionalization of Indian politics had saved Indian politics. No such savior is at hand to remove the destructive impact that the obsession with caste and religion in politics has on the prospects for social equality. As I have shown, this obsession now infects the civic sphere as well. Critics would argue that it need not be so because democracy ultimately will save India. They point to the defeat of the BJP-led government in 2004 at the hands of a more secular Congress-led government as evidence. But in reality this is no evidence at all. The defeat of the BJP in 2004 had much more to do with poor rural development and low job growth than concerns about secularism. If the Congress Party fails to deliver on its promises, the BJP will be back.

Eminent scholars such as Meghnad Desai and Amartya Sen have argued that secularism has failed to take root in India not because of an inappropriate model, but because of a lack of popular debate. They note with some bemusement that politicians are scared to raise the subject in public despite the likelihood that doing so would give them the moral high ground.

Periyar Thidal, the founder of the Dravida Movement in Tamil Nadu, a movement for the uplift of the middle castes, once said (and it is inscribed under a statue of him in Tamil Nadu): "There is no God. There is no God. There is no God at all. He who invented God is a fool. He who propagates God is a scoundrel. He who worships God is a barbarian." Foolish words, some people may say. These would probably include his many followers, who now rule the state of Tamil Nadu and yet are deeply religious. But Periyar, who fought all his life to uplift the middle castes, saw the folly of bringing religion into politics. The current politics of Tamil Nadu, which centers on the iconization of its leaders, would be a bitter pill for him to swallow.

Lord Acton presciently warned that if (as was not unlikely) liberty and democracy were thwarted because of the progress of nationalism, nationalism would inevitably lead to a nation's downfall. Thanks to the politicians' obsession with religion, the Indian state today faces its gravest challenge.

CHAPTER 11

The ABCD, NRI, and Other Species: Indians Living in America

THE WORD *DESI* IN HINDUSTANI means "a native". The nonresident Indian (NRI, to use the Indian government's term) is sometimes referred to as an ABCD, an American-Born Confused Desi.

Nearly two-million American NRIs have arrived in waves. Their origins in the United States go back to the economic opportunity that came with building the West in the early twentieth century. About 8,000 South Asians migrated to the United States and Canada between 1899 and 1920, the largest ethnic group being Sikhs (85 percent) and Muslims (13 percent) from the Punjab. The seemingly disproportionate number of Sikhs may be connected to the enhanced presence of British troops on Canadian soil at the time of the celebration of Queen Victoria's Diamond Jubilee in 1897 (the Sikhs were the largest contingent of South Asian troops in the British army). Once in the United States, the majority worked as farmhands, loggers, and steelworkers. They braved the discrimination common to such groups at the time and slowly moved into businesses they had been comfortable with in India, such as farming. Especially worrisome to the white natives of California was their transformation from common laborers to landowners.

Over time, the Sikhs established large farming enclaves in northern California. Today, their descendants make up about 15 percent of the total NRI population in the United States, as much as the Gujaratis, who hail from western India. The remainder of today's NRIs came to the United States in waves—people of diverse age groups, origins, and with different destinations in mind. So it should come as no surprise that they differ in political orientation and culture as well. In recent times, they have come together for common causes—lobbying for the U.S.–India nuclear fuel agreement, for example—but in many other ways they remain different from one another.

MODERN TIDES OF IMMIGRATION

In the mid-1960s, as the promise of India faded into the socialist embrace from which it would not emerge until 1991, the country's technically skilled professionals first began migrating to the United States. Initially, they consisted mainly of medical doctors, due to the availability of immigrant visas for this category. These Indians were from wealthy backgrounds at home. Though disgusted at India's failure, they were rooted in its culture. Hence, they became Americans outside while remaining Indians within. Their homes were perfect replicas of the India they had left behind, with cane chairs, dark curtains, and ornate wall hangings favored by the wealthier Indians of India. This gave an anachronistic, outdated feel to a more recent visitor from India, because India had changed even though their homes had not.

Their politics had nothing to do with India; they wanted themselves and their children to grow up rooted in the United States—a near impossibility as they found glass ceilings for themselves and their children, and other barriers. Some were of their own making, such as the desire to have their children wed within the community. Given the sparseness of the NRI population, this sometimes meant that a daughter had to be wed to a man living in India—not necessarily her choice of groom or location. They located themselves mostly in the big cities—New York, Chicago, Boston, and Washington, D.C., but—due to the nature of the medical profession rather than by choice—some could be found even in small-town America.

In the early 1970s, the doctors were joined by a third wave: students graduating from the best Indian undergraduate engineering and management institutions who entered the upper tier of American universities with a desire to stay on in the United States. The motive was again economic opportunity, but this wave included émigrés from more diverse backgrounds. With less openness to new immigrants, direct employment in the United States was difficult. Like students from many other countries at the time, Indians recognized that higher education was the easiest route to immigration.

Although younger at arrival than the earlier migrants, they embraced the "we don't care about India" attitude of their India-educated elders; they felt left out of economic opportunity in India due to its stifling bureaucrat-led culture that rewarded only mediocrity. But not having worked in India and being younger, they were less tied to the atmosphere of India in their culture, more willing to experiment, and more liberal in their politics. They tended to look on the older migrants as unduly conservative, which they ascribed to mixed identities. This group was willing to embrace America more fully. Of course, like the earlier group, they largely could not due to the glass ceiling of color and sometimes faith, even though many married outside the community.

At about the same time, a fourth wave of immigrants extended into the 1980s. These were less educated and came from relatively underprivileged backgrounds in small-town India, particularly from

Gujarat. Primarily, they were in search of a decent living. Their aspirations were simpler than the Indians' of the 1960s and 1970s: to work hard at a restaurant, store, or security company, earn a good living, send money back to the parents, and, finally, become shop owners themselves. Often, they arrived as tourists without the necessary immigrant paperwork and overstayed their official welcome. It was relatively easy to do so in those days—easy even to buy businesses and own homes as illegal immigrants while waiting for an immigrant amnesty program (usually targeted at Hispanics but that would necessarily include them) that would allow them to become legitimate residents.

Initially landing in New York, where jobs were easy to find and support groups were extensive, this group migrated over time for lower business and living costs to the south, particularly Florida, Georgia, and Texas. The climate in the South was also more familiar, and it was possible to live in large Indian enclaves and build businesses in the dry-cleaning, fast-food, and convenience-store industries.

Culturally, too, the rising conservative climate of the South suited these migrants. It matched their humble origins to rub shoulders with southerners with small-town roots, including strong religious backgrounds and family ties. Although they shared little in common with the liberal Indian student communities that were building up around the country, they integrated very quickly into their local communities.

I recall a conference that I helped organize for small South Asian businesses in the early 1990s in the South. By then, the small-business network of Indians in towns like Atlanta and Houston was well entrenched. Organizations such as the Asian American Hotels Owners Association (a somewhat presumptuous name: their membership is almost entirely Indian and excludes the extensive hotel interests of, say, the Chinese community in San Francisco) were formed in the late 1980s. AAHOA, for instance, represented a large network of hotel owners.

The objective of the conference was to expose small-business owners to trends in business that they could leverage, such as franchising, new technology, and access to capital markets. One of the organizers' worries was that, living in Indian enclaves, they were not mainstreamed. So we called in the CEOs of large firms to talk about franchising, the software engineers to talk about technology, and the investment bankers and professors to talk about risk management and capital markets.

To my surprise, I found that there was too little in common for any meaningful exchange of ideas. The audience didn't feel comfortable talking with the likes of an East Coast CEO of a publicly listed company. Their accent was a mix of southern U.S. drawl and *desi* Indian, which was difficult for the CEO to understand. In some cases, their English grammar was of poor quality. And their thoughts were focused on buying the next store cheaply. Concepts such as franchising made little sense to them. Why pay extra for a franchise label and suffer the burden of being answerable to some corporate yuppie about royalties due? They had come to America to own their own businesses, not to answer to someone else after having made it.

More striking was the divide between these Indians and the more educated Indians attending the conference. For example, on politics, while the small-business owners' political concerns were centered on the latest environmental regulations for gas stations and how they could lobby local politicians for support, the educated Indians were talking about national and global issues. The small-businessmen heartily supported the faith-based views of various U.S. presidents and the general religiosity of the South, something that the more educated Indians shrunk from.

THE LAST WAVE

The fifth wave (and I believe this *is* the final wave) were the trained engineers. This wave began with the outsourcing of software to

India in the mid-1970s but really grew in the late 1980s and 1990s. These people were largely trained in India and had jobs with IT firms in India before coming to the United States. They were sent overseas by their Indian employers to undertake software projects for their firms' U.S. clients. Over time, a number of them stayed on, working for high-technology firms. A few found their way to Silicon Valley and absorbed its entrepreneurial culture.

These were the first migrants to come from an India that had already economically benefited them. Their decision to work and live in the United States came out of a desire to experience an even better lifestyle and work style than was possible in India—to do cutting-edge work in information technology, for example. But they saw themselves as much Indians as Americans and retained their Indian connections by frequently traveling back and forth.

Sabeer Bhatia, the founder of Hotmail, is an example of such a culture. Educated at the Birla Institute of Technology and Sciences (in the western state of Rajasthan in India), Caltech, and Stanford University, he dreamed up Hotmail after a brief stint at Apple. To develop Hotmail, he actively sought venture capital support from established fellow Indian techies in Silicon Valley. This effort did not succeed, so he turned to the mainstream venture capitalists of Silicon Valley, one of whom, Steve Jurvetson of Draper Fisher Jurvetson, supported him. The point of noting Bhatia's failure to obtain funding from fellow Indians is not to suggest they had poor judgment, but to show that he was then able to tap mainstream venture capitalists.

Once Hotmail was sold to Microsoft for a reported $400 million in the late 1990s, Bhatia turned his attention to India. His first venture, Arzoo.com, was a Web-based job exchange system that utilized a large number of engineers trained and working in India. As Bhatia tells the story, he asked a team working in another company in Bangalore to come over and work for him in Silicon Valley.

At the time, I was working on a case study of Hotmail for the Stanford Business School. One day, Bhatia and I were scheduled to meet to discuss the case at his Arzoo offices. Unfortunately, I had noted his office number incorrectly and landed up at the wrong office suite in the industrial park where Arzoo had his offices. Wondering what to do (this was prior to the age of mass cell phone use), I noticed a group of young Indian men a short distance away standing in the parking lot. All of them were smoking cigarettes, a trait common to men in India. I was sure now that I was hot on the trail. Confidently, I went up to them and asked if they worked for Arzoo. They confirmed this and directed me to the correct office.

When I told Bhatia how I had found his office, he was amazed: How did I know they worked for Arzoo when the valley was dotted with Indian techies? I told him it was obvious: No other office in northern California would have such a large number of Indians smoking cigarettes unless they were fresh off the boat from India!

Bhatia has since done several projects that leverage India, either by using Indian workers for global projects or developing products for the Indian market. His latest project, Nano City, is an ambitious attempt to create a Silicon Valley in India. In 2006, Bhatia made a dozen trips to India to work on this and other projects. He counts himself among the luckiest of Indians, able to maintain a Silicon Valley lifestyle while helping his country of birth.

THE IMPORTANCE OF NETWORKS

Bhatia's experience with mainstream venture capitalists is not unique for Indians in Silicon Valley; it is a marker that sets this group apart from other ethnic groups, notably the Chinese. Although larger in number than Indian IT professionals in Silicon Valley—there are estimated to be about 75,000 engineers of Chinese origin (including Taiwan and other parts of Greater China) compared with about half as many of Indian origin—they have been less successful in many aspects that are considered core to Silicon

Valley—for instance, starting new firms and accessing venture capital funds.

In a survey of more than 2,000 Indian and Chinese engineers in Silicon Valley that I undertook in 2001, I found that over two-thirds of those born in the People's Republic of China occupied technical, nonmanagerial jobs and 23 percent were executives or managers. By contrast, 65 percent of the India-born were executives or managers. This was despite the PRC-born having arrived in the United States earlier (two-thirds had come by 1999 compared with less than half of the Indians) and having overwhelmingly obtained their highest educational qualification in the United States (81 percent for the PRC-born versus 63 percent for the India-born). I also found that when it came to founding and running startups—arguably the lifeblood of Silicon Valley—60 percent of the India-born were doing so compared with 30 percent of the Chinese.

Since 2001, the importance of the Indians in Silicon Valley has increased significantly. This is because many of the successful engineers have gone on to join mainstream venture capital firms as partners, an important step toward complete participation in the Silicon Valley habitat for entrepreneurship.

There are several reasons for the Indians' success. Knowledge of English is important but cannot be assumed to be the main reason. There are several ethnic groups with equal or better command over English—the Irish and Filipinos are obvious examples—who have not had the same success in Silicon Valley.

Another reason is that they have formed extensive ethnic professional associations. The Indus Entrepreneurs (TiE) and the Silicon Valley Indian Professionals Association (SIPA) are the two main networks around which the engineers tend to coalesce. TiE is primarily for the older (30 + —these things are relative!), more successful engineer experienced in startups. SIPA is for the younger professional employed in a large IT firm in the valley—but, like all the others, with serious ambitions of doing her own startup. There is also an active U.S.–India Venture Capital Association.

The ethnic professional associations are important, especially for the newcomer to Silicon Valley, because they enable rapid entry into the ecosystem of Silicon Valley. In a regular meeting of an association like TiE or SIPA, the new arrival to the valley can meet with potential venture financiers, cofounders, and employers, all via an evening of sharing ideas. The more experienced members find the newcomers, in turn, useful. This is because an ethnic association helps to resolve the problem of *trust in entrepreneurship*—a financier and the founder of a startup might trust each other more if both are of the same ethnicity.

Again, while the associations are important, they cannot be assumed to be the main cause of the Indians' greater success. This is because the Chinese have formed even more extensive professional associations than the Indians. For example, there are separate Chinese associations for software professionals and hardware professionals, as well as associations that offer platforms to both types. Attendance at the networking events of these associations rivals those of the Indians.

So, the unusual success of the Indians in Silicon Valley remains a puzzle to academics and other commentators. Perhaps it is a combination of factors that they possess—English speakers, well educated, and associational—that together provides the answer. Whatever the cause, the impact of this wave is likely to be tidal with time. They have already gone on to create an infrastructure for themselves in Silicon Valley that, apart from professional associations, includes purpose-built community centers, senior citizens' advocacy groups, and charitable foundations. They have networks with their country of birth that far exceed in scale and ambition that of any other ethnic group. As I have discussed in Chapter 9, after years of being marginal participants in India's software story, the NRIs of the fifth wave are now the primary carriers of innovation in the Indian IT industry.

MAINSTREAMING

The rise in Indian-American influence in national politics is due to the fifth wave of immigrants. Their experience of successfully working in India has given them the commitment and knowledge to further India's prosperity in a way that the frustrated migrants of earlier waves never had. Their immense wealth and understanding of globalization of economies led to their sponsorship of influential associations like the American India Foundation and the US India Political Action Committee. The Indo-U.S. nuclear energy supply agreement is an example of their clout.

In this project of supporting their home country, they have been encouraged by the Indian state and its citizens. For example, Sabeer Bhatia's Nano City project, which aims to cover 5,000 acres of land outside the city of Chandigarh in North India, was the result of a request by its local government to Bhatia to undertake such a project.

This bespeaks an unusual change in attitudes. Through the 1970s and 1980s, it was common for the media and politicians in India to speak disparagingly about the NRIs visiting their home country. The media would mock them for their insistence on drinking only bottled water, their complaints about the heat and bad roads, and their ostentatious displays of wealth while in India.

But now India has changed: Its wealth is catching up with richer countries and the opportunities at home are as good as abroad. One can see in the American universities the decline in enrollment by Indian engineers, a trend likely to continue as India continues to grow—which is why I believe it is the last wave. Now on par, Indians in India have finally accepted the NRIs as their own, even as the NRIs increasingly view India as their real homeland and one that they plan to return to throughout their lives. India even has a big state-sponsored event in Delhi each year that celebrates the *overseas Indian,* as they are now increasingly termed.

Such globalization is creating its own challenges of fitting into America. In the old days, the overwhelming economic lure of America forced migrants to adjust to life here. In some respects, it was an easy adjustment, especially when it came to political life. It was a truism until the 1990s that Indian Americans were either highly educated and liberal or poorly educated and conservative. There was a divide, but a satisfactory one: The aging conservatives lived in the South and voted Republican; the younger, educated ones lived in the East, Midwest, and West, and voted Democrat. It was generally expected that the next generation from the South would most likely choose education-based careers and become more like the young professionals than like their parents.

But now globalization has created some interesting dilemmas. Consider the Indian student body at the University of Illinois at Urbana-Champaign (UIUC), a premier state university located 150 miles south of Chicago. Indian students, 4,000 strong, make up 10 percent of the total student body. It is a mix of U.S.-born undergraduate students and largely India-born graduate students. The U.S.-born undergraduates were educated at very good public and private schools, mostly in the Midwest. Their friends in school were mostly the white children who would also, like them, attend elite schools like UIUC. In accent and thinking, these young NRIs may be considered mainstream Americans.

It is interesting, then, that as soon as they leave the confines of high school, typically in an upscale suburb of Chicago, and enter UIUC, their peer group changes sharply and quickly, becoming all Indian or, more generally, South Asian. Their music and movies now include a substantial mix of Bollywood fare, and they follow the cricketing fortunes of the Indian team. They spend junior year in India. Many want to live and work in India. Their domestic political views are increasingly colored by how India might be affected.

This is an unusual development in the sense that it did not happen to Indians elsewhere. In Canada, the United Kingdom, Australia, the Caribbean, and other English-language locations with a substantial Indian population, second- and third-generation Indians are more culturally similar to the majority than in the United States. Ask a UK-born, young, ethnic Indian male about his sports team and you will find that the red cross of the English soccer team means as much to him as to a white Englishman; only one other team evokes even more emotion in him, and that is the local soccer team of whichever part of England he hails. The complex politics of India are of minor interest. In the United States, by contrast, it appears that after mainstreaming—in different ways in the South and North, there is a trend toward demainstreaming, or, at least, a transnational identity.

Even when compared with other Asian migrants to the United States, this trend is somewhat unique. For instance, second-generation Japanese and Koreans see themselves as primarily and increasingly American. This may be because they are not as welcome in their parents' countries of birth as the second-generation Indians. The Indians' experience is probably most closely paralleled by the Chinese in the United States, who feel as proud of China's many successes as those of their adopted land and want to help that success and participate in it.

So far, the NRIs' mixed loyalty that has come from demainstreaming has not been tested. For one thing, Americans do not play cricket, so they can safely cheer their beloved Indian cricket team. Second, India and the United States are moving closer to each other politically, unlike China and the United States.

But these are only the facts of the moment. The reality is that, with any two states with global ambitions, it is a matter of time before national interests diverge. What then? The answer may well lie in the rapidly evolving identity of the NRI and how it interfaces with America's evolving identity in the age of globalism and terrorism. In either case, the NRIs who have assimilated better into the local cultures, as those in the American South seem to have, will probably fare better than those who have not.

CHAPTER 12

The Stock Exchanges of India

ONE CAN HARDLY JUDGE THESE THINGS from the quiet clicking of terminals inside the twenty-eight-floor building that houses the Bombay Stock Exchange or the bedlam that characterizes the aptly named street outside, Dalal Street (*Dalal* is Hindi for *agent* or *stockbroker*), but the stock exchanges of India are among the world's busiest and well-run. Two of the Indian stock exchanges—the state-sponsored National Stock Exchange (ranked third) and the privately owned Bombay Stock Exchange (ranked fifth)—make it to the world's top five, measured by the number of transactions (the New York Stock Exchange and NASDAQ top the list and Shanghai is fourth).

The key to their success is efficient regulation. As is well-known, financial markets are among the hardest entities to regulate. The incentives for misusing confidential information are high and the misdemeanors hard to track. Even the most highly developed stock market, the New York Stock Exchange, continues to experience episodes of insider trading. Some stock markets in developed countries, such as the Toronto Stock Exchange, are almost bywords for poor regulation.

Effective stock-market regulation requires technological smartness and a regulatory body that is independent, empowered, and capable. On all these counts, developing countries may, therefore, be expected to have a tough time achieving a high regulatory standard. Yet, in India, good regulation is now in place, converting a murky environment that existed up to the early 1990s into a much more efficient marketplace. Interestingly, this happened within a couple of years. The story is, therefore, one in which the institutionalization of professional governance happened in a remarkably short time. How it happened is a fascinating and necessary part of understanding institution-building in India.

THE BEGINNINGS OF SECURITIES TRADING

Prior to independence, the Indian stock markets, whose origins date to the 1870s, were subject to global influences. This was for the reason that the companies listed on them were typically local firms that catered to local and global markets, such as textile firms, and because the Indian rupee was globally tradable. The crash of world stock markets in the 1930s was duly echoed in Indian markets and the leading textile firms crashed into bankruptcy.

In newly independent India, a priority was the raising of capital to finance growth. As we have documented in Chapter 3, the state quickly came to control the banking system as a part of its strategy of industrialization. It also controlled, through a licensing system, how much a firm could produce, thus guaranteeing profits to licensed firms. It could not, however, prevent already wealthy industrialists from cornering these licenses. These were the most creditworthy, and the state did not want to risk capital on new entrepreneurs. The corruption of the system also favored established entrepreneurs, as these were the most able to bribe their way into a license.

In order to prevent such industrialists from grabbing up the easy money to be made in such protected markets, the state created rules that limited a promoter to hold no more than 40 percent of his firm's equity in case the firm wanted to access bank capital beyond a certain amount. Given this, the best way for a promoter to retain control of his firm was to have the remaining 60 percent of the shares widely held via listing the firm on stock exchanges. Thus, a wave of listing of large industrial firms followed the new rules in the 1950s. Ironically, it was the socialist impulse of spreading wealth that rooted this most capitalist of institutions.

Privately, promoters often fumed at the logic of sharing their wealth with the idle public. After all, the firm's profits were protected once the promoter had the needed licenses and had implemented the projects. The firm's growth was steady due to license constraints. There was no need for the public's risk capital because the banks were willing to fund such guaranteed growth. As such, the public was usually viewed as the fifth wheel by corporate promoters, to be dispensed with when possible.

With the exception of a few ethical industrial groups like the Tatas, it is perhaps not surprising, therefore, that the mass of listed companies were run by promoters who, given the lax regulatory environment, ran their listed firms as hereditary fiefdoms. They concealed large amounts of the firm's income from public scrutiny, distributing this to themselves. The markets priced in these irregularities, of course, leading to a generally moribund market.

Another piece of regressive legislation—the Foreign Exchange Regulation Act of 1973 (FERA 1973)—changed this. FERA required multinational firms to reduce the shareholding of the foreign parent to 40 percent. Although some firms, notably Coca-Cola and IBM, refused to do so and preferred to close their Indian operations, most foreign firms complied. They concluded that they would rather sell into Indian markets on those terms than not at all. Like the large Indian firms, these preferred to list on domestic markets as a way of complying with the restriction. A new wave of listings of such firms occurred in the mid-1970s in consequence.

The impact on stock markets was electric. Suddenly, John Q. Public could now invest in a large number of listed firms whose managers did not cheat shareholders—because their foreign parents would not allow it. A hierarchy of investor preferences resulted. At its apex were the foreign firms. These were mostly in areas with limited domestic competition, such as tea plantations and patented industrial products. As such, their growth prospects were the most ensured. Next up were the few ethical Indian firms whose growth prospects were not quite as ensured as the foreign firms (as they were in industries such as steel and chemicals with more cyclical growth and competition). Finally, along came the rest—about 90 percent of the listed firms.

Interestingly, because the overwhelming proportion of firms were valued on the worst possible assumptions about managerial behavior, it was not easy for the corrupt promoter to manipulate the firm's share price to his advantage. I know. I spent seven years as a broker trading on the floor of the Bombay Stock Exchange. If there was a corporate announcement, we first tried to figure out what was in it for the management before reacting to it on the trading floor. Our starting premise was that the management must have an angle and was trying to make money for itself. Under that assumption, all news was considered negative for shareholders, making it hard to move the stock price through rumor.

This did not stop promoters from trying and sometimes succeeding. A textile company out of Mumbai—one of the country's largest—was well-known in the investment community for making misleading announcements about the firm's functioning just prior to announcing its semiannual results; the brokers expected that the announcements would imply the opposite of how the results would actually be. In one that I recall from the mid-1980s, the firm announced that there had been a major fire in one of its plants. No other aspect, such as earnings impact, was discussed in the announcement. There was just an official press release noting the fire.

The stock price plummeted. A few days later, the chairman of the company released the results, which were as expected prior to the press release. In it, he noted that the fire had been quickly contained, had no impact on the year's outcome, and was not expected to have any future impact. The stock price recovered. Undoubtedly, the promoter made a lot of money trading in his shares through trusted brokers.

Perhaps the worst news for the hapless investor was therefore not that a domestic firm had declared bad results—over time, he had come to recognize that such events would happen and priced this in—but that a foreign firm had been sold to a domestic promoter who belonged to the "corrupt 90 percent" category. This was not infrequent, because the smaller foreign promoters, such as plantation owners, had been family-owned for generations. They had little long-term interest in continuing with their India operations. The takeover of such firms by a domestic promoter almost immediately led to a decline of at least 30 percent in the share price, indicating the extent of the "clean" premium.

Because the quality of the information from the typical firm was suspect, one might have expected the few honest firms that remained to cash in on this by being forthright about corporate events. However, even the honest firms offered little information on their performance. This was because the government—represented by bureaucrats also on the make for themselves—was always on the prowl for ways to enhance its revenue. Any good news was sure to attract their attention and lead to special official levies and taxes and "personal takes" by bureaucrats.

If promoters were generally corrupt, they found their match in the members of stock exchanges. Up to the formation of the Securities and Exchange Board of India (SEBI) in 1991, the exchanges were self-regulating. However, there was almost no such self-regulation in practice. Contrary to many people's belief that institutions work best when self-regulated, the stock exchanges' members, led by the Bombay Stock Exchange—Asia's oldest exchange founded in the mid-nineteenth century—was a den of thieves in which insider trading was rampant, crises were manufactured to enable powerful speculators to defer payments, and corporate insiders were part of the game.

MAKING MONEY ON INDIAN STOCK MARKETS

SEBI's arrival in 1991 coincided with the arrival of the first foreign institutional investors. Before then, the honest broker and the financially successful broker were nonoverlapping categories. I know because my partners and I were honest. The results: Our brokerage firm lost money every single year that we operated in the 1980s, until we finally sold our broking license in 1989.

It was impossible for honest brokers to make profits because brokers made income primarily by getting the large public financial institutions to place orders through them. As in developed countries, institutional business was where the money was, and those brokers who relied solely on what little retail business existed lost money.

The public financial institutions consisted primarily of the big four: the Industrial Development Bank of India, the Industrial Credit and Investment Corporation of India, the Life Insurance Corporation of India, and General Insurance Corporation of India. They were government controlled, with a mandate to support the development of an orderly market. They understood this to mean that a market rose steadily over time. Their management was chosen from the public-sector bureaucracy, and the managers served at the whim of the minister in charge of the company; hence, there was very little interest in understanding their sector.

For example, the Life Insurance Corporation of India (LIC) was a state-owned monopoly issuer of life insurance policies. As a monopoly, it always made some money and had a regular flow of cash from sales of new policies. Its premium income was mostly invested in government securities, but a small proportion was invested in the stock markets.

LIC and the other public financial institutions would only give their business to a few brokers who were registered with it. Getting registered was the hardest part of doing business with LIC. It was a thoroughly corrupt process that involved paying off the bureaucrats involved.

Those brokers who were registered with LIC viewed their registration as an annuity to be handed down from father to son. This was because the LIC was obliged, as a state-owned company, to be equitable to its brokers; so each of them received a percentage of its business in proportion to the broker's past tenure of service and to his record of bringing in business below the price limits set by LIC. This business was given as nearly as possible on a daily basis. Naturally, for a broker, registration with LIC was highly sought after.

Later, when foreign brokers arrived on the scene with higher standards in most (but not all) cases and sought registration with LIC, their calls for a normal registration process initially went unanswered. Because they would not enter the payoff game, they complained to someone high up in the organization or the finance ministry. If they had enough clout, the institution would come through and register them.

I remember a time during my later years in the stock markets, as head of a foreign broking firm, when the head of the LIC trading desk refused to meet anyone in our firm for several months after we applied for registration. We complained up high and one day, unexpectedly, received registration.

Thereafter, doing business was a piece of cake: Our trader had only to get through by phone to LIC's trading desk to receive an order. The only difficult portion was connecting to LIC's trading desk, since it had a limited number of phone lines. But once we got through, invariably we got an order to buy some stock—often curtly stated, with little interest on their side in discussing the deal or any recent research we might have done on the stock. Beyond giving us their orders, the LIC staff had no other interest in us because their raises were based on tenure, not on performance.

After a while, we realized that this largest of financial institutions was the easiest to service. The LIC traders were merely fulfilling a quota of orders to foreign brokers that had been decided at a level far above theirs, probably in a joint discussion between the CEO of LIC and the Finance Ministry. We responded to the opportunity by cutting our costs: We assigned our most junior staffer in the office, a peon (or messenger boy, whose normal task was to serve tea to traders during the day), to the task of repeatedly dialing the LIC's number until someone answered. He then simply had to say, in Hindi, that he was calling from J＿＿, and immediately was given an order to buy shares.

The brokerage firm usually received an order from LIC or a similar institution at a price limit marginally above the closing price of the previous day. This was because the LIC believed in an orderly, gradually rising market. Hence, the chances of getting stock at the same price as the previous day was, on average, less than half. Because they regularly coordinated strategies with the rest of the big four, and because these four accounted for the majority of trades on the BSE, they usually got it right. This must undoubtedly have pleased their bosses in the Finance Ministry.

For the broker, several games were possible in response to the institutional strategy. The simplest was to satisfy the demand at the price limit set by LIC, provided the broker could obtain stock at or below that price. The difference was usually retained as the broker's private margin. Since it was likely that a proportion of the gain would be shared with someone in the LIC trading office, the brokers were not worried about being found out.

The more sophisticated brokers would work with LIC's traders to understand how much of a particular stock LIC intended to buy over the next several days. They would then purchase a large quantity of a stock and ramp up the price on the previous day in anticipation of the LIC order. This could be done simply and cheaply. The stock exchange had an official "price-recorder," an underpaid officer whose job it was to go around the trading floor at the time it was closing, a notebook in hand, and ask jobbers the closing price. For a small fee, he would record a higher price than actually was the case.

Some brokers would also direct made-up research or "late breaking news" to the LIC trading office the previous day recommending that stock. Then, armed with the stock and a high price, they would offer large blocks to LIC at the high price.

The publicly listed Indian firms smelled profit in joining in with brokers in this game, and the dishonest ones would make up announcements and time them to benefit their brokers. Even some foreign firms played this game. A favorite time to do so was at the time of announcing the firms' results, which, until the 1990s was done twice annually (they are now announced quarterly). I recall that a large multinational firm that made consumer products once made an announcement in 1987 that it planned to announce a bonus (equivalent of a stock split). As is the case in western markets, this was taken to be news of good underlying performance. Because this particular firm had a record of good performance and of announcing regular triennial bonuses (the maximum permitted under extant regulations), the stock price went up from Rs.160 to Rs.190 on the announcement.

It remained at that level until the announcement of the corporate event. Based on past events and its analysis of the firm's performance, the market's expectation was that the firm would announce a

4:5 bonus—that is, four new shares for every existing five shares, equivalent to a 9:5 stock split. On the afternoon of the actual announcement (which was to be made after the close of trading) a broker for a firm that I dealt with received a call from a client who worked for the multinational firm in question. He revealed that the actual bonus would be 1:1 (equivalent to a 2:1 stock split). This was the maximum allowed under the law and was above the market's expectations. The client said that he wished to purchase a large number of shares.

Upon receiving such insider information, the firm's ethical owners disregarded it and refused to execute their client's trade. It was fascinating that when the bonus was announced (it was 1:1, as the insider had correctly called), the stock price fell from Rs.190 to Rs.180. I was intrigued when I heard the tale and investigated it further with the most active traders on the floor. I found that enough insiders who knew the true ratio had traded up prior to the news and were selling on the news, leading to the fall. Perhaps it is fitting that the insider who gave us the information took his trade elsewhere and made a large purchase at Rs.190.

THE IMPACT OF THE EARLY LIBERALIZATIONS

The 1980s saw the first qualitative change in Indian stock markets since FERA 1973. The government of Rajiv Gandhi liberalized industrial quotas from 1985, for the first time enabling firms to plan very large projects. This meant large requirements for capital. Where, up to 1985, the announcement of even a Rs.200 million public issue ($20 million at the time) could sink the stock price of a firm by 10 percent or more, by the late 1980s, firms were routinely issuing additional capital of $100 million with only modest impact on the stock price. The volume of trade soared and the value of a broking license rose with it, from less than 200,000 rupees in 1984 to nearly 10 million rupees by 1990.

Because trading was still done on paper on the floor of the stock exchange, the high volume of trade often meant that it was difficult to make a trade. Brokers were entitled to also be jobbers. That is, they were allowed to execute two-way trades on a voluntary basis. This is unlike the specialist on the floor of the NYSE who is obliged to quote two-way prices. Some jobbers covered as many as fifty shares, usually including some thinly traded ones, and were the only ones who would make a market in such shares. However, for some large firms, such as Reliance Industries and Tata Steel, there would at any point be more than one jobber. During the periods when its results were to be announced and speculation was rampant, there might be as many as twenty jobbers.

During such busy times, even reaching the primary jobbers located at the center of the action was difficult. Outsiders in the mid-1980s would often derisively refer to the stockbroking community as "working as hard as schoolboys on summer hours" since the exchange would open for only two hours a day, from 11:30 A.M. to 1:30 P.M. But there was a good reason for such short hours: The rest of the time was needed to reconcile trades manually, a big problem in those nonelectronic days when all contracts were initially agreed to by verbal exchange on the floor, and discrepancies on volumes or price were common.

It also took hours to recover from the intense action on the floor, where merely reaching the location for a trade often required fighting one's way in. Some jobbers made a living by locating themselves at the periphery of a counter (a virtual counter, one should add, because it was wherever the main jobbers chose to locate themselves) and offering a higher spread than available at the center of the crowd. They would do the fighting into the center on behalf of their clients later.

It was a man's world in those busy days. The arrival of the first female stockbroker on the floor of the stock exchange in the late 1980s created a sensation. A tall woman in a sari, she confidently strode toward a particular counter to make her first trade. I was on hand and, to my consternation, the brokers treated her like one of their own. Like any male newcomer, she was disregarded initially; when she tried to force her way into the center of the counter, she was again disregarded, meaning that she had to fight her way in along with two dozen others competing for the jobber's attention. As I watched her getting pummeled along with the rest as she drilled into the center of the crowd, I wondered how she felt and whether she would be back the next day.

She returned and had her strategy perfectly worked out. She came with a megaphone in hand. Her sari was firmly draped around her so it would not come undone! Standing on the periphery of the counter, she calmly turned on the megaphone to full volume and called on the jobber. The jostling crowd was momentarily stunned into silence, the jobber called out the information she had sought and she made her trade. Since then, she has become a very successful broker.

It was relatively easy to make money in the stock markets of the Rajiv Gandhi era. This was because this was an environment in which inflation ran at 10 percent per annum and the government still licensed industries in order to conserve resources. As such, large industries continued to operate as monopolies or near monopolies. Hence, profits were predictable for the more transparent, well-run firms. There were several of these by the late 1980s, though still a minority of the total. The stock market thus offered long-term investors steady returns.

A REGULATOR IS BORN

Within a year of SEBI's arrival in 1991, and before foreign participants arrived, the stock exchanges were hit by a scandal of unprecedented proportions. A set of money-market brokers in Mumbai and Kolkata, in league with officers in both foreign and domestic banks and led by a kingpin named Harshad Mehta, borrowed large amounts from the banks through fraudulent transactions.

Their method was as follows: The broker would deliver a contract to Bank A showing that Bank A had bought government securities from Bank B on account of Bank A. Bank A would issue payment to the broker. The payment was supposed to be paid to Bank B after deducting the brokerage commission. The broker would, however, keep all the proceeds.

Because Bank B was unaware of the transaction, its books did not reveal any discrepancies. However, Bank A's books, when reconciled, would show that it had not received the securities. The records were maintained in a reconciliation ledger with the central bank. Given the poor state of computerization of such transactions, lax procedures for reconciliation, and corrupt bank officials, the brokers generated large sums, which were then deployed on the stock markets for several months before they had to be returned.

For a while, the profits from such transactions were large. Mehta played in many stocks, and the volume of his trades was so large relative to the rest of the market that he was able to influence prices. The market became enamored of Harshad Mehta. Pages about Mehta in the financial press (to which this author regrettably contributed while a business journalist in the 1990s) were devoted to analyzing his success. That his source of funds was dubious was not initially known. The assumption was that he had a hidden backer for the initial investments and that profits from his shrewd initial investments funded later forays.

Mehta's favorite investments were asset plays. For example, Scindia Steamship, a company whose assets consisted of merchant ships, was once rumored to be on Mehta's list. The firm's ships had long been grounded for lack of maintenance. It was on the verge of closure, kept alive only because someone in management had "persuaded" the government to take over the firm and keep the employees' payroll current—thus releasing management from this liability.

The firm's shares had languished at less than ten rupees for some years. A friend of mine had once bought a thousand shares at ten rupees a few years earlier. When I asked him why he had bought an apparent dud, he responded, "I figured, how low can it go?" He soon found out, for by early 1991, the shares traded at Rs.2.

The Mehta rumor mill then struck and, overnight, the shares went from Rs.2 to Rs.160. As I was then in the business as a journalist, my friend called me and asked if I thought it would go higher. I laughed and said that it was impossible that even Mehta could move the price of such a dud. I suggested he should sell. He did so, while the stock price was on the way down, at Rs.125. A few days later when Mehta announced that he was not an investor in the firm, its price, like its grounded ships, returned to its old moorings.

When Mehta's wrongdoings were finally discovered, the stock markets sank—and Mehta with it. Most of the other wrongdoers, including several foreign bankers who profited mightily for themselves and their firms, remain at large and have reinvented themselves in related businesses.

The Mehta scam came at a time when SEBI was too embryonic to help markets manage the crisis. A second scam, again fueled by bank money, surfaced in 2001. Although of similar proportion, a much stronger SEBI was able to deal with it without significant repercussions on the market.

The advent of foreign participants was the principal cause of a change in the rules of the game. This is not to state that all foreign investors, bankers, and brokers were clean, though most were. One out of the Middle East and another from the West Coast of the United States come to mind as firms that refused to give my firm business (I had rejoined the investment banking industry after my stint as a journalist) until we came through with favors. In one case, a request was made for a prostitute. When my salesperson came to me with this request, I was appalled and asked for the recording of the conversation. And there indeed it was, in the crudest Hindi, a request from the fund manager, a man of Indian origin who headed the multinational's Indian operations from overseas.

Under my advice, my colleague called him back saying that our firm would be glad to come over and treat the fund manager to a sumptuous dinner but that complying with his particular request was not possible. We never received any business from that firm. Yet we know of many others that did.

Foreign brokers and bankers brought with them the rules of the game as it was played overseas. Initially, SEBI had no idea of these rules. SEBI's bureaucrats were led by persons who came from diverse backgrounds, including a physicist and an electrical engineer, and lacked an understanding of disclosure-based regulation.

The advantage was that they were not dyed-in-the-wool bureaucrats. My guess is that they were chosen not because of their competence but because they were known to be honest. Being ignorant turned out to be a blessing. They were forced to rely on foreign firms for guidance because the domestic brokers, who were largely corrupt, did not understand the meaning of the term *rules*.

Dealing with foreign brokers was initially difficult for the SEBI regulators because of the problem of hierarchy. The foreign broking firms operated in the way common to their approach in developing countries. Their CEO was usually a generalist, more skilled in relationship management than in financial markets. The *content* people who were left to run the business were a step lower in the corporate hierarchy, with titles such as *manager, sales,* or *dealer*. SEBI's executive directors found it extremely difficult to even talk to specialists, let alone accept advice from them. After all, they were a step below them in their perception of the corporate ladder.

However, over time, both sides learned—the foreign firms by allocating fake divisional titles to specialists (also very useful for approaching the public financial institutions for registration) and SEBI by focusing on content.

As the rules of the game became established, foreign brokers applied to join the Bombay Stock Exchange. This was stoutly resisted by the BSE, which welcomed foreign investment but did not want to share the commissions with foreign brokers. Also, it realized that foreign entry would end its corrupt style of business.

Because the BSE was a private institution, there was little the regulators could do. The BSE was also extremely powerful with government higher-ups—hardly surprising, given its murky past—and with the media. The regulators were constantly chastised by both for pushing reform too fast.

Once, after several months of pressure from SEBI, the BSE announced that it would accept a new category of *professional members*—members with professional qualifications to be brokers. One might normally assume that the BSE would have had such a requirement from its inception, but this was the BSE, a club that existed for its members, their families, and close friends.

After about a year of framing the rules for professional membership (a delaying tactic), the BSE finally began the process of admission. Would-be professional members had to first sit for an examination—something that applicants who were sons and daughters of brokers did not have to do. They were then interviewed by the BSE board on their suitability.

It so happened that someone who had ranked first in the examination and had strong professional qualifications had, in the meanwhile, joined a foreign brokerage. At the interview, the BSE board refused to let him join, stating their worry that the interviewee would bring his foreign employer in as a member through him. When the interviewee later petitioned SEBI for redress, SEBI wrote a letter to the BSE asking for the reason that the applicant was turned down. The BSE merely responded that the interviewee was found unsuitable and gave no underlying reason. How do I know this? I was that applicant!

Through such incidents, and there were several, SEBI found itself stymied in seeking to introduce real change at the BSE. Nevertheless, a breakthrough was at hand.

THE NATIONAL STOCK EXCHANGE

The real breakthrough in regulation happened once the head of SEBI in the early 1990s, G. V. Ramakrishna, realized that working to reform the BSE was not going to bring about real change. Frustrated by the delaying tactics of the BSE, he realized that the quickest way to change the BSE's course was through promoting a competing stock exchange. Since all the others in existence, such as the Calcutta Stock Exchange, had the same ideas about stock broking as the BSE, another way had to be found.

Thus was born the government-sponsored National Stock Exchange. Heavily supported (after some initial hesitancy) by the foreign firms that were thoroughly fed up with the BSE's opacity and corruption, the NSE quickly became the leader in transparent functioning and business.

The NSE was both an unexpected and an easy success—unexpected because no one really believed that the state could establish a stock exchange. After four decades of failure, there was deep distrust of state action. In addition, there was the experience of the failure, years earlier, of a state initiative known as OTCEI (Over the Counter Exchange of India), designed to enable trading in small-company stocks.

SEBI favored the NSE with a national license, whereas the BSE was only allowed to operate in Mumbai (SEBI had been willing to do the same with the BSE provided it reformed). This, however, was not a crucial factor. The main thing that made the success of the NSE easy was that there was a sustained effort for it to achieve global best practices. So, while the members of the BSE continued to shout their trades on the BSE floor, the NSE began life as a fully digital exchange. Its members, connected by satellite links, could trade from their offices. There was no trading floor and no counter for shares. In other words, it was even more advanced than the New York Stock Exchange, which had continued with these traditional methods at the time. BSE brokers spent more time resolving differences in prices and volumes than they did on the trading floor. But this problem did not even exist under the electronic system. The NSE also pioneered the conversion of shares into electronic form by creating an electronic depository. Within three years of its commencing operations in 1994, the NSE overtook the BSE in market share and has not lost leadership since.

For students of institutional development, the creation of a state-sponsored stock exchange that could successfully compete with a private, 120-year-old stock exchange, many of whose members had been in the business over several generations, provides a new paradigm. When the NSE was formed, many pundits forecast an early demise on the grounds that a public-sector creation would never be able to stand up to the BSE, despite its corrupt ways. At the very least, it was thought, the BSE would respond to the NSE's pioneering moves with great rapidity and with better quality.

In reality, monopoly had weakened the BSE, and extensive corruption had corroded its own workings. For example, on simple decisions such as the computerization of trading, the BSE could not bring itself to take action for some years after the NSE introduced paperless trading. A member of the BSE computerization committee told me that this was because more than one IT vendor had bought the loyalties of the committee members, making it impossible to choose a vendor.

Foreign participants fully supported the NSE. As we noted, foreign brokers were initially disallowed by the BSE, which had wanted to retain all the lucrative new business coming from overseas for its own (domestic) members. By contrast, the NSE opened its doors to foreign brokers from the beginning. I know this well, too: The foreign firm that I led was admitted as its first member, and I worked closely on some parts of the rule-making with the NSE.

Thus, it was the combination of ingrained weaknesses on one side and an open environment with quick learning due to foreign participation on the other side that made this possible. The history of SEBI is very similar: It succeeded because it decided to adopt the best global practices. Playing by the rules made it difficult for the normal disruptions that characterize the public sector to destroy SEBI.

The lesson is that catching up is relatively easy to do. It is heartening to know that the public sector can add significant value. It could be argued that the state had other options: It could have allowed a new stock exchange to come up from the private sector, as well. However, it feared that any such organization would be staffed largely by the BSE's members due to their superior domain knowledge. It would end up being equally resistant to change. It feels good to report that the BSE finally was forced to clean up its act and, though unable to overtake the NSE, is now a more professional organization.

In conclusion, the history of Indian regulation and stock markets offers a new paradigm of successful institutionalization, one unavailable in the West or in any other country. It is a useful lesson on how regulators and the public sector can work together fruitfully.

CHAPTER 13

Rural India

THE STARK FACT IS THAT INDIAN FARMERS have successfully fed urban India but have failed to feed themselves. A telling statistic is that the poorest third of the population, mostly rural, consumes about 1,600 calories per day from various sources. This is about a third below their requirement. As a result, one-third of Indian children are born severely malnourished, and 50 percent of rural children below five years of age are underweight. Over a third of rural children are severely stunted as a result.

According to the World Bank, the Indian problem of undernutrition is worse even than sub-Saharan Africa. Nobelist and Harvard economist Amartya Sen has calculated that general undernourishment is nearly twice as high in India as in sub-Saharan Africa on average. The reasons appear to include poorer hygiene standards and a lower social status for women. Minorities and lower castes are more likely to suffer from malnutrition than upper castes. Meanwhile, in urban areas, although malnutrition remains a problem, it is limited to the bottom 15 percent of the population.

It is fashionable to blame British rule (the *British Raj*, as it is often termed) for many of India's problems. The rural deprivation problem is no exception. There is truth to the argument that the rural condition in states that were under British rule the longest ended up as the worst. The comparison between the Malabar and Cochin regions in the southern state of Kerala is instructive because initial conditions prior to British rule were similar. Up to the nineteenth century, the literacy rate in these two regions was about 13 percent. During British times, Cochin remained a princely state. Malabar became part of the British presidency system and was directly ruled by the British. By 1931, Cochin's literacy rate had doubled, while Malabar's was unchanged. Cochin's literacy rate was to double again in the next decade, while Malabar lagged far behind.

Nevertheless, it remains unfair to blame British economic policy for the *current* state of rural India. Several countries began in the 1950s with the same legacy of rural underdevelopment as India and subsequently did much better. For instance, by the end of the 1970s, when China had yet to begin its economic reforms, Jean Dreze and Amartya Sen point out that "almost the entire rural population had access to essential health services at a reasonable cost," while Indian rural areas' access to health care was negligible.[1]

This suggests that the current rural problem may have had political rather than economic causes that are proving resistant to change. It was perhaps not because of the extortionate rates of tax or neglect of agriculture during British rule that India today has a rural problem. Instead, I argue in this chapter that a key factor was that the British introduced a system of governance of rural areas based on a private patronage system. In independent India, this has proven more destructive and difficult to dislodge or reform than the most pernicious forms of bureaucracy that the British or Indians have devised.

THE RAJ'S RURAL PATRONAGE SYSTEM

During British times, agriculture was the most important source of revenue to the Raj. The extant system of agricultural taxation prior to British rule was the payment of an agreed share of the revenue earned during the year. The village was represented by a committee of elders who were responsible for making the payment to the village's urban protectorate.

The British found this system unsatisfactory because the tax varied by year, depending on the rains. This made the tax dues uncertain and hard to monitor. The British replaced the old system with a new one in which the tax was a fixed sum. They appointed the largest landowner as their collection agent. This sum was based on acreage and long-term productivity. The landlord became the patron of the village and, in turn, was part of the Raj's patronage network.

If the crops were weak in some years, no tax relief was afforded. Instead, peasants were expected to borrow in order to pay the tax. If there was a shortage of food, almost no relief was provided by the state to stave off famine. A persistent shortage of rainfall over some periods, particularly during the last twenty-five years of the nineteenth century, led to the rising impoverishment and indebtedness of the rural areas.

One consequence was the wholesale transfer of land to richer farmers. India also had regular incidences of famines during British rule, during which the Raj did very little. As Amartya Sen's studies have shown, famines in India were not caused by lack of food, but by lack of entitlement to food. Over 30 million are estimated to have died in famines during British rule, largely as a result of callous administration.

Upon observing the devastating effects of the Orissa famine of 1865 to 1866, Lord Salisbury, secretary of state for India, said the following:

> I did nothing for two months. Before that time the monsoon had closed the ports of Orissa—help was impossible—and—it is said—a million people died. The Governments of India and Bengal had taken in effect no precautions whatever. . . . I never could feel that I was free from all blame for the result.[2]

As Jawaharlal Nehru pointed out, by independence, hunger and mass poverty were worst in the parts of India that the British had governed the longest. Bengal, the richest part of India during Mughal times, had become one of the poorest after nearly 300 years of British rule. And the Raj never changed. At the end of 1942, even after a large shortfall in grain production, the viceroy was still arguing that any attempts to intervene in the business of foodgrain production and distribution were "not likely to yield results comparable to the panic they would create."[3] This helped to precipitate the terrible Bengal famine of 1943, in which 3 million persons died of food shortage and poor distribution.

By independence in 1947, agriculturists' exploitation for centuries at the hands of the "rentier, the usurer, the carpetbagger and the state," in the economist Christopher Baker's colorful phrase, had led to chronic indebtedness and, worse, uneconomic land ownership. Over three-fourths of landholdings were below five acres, and per-capita availability of grains had declined from 1,800 calories in 1921 to 1,400 calories in 1951. Even the five-acre figure does not give a sense of the unviability of landholdings, since many landholdings were divided up to ensure roughly equal land quality among the heirs, often into five or more strips of land of uneven size, contour, and water availability.

THE INDEPENDENCE REFORMS

With independence came a removal of the tax burden on agriculture. Under India's federal constitution, agriculture was handed over to the individual states to administer and tax; the states withdrew all the taxes that had hitherto been levied on agricultural production. The political impetus for this came from wealthier farmers.

The incidence of famines declined after independence, both due to the removal of tax and greater administrative responsiveness to monsoon failures. The latter was as may be expected of a democratic regime. Despite no systemic change in the pattern of rainfall, there has been only one "near famine" in 1966 (that one was averted by U.S. aid) in independent India's first six decades. This compares with four famines during the last six decades of British rule.

Jawaharlal Nehru, however, had little interest in agricultural development. Even politically easy initiatives such as creating cooperatives and providing finance were neglected. This was because Nehru's economic growth model was based on industry.

Nevertheless, the Congress Party needed the votes of rural India. It turned to the same network of landlords created by the Raj for collecting revenue. These became the Congress's political network in rural areas.

Under the Congress Party's patronage system, the rural elites were left alone—primarily, their income was not taxed and land was not redistributed to the poor—so long as they delivered the vote. This they could do because of the overwhelming economic dependence of the poor on the rich. Hence, the Congress Party saw no political pressure for programs that appealed to the rural masses. In consequence, during Nehru's rule, the states were deprived of funds to support agricultural development, and the condition of agriculture continued to deteriorate.

The economist V. Ramachandran provides an example of Nehru's weak commitment to land reforms.[4] Faced with a radical land-reform act (that took control of land away from absentee landlords and gave it to tillers) passed by the Communist government of the southern state of Kerala in 1959, the Congress Party began a violent campaign of social disruption in the state. Nehru used the violence to argue that the Communists were disrupting civic peace and dismissed the state government. The state then passed a new land act, largely undoing the gains of the earlier act.

This was the situation that the populist government of Indira Gandhi encountered in the late 1960s when it turned its attention from Nehru's first love, industry, to agriculture. Mrs. Gandhi's interest in agricultural development stemmed from her political style. Her style, as I have documented in Chapter 3, was populist and anti-patronage. She wanted to go over the heads of the patronage networks directly to the people. She realized that, just as she was doing for urban areas, a more equitable distribution of wealth had to be attempted. Whereas in urban areas this was sought to be accomplished by a large expansion of the state-owned industrial sector and the creation of strong trade unions, in agriculture a different strategy was needed.

A program of providing subsidized inputs, including fertilizer, power, and capital, was accordingly planned. Although fertilizer and power were under state control and relatively easy to subsidize, the banking system was largely privately owned. When the banks did not heed her informal requests to lend more to agriculture, Mrs. Gandhi imposed large lending quotas for agriculture. When they still did not lend to farmers, she accused them of colluding to prevent national development. Then she nationalized all the large banks in 1969, bringing more than 75 percent of the banking system directly under state ownership.

The 1970s was a decade of massive bank lending to agriculture. The lending began through a rural branch-opening program, followed by liberalized conditions for rural lending. Corruptly run, it was to bankrupt the banking system as a whole, from which it would not recover despite large-scale debt forgiveness and recapitalizations, until the 1990s.

Also during the 1960s and 1970s, with support from American foundations, the Green Revolution of Mexico was introduced to India. This consisted of the introduction of high-yielding varieties of grains, primarily wheat and rice, into already irrigated lands. It resulted in a rise in the productivity of such land by 30 percent on average.

The Green Revolution appears to have happened despite rather than because of Mrs. Gandhi's populist instincts. Atul Kohli and

Rani Mullen have pointed out that the Green Revolution concentrated production inputs in the hands of landowning classes in some regions of India (notably Punjab and Haryana, due to their high levels of irrigation) and so did not readily fit Indira Gandhi's populist, anti-elite designs. They note that Mrs. Gandhi was forced by the monsoon failures in the mid-1960s to ask the United States for food aid, which it did in return for India accepting the Green Revolution. They provide evidence on the political sensitivity of the potentially maldistributive impacts of the Green Revolution: The policies were adopted by a handful of the political elite, nearly as executive decisions, far from open political discussion. This was a far cry from Mrs. Gandhi's very public process of bank nationalization.[5]

Despite the Green Revolution and despite the rise in bank lending to agriculture, agricultural growth rates fell during Mrs. Gandhi's regime to 2.3 percent, compared with 3.1 percent during Nehru's rule. The continuing impoverishment of farmers pointed to the ever-deepening problem of the rural income divide. This forced Mrs. Gandhi to reconsider land reforms.

If there was one policy that would change the rural masses' view of her government, this was it. Nehru's failure on this front had cost the Congress Party in terms of votes, as we have documented; to the extent that the late Harvard sociologist Barrington Moore's description of him as "the gentle betrayer of the masses"[6] seems apt.

Mrs. Gandhi certainly spoke extensively about the need for land reforms. She imposed landholding ceilings in rural and urban areas, and even pushed through a law removing property ownership as a fundamental right enshrined in the constitution. However, she did not follow up with the implementation of land ceilings in rural areas. Some states, notably Kerala and West Bengal, were able to legislate some land redistribution, largely of unallocated or common property to poorer farmers. But this was not to Mrs. Gandhi's credit; she opposed the reforms because they were undertaken by opposing political parties.

There is a reason behind Mrs. Gandhi's inability to effectuate rural land ceilings: Her deinstitutionalization of the patronage networks was not her only act of deinstitutionalization. In her quest for personal popularity, she deinstitutionalized the Congress Party, the bureaucracy, the judiciary, civil society, and even other political parties. We have documented this in Chapter 3. The result was that the state's capacity to implement land reforms was severely curtailed.

Thus, during her rule, with the exception of the few areas brought under the Green Revolution, nothing significant changed in India's vast agricultural hinterlands. These continued their gradual decline into poverty and indebtedness. Later, in the name of the suffering masses, the state would forgive rural bank debt and increase subsidies on inputs such as power and fertilizer. But neither the capacity of the land nor the capabilities of its people were changed. A. K. Ramanujan, translator of U. R. Anantha Murthy's 1965 novel, *Samskara*, could accurately, if mockingly, write about the unchanging nature of rural India: "Indian Village Time: indefinite, continuous, anywhere between a few decades ago and the medieval centuries. The cycles of natural season and the calendar of human ceremony are interlocked in Village Time."[7]

THE MONEYLENDER'S ROLE IN AGRICULTURE

I came face to face with the systemic social problems of Indian agriculture in the early 1980s. I was, at the time, attempting to set up a project to grow tomatoes in water (using a technique called *hydroponics*). My project took place in the village of Karnala, a two-hour drive from the megalopolis of Mumbai. Karnala's villagers relied on two rice crops a year, one planted in time for the heavy rains during the monsoon season and the second to benefit from the still-wet soil immediately after the monsoon harvest.

I had several problems getting the project off the ground, not the least of which was that my project required peat moss. Peat moss is a natural soil-like product that is available in peat bogs in the northern hemispheres but is not found in India. The government's stringent import rules at the time listed each item that could be imported and the import tariff associated with the item. However, peat moss was not listed, probably because no one had imported it until then. At the same time, the customs inspectors were reluctant to classify it under the residual "other" category, in which event it would be taxed at 65 percent. This was because they did want to miss out on collecting a higher duty under some other category, assuming they could find one. So, they spent several months thinking about it. Their most helpful comment during this period was in response to pictures I showed them of what peat moss looked like. It was, "But why do you want to import mud when there is so much available in India?"

Finally, after peat moss was allowed under the "other" category, we set up the greenhouse and began planting our tomato seeds. One day in April, a farmhand, Hasuram, asked for a few days off. Since we were about to begin our tomato harvest the next day, I asked him if he could wait a few days. He said he could not do so, as he had urgent work on hand.

It emerged that the local moneylender, who was also the area's largest landowner, needed Hasuram to help him harvest his own land. The moneylender also planned to recruit several other villagers for the purpose, many of whom were beginning to harvest their own rice crops.

This seemed like the worst time to offer one's services to the moneylender. Were they paying off their debts to the moneylender in this way, I wondered? "Oh, no," said Hasuram, "We don't charge for this service. It is given for free," adding, cryptically, "We never pay off the moneylender's debt." It turned out, in further conversation with him, that the moneylender regularly took the season's best days for sowing and harvesting from Hasuram without payment.

The interest the borrowers paid him, a 15 percent rate, was separate.

Hasuram told me that he owed the moneylender just Rs.3,000 (about $300 in the exchange rate of the time). I was appalled: just $300, and his best business days were being given without compensation! I immediately offered him the money and urged him to repay the debt. I offered, too, to adjust his loan without interest against his future salary, something he could comfortably do, since he was being paid Rs.100 ($10) a day by me.

To my surprise, Hasuram refused. He said, "If I pay him off, he will be very upset with me as he can no longer claim my free labor." This made no sense to me. It made him debt-free and liberated him from supplying his labor during the critical periods, I argued.

He looked at me with perplexity as if the matter ought to be obvious. "Sir," he said, "You will employ me for some more time—one year, two years, maybe five years, ten if I am lucky. Who will I turn to thereafter when I need money? Unlike you, the moneylender and his family will be here forever."

THE TOLL OF SUBSIDIES

Eventually, Mrs. Gandhi's populist policies took a heavy toll, not only on the banking system but also on the rest of the economy. In particular, subsidies on power and fertilizer proved to be heavy burdens on the treasury. Its beneficiaries were both the rich and poor farmers, but the richer farmers were by far the bigger beneficiaries. This was because the subsidies were paid to the producer of power and fertilizer rather than to the user. Hence, the larger the user of these inputs, the bigger the benefit.

In retrospect, Mrs. Gandhi would no doubt be upset that her populist schemes were permanently captured by the very elites she was trying to bypass. By the year 2002, subsidies to meet the costs of power supplied to rural areas were 1.1 percent of GDP, and subsidies for the cost of fertilizers were another 0.5 percent. On average, agriculturists today pay about a half cent per kilowatt hour of power, or less than a tenth of the real cost of power. For many states with large rural populations, such as Andhra Pradesh, rural subsidies for power and fertilizer account for more than a third of the states' budgets, leaving too little to support rural education and health services.

As the rich farmers/moneylenders have captured the best land (and the benefits of subsidies), poorer farmers have moved to the tilling of smaller lots and poorer-quality land. In 1970, the median holding of land was sixteen acres. By 1995, it had come down to eight acres.

This has created a perverse situation: While rich farmers have used their clout to ensure that subsidized inputs will be continued (and some could survive if subsidies were reduced), the subsidies are crucial to the survival of the poor farmer. Urban analysts have long bemoaned the fact that the political power of rich farmers is stalling more rational pricing. This is true, but, if prices are raised, the poorer farmers will starve.

A better solution, of course, is to provide bigger subsidies to poor farmers than to rich ones. Unfortunately, this is a nonstarter in the current environment. It requires a fundamental change in how subsidies are delivered. Currently, subsidies on power, fertilizer, and finance are paid by the state directly to the utility, fertilizer producer, and bank. This will have to change if subsidies are to be targeted to farmers with low incomes. At the very least, the poor farmer will have to be identified. How will one do so, given that agriculturists are not required to pay taxes and keep no records of their income? So, even if politically possible, which is itself unlikely, it will be far messier with significantly more room for corrupt practice than the current system.

EVERYBODY HAS LOST OUT

But how rich is the rich farmer, and how badly off is the poor farmer? To study this more closely, Professor V. Ranganathan of the Indian Institute of Management, Bangalore, and I surveyed the land usage of more than 400 farmers in the southern state of Andhra Pradesh in 2000.[8] The farmers were distributed across the state and our study covered both irrigated and dry areas of the state. Most produced rice as the main crop. They typically harvested two crops a year from the land.

To our surprise, we found that, on average, the revenue farmers earned from the land was so inadequate that, had they been asked to pay the true cost of power and fertilizers, these costs would exceed their revenue. The bleak fact was that, for the average farmer, the land he tilled was so unproductive that he could not afford to pay the full price of inputs. We found that the average annual revenue per acre was Rs.2,300 ($50). For the average farmer with eight acres of land, the annual revenue was Rs.18,400 ($400). For the typical rural household of 5.5 persons, this is the equivalent of less than 25 U.S. cents of revenue per person per day.

Note that this is revenue, not income. Against this revenue, the farmer had to pay for fertilizer, seeds, and power, which accounted for 30 percent of his revenue. For the average farmer, the true cost of electricity (not the subsidized cost, which, as noted, was below 10 percent of the real cost) alone was Rs.21,000, that is, more than his income! We found that even the wealthiest 20 percent of farmers were only earning revenue that would allow them to pay up to 1 cent per kilowatt hour, or about a fifth of the true cost. *None* would be able to afford the real cost of power, which was about 5.5 cents per kilowatt hour.

In other words, even the rich farmers were no longer rich, and the poor farmers were much worse off. How had this happened?

The answer is that the patronage system ultimately chokes itself if it contains inadequate incentives to produce efficiently. The patronage system had prevented land reform in the first place and had thus created a deeply indebted and impoverished population that tilled its land. The combination meant that the land was increasingly tilled by an underfed population whose incentive to maximize production reduced with every generation. If the small farmer worked hard because his five acres of land could just about feed him and his family, then his sons, who inherited just half that amount because of the moneylender's debt, might work twice as hard. But, there would come a time when the sons would realize that no matter how hard they worked the next generation would be worse off than they. At that point, they would rather benefit from trying to cheat or upturn the system than by working hard.

The rich farmer saw this happening and understood the effect it would have on his own income. So, he persuaded the government to subsidize him; but this was just a purchase of time and not efficiency. So, finally, it has led to an inefficient, subsidy-driven agricultural-production system that is slowly bankrupting those it was meant to benefit.

POLICIES FOR AGRICULTURE

Here, then, was our bleak finding: Agriculture is a losing proposition. Ironically, Nehru, who rejected so many things that were rational simply because they were also British, retained the one institution—the rural patronage system—that was a disaster in the making.

Without pursuing land reform, if Indian policy makers pursue the apparently rational strategy of pricing inputs at cost, it will simply lead to a large rural exodus to urban areas unprepared to receive them. As it happens, the subsidy program has, to an extent, stabilized the rural population. The population in rural areas has declined very slowly from 82 percent at independence to 72 percent in 2007. By contrast, over the same period, China's rural population, despite its highly controlled closed-city policy (implemented through the *hukou*, or household registration system) declined from 88 percent to 60 percent. Worse still, today, per capita grain output in India is 160 kilograms compared with 380 kilograms in China. Meanwhile, the rural sector's contribution to the national product has fallen during this period, from 55 percent to less than 20 percent now.

A better policy than subsidies, absent land reform, would have been to spend more on rural health and education. This might, slowly, create the capacity for more productive rural activity, including rural industry. Even a policy of redirecting development money to create urban infrastructure to enable rural migration would have been a superior policy. Instead, the policy of directing funds to subsidies enriched only a minute proportion of the rural population and created a large class of impoverished agriculturists. It has led to an impossible social situation where the reduction of subsidies will lead to widespread bankruptcy (although this is not the right term, because the poor are not bankable), and so cannot be done.

After I completed the study with Dr. Ranganathan, the regular and disheartening news reports of farmers resorting to suicide whenever the states raised the price of subsidized inputs suddenly became explicable: These farmers were so poor that they existed only because of the subsidy. It would be cheaper for the state to force them to stop farming and receive a subsidy that fully compensated them for the lost income! And there is no respite: In 2006, on average, four farmers committed suicide every day.

Since the reform era began in 1991, the rural elite have become even more powerful. This is because of the new age of coalition government that was discussed in Chapter 3. They are now wooed by all the political parties, with the exception of the Communist parties. In some future era, it will take a leader with the charisma of Mrs. Gandhi, the sincerity of Nehru, and a party with a deep interest in the rural poor to reduce the power of the rural elite; no such combination appears likely to emerge from the current set of parties, all of which have other, largely urban, agendas.

Hence, the political dynamics of the rural areas are such that India must either build up very quickly an urban infrastructure that can receive large numbers of the rural poor, or it will happen that the rural poor will continue to keep India's development lopsided and, ultimately, well below its potential. The former is an unlikely outcome, at best. China, after decades of infrastructure buildup unfettered by urban political concerns, now has an urban infrastructure capable of absorbing ten million new rural migrants a year into the urban economy. This is beginning to have a substantial impact on the rural-urban mix. Combined with its low birth rate, China can expect that by 2050 its urban population will be 75 percent of the country's total, compared with 40 percent now.

India, by contrast, will be unable to accommodate more than two million persons a year into urban areas, a rate lower than the rate at which the rural population is growing. Hence, even by 2050, India will still have largely a rural population. What else can be done?

A ROLE FOR TECHNOLOGY

Can technology solve what seems an otherwise insoluble problem? In a study that I did with the state-owned National Informatics Center (NIC) in 2004, we unexpectedly came to grips with this problem. Our objective was supposed to be to study how rural users might best use information technology. Our expectation prior to the study was that rural users would be interested in keeping in touch with migrant relatives through e-mail and buying and selling agriculture-related items through the Internet. This suggested that, perhaps through installing public Internet kiosks, it might be possible to use technology to fulfill this need.

Instead, our project turned into an exercise in understanding how to develop rural areas. This was because, to our surprise, we found that existing IT services, which mostly provided e-mail and Internet access, were hardly used by villagers. They preferred to keep in touch with relatives using the humble postcard. This accounts for two-thirds of total mail in and out of a village and costs only 50 paise, or about one American cent (this is a heavily subsidized rate, though; the real cost being Rs.6.60).

With regard to using the Internet to undertake business, we found that services such as information on grain prices or using the Internet to distribute agricultural goods were largely unavailable. Even when available, these services were mostly unused. The villagers were well connected through middlemen to all the villages in the surrounding area with which they did business, and there was little added value to posting prices on the Internet.

When middlemen cheated them, as they often did, by colluding amongst themselves to set prices below market rates, the villagers accepted this. They did so not because they did not know better but because they could not surmount the grip of the middlemen, who were also their moneylenders and part-time employers.

Instead we found that the primary need of rural users was for government services. This surprised us, perhaps because those who conducted the study were urban dwellers. The typical urban dweller does not realize how much he takes government services for granted—to the point where it is common to say that government does not play a significant role in urban lives. In reality, in urban areas, services such as water supply, electricity, legal services, health care and education at all levels, welfare services, the postal system, tax payments, and official records are either owned by the state or closely regulated by it. They are part of the urban air we breathe that is taken for granted. Were these services not available—as is the case in India's villages—urban residents would complain of suffocation.

Even the minister for Information Technology was surprised by our findings and insisted we were wrong when I presented our final report to him and his team. It was only when NIC's respected departmental head, Dr. Vijayaditya, firmly stated that he stood fully behind the report was the minister willing to accept our findings.

We found that, most important of all, villagers want information on and access to employment projects in their areas. These are usually public projects such as road building, building construction, and infrastructure maintenance projects, and also include services such as employment in the postal system, state-owned banks, and state administration. Such information, in principle, can be posted on village or district Web sites. We termed such information *generic information* because it is potentially valuable to any Internet user.

Second, rural users need information specific to themselves, such as land records and birth and death certificates. These are needed primarily for business transactions, such as applications for bank loans and establishment of land claims.

They also need the government to speed up approval of claims, such as registration under various categories that entitle them to financial benefits, for instance, "below poverty line" (BPL) certificates and grievance redressal. Currently, issuing a BPL certificate takes a long time, and it is a corrupt process that involves intermediaries. Often, the claimant's poverty level frustrates her from completing the process. At the very least, a share of the proceeds must perforce be given by her to middlemen at all levels. This process needs to be simplified through a single-window application at an Internet kiosk and speedy disposal through electronic funds transfer to the local post office (which is typically close by and has a good distribution network). Further, the state's claims on its villagers for finance, such as water taxes, and information, such as the census or updating of land records, could be done through the Internet.

Third, services such as banking and postal services can be provided through the Internet. Consider, for example, the simple postcard, 255 million of which are mailed annually in India. This is a public document that, as noted, is the staple of postal communications in rural areas, accounting for about two-thirds of all such communications. As already noted, the postal service subsidizes the real cost of the postcard, Rs.6.60 (about 15 U.S. cents), and the user pays Rs.0.50 (a little over a penny), or less than 10 percent of the true cost. It takes seven days, on average, for a postcard sent from a village to reach a town in another state. And it takes even longer for a postcard to travel from one village to another village out of state.

Since the postcard is a public document, there is no reason why technology cannot be used to speed up the process while cutting costs. The user can write her postcard on a piece of paper or enter it directly into a kiosk from where the post office can transmit it electronically to its destination, print it out, and deliver it.

Happily, in this case, the postal service has already gone electronic, launching the ePost in 2004, although the service, which costs Rs.10 per mailing, is too high compared to the paper postcard, to be of much use in rural areas.

Finally, social services such as health and education need to be provided to a greater extent through the Internet, using already available tools such as distance learning and medical chat advice. This, incidentally, raises a policy dilemma for the state. Its long-standing policy, implemented at considerable cost, has been to create bricks-and-mortar institutions for the provision of health and education services. This policy is generally considered a failure, as already noted. Is it worth replacing it, or at least substantially supplementing it, with virtual learning via the Internet?

THE DILEMMAS OF RURAL EDUCATION

As I found out firsthand on a visit to a village school in southern Gujarat some years ago, the real problem with rural education lies with the system's structure. The secondary school I visited had not had a visit by a teacher for a week. There were a few children in the classroom being tutored by an older student.

According to the villagers, this was typical: The schoolteachers would visit just once a week, on average. The reason was that it was inconvenient for them to travel daily to work from their homes, which were always in the nearby towns. In these towns, the teachers were able to live the "normal" urban family lifestyle that they had grown up in. Their children went to urban schools, and most of the teachers had second (full-time) jobs in town.

It made no sense for the villagers to send their children to sit in empty classrooms. After talking with them, I finally understood something that had long puzzled me: why national statistics show that attendance rates drop sharply when rural schoolchildren transition from primary to secondary school. It goes from well over 75 percent of the eligible population to less than 40 percent. The popular wisdom, bolstered by studies by respected multilateral organizations, had been that rural schooling was viewed by illiterate villagers as a babysitting project. Once primary school was completed, the child no longer needed babysitting but could, on the contrary, be useful at home or on the farm.

I had never been convinced by such popular wisdom because I had observed during my field trips the deep desire of rural populations for education. In one village, I had seen that when an English-speaking school that was coming up in a nearby town was discussed, some parents said that they would be very keen on such a school in their village. One mother had told our team that she would be willing to sell her jewelry to pay for an English education for her children. During other field trips, I saw how popular privately provided computer education in the villages was.

The fault lay with the state, despite its good intentions: It could implement the "hardware," that is, the bricks-and-mortar part, but not the "software," the teaching. Now, with the Internet as a tool, the state has more choices but also more dilemmas. Should it (at high political cost) redesign the governance of village education? In Chapter 5, I noted that the state is trying this route by empowering the village administration so that it, rather than some absentee bureaucrat in a town, oversees the teacher.

Or, should it spend on Internet-based education? In the more remote areas, the state will probably have to make the sacrifice of forgoing the concept (but not the reality, given the absentee teacher) of face-to-face service provision in return for providing remote education to greater numbers.

In summary, rural "e-government" services should include:

◆ *Generic information* on and employment in government projects

◆ *Customized information* such as land records and birth certificates

◆ *Approvals*, such as for "below poverty line" status, and grievance redress

◆ *Social services*, such as health, education, entitlements, and other social services

◆ *Mandatory services*, such as taxation, updating land and population databases

◆ *Exchange services*, such as postal, banking, and utility services

DEMOCRACY AND THE  FUTURE OF AGRICULTURE

Although technology has a role to play in improving the rural condition, one should not be too optimistic about the impact of these solutions. They will probably make a difference, but not a transformative one.

What to do with rural India remains the enduring India problem of the century. Indian policy makers thought about rural industrialization but soon realized, like China did three decades earlier, that it made better economic sense to provide the resources in large, urban agglomerations. India, as we have noted, cannot pursue China's solution of mass urbanization as it will take several decades to build an urban infrastructure that can support large-scale rural migration.

If India's policy makers do not solve the problems facing rural India, will rural India revolt? This was Nehru's big fear: that the oppression of the people, particularly in rural India, might prove intolerable. But Nehru underestimated their tolerance. Of course, when he found that his policies on rural India, which were really anti-poor, had no impact on the poor's willingness to tolerate the system, he forgot about them.

So why don't the rural poor revolt? Instead, in every election since the mid-1970s, they go to the polling booths in large numbers. Indian voting rates are 55 percent of the eligible voters. But the urban poor and the rural areas have higher voting rates—up to 80 percent—than the wealthy urban residents, whose voting rate is 40 percent. This is the opposite of western trends. It seems inconsistent with findings in many other countries, where the poor are believed to lack the will to vote due to their state of poverty.

It also seems inconsistent with the other reality that we have spent this chapter discussing: the nearly hopeless state of rural India. Thus, the paradox is that, in a situation where over half the voters are illiterate and there is little hope for change, villagers still converge *en masse* on the polling booths come election time.

Popular commentary focuses on nationalism as the reason: Poor people in rural areas, we are told by urban analysts, vote because they want to register their presence as citizens. In other words, the vote is a *consumer good* from which pleasure is derived for its own sake. Such commentary, it should be noted, is usually accompanied by photographs of gaily colored voting booths and people dressed in their best for the occasion.

In reality, concepts such as pulling together for the nation's sake and collective action, which seem to be powerful forces in the development of China, ought to mean very little when one's livelihood depends entirely on toiling on someone else's land for a starvation wage. So, one should dismiss this explanation as something bordering on fiction.

I propose, instead, an alternative explanation based on an experience I once had of the democratic process in the Gujarati district of Anand, in western India. In order to understand the problems involved in marketing milk through the famed cooperative society, Amul, I attended a meeting between a local legislator and farmers.

I should note here that I grew up in an urban environment in which politicians are respected by their constituents because they are the most powerful bestowers of favors. Hence, I was thoroughly puzzled to observe what, even with my limited understanding of the Gujarati language, was obviously a verbal mauling of the legislator by his voters. Essentially, they told him, in no uncertain terms, that he had disappointed them. They added that if he did not solve their problems in short order, they would all vote him out in the next elections.

So here is my hypothesis: In urban areas, the Indian situation is no different from a typical American election where a candidate's true competence and inclinations are only revealed if he makes a mistake or if an opponent ferrets out a weakness, perhaps with the help of the press. This, over time, imbues urban voters with a certain cynicism of the electoral process. Urban voters assume that the candidate will reveal as little as possible about his own capabilities and as much as possible about the beliefs that he would like the public to know. So, many urban voters abstain from voting because they do not know enough about the differences among the candidates to care about the outcome. In addition, there are two more factors. Being wealthy, an urban voter will not suffer as much from a bad choice as would a poor voter. This makes him even less likely to vote. Being more homogeneous with the rest of the urban middle classes, he counts on others' percipience and energy to represent his interests.

By contrast, the poor, by virtue of their condition, have much sharper and accurate antennae as to which candidate can best help their situation. They also have the social networks that are missing in urban areas. These factors enable them to share information accurately and honestly among fellow voters and come up with a more accurate assessment of a candidate and the party he represents. Their higher voting rate is simply an outcome of the better quality of their assessment.

Put this way, a cynic might conclude that democracy is the ultimate opium of the masses. It fools them each time, convincing them that it is worth participating whereas they might do better with a revolt.

But this misses the point: It is not democracy that is an opiate. Many countries have found that they need to go through several cycles of democratic elections before the candidates become responsive to voters' needs. Among those countries that are genuine democracies—at least in the sense that candidates can freely stand, voters are allowed to freely vote, and the vote is fairly counted—India is the world's youngest. If the United States could take centuries of such a genuine democracy before its black citizens were fully empowered to participate, India's situation should be given a similar understanding. Perhaps not deliberately but certainly definitively, India's rural voters are saying through their vote that, if not for themselves, they are buying time for their children. They realize that a revolt would move that time further back, but a vote brings it—however infinitesimally—closer.

CHAPTER 14

The Media in India

INDIA'S LOVE OF READING seems hard to dispute. The literacy rate is about 60 percent; that is, about 600 million Indians are literate. More than 45,000 newspapers are published in India, including more than 7,500 in English. By comparison, literacy in America is nearly universal. There are around 300 million literate Americans— about half the number as in India. But there are only 1,500 newspapers. China, which has a literacy rate of 90 percent (or, over 1 billion literates), has 2,000 newspapers. In short, India, despite its poverty and illiteracy, is a nation of exceptional readers. Delhi alone has nine daily newspapers in Urdu and nearly 500 in Hindi.

A perfect place to observe the love of reading is on the trains. Mumbai's metropolitan train system, consisting of first-class and second-class travel, is always crowded, with standing room only at any hour of the day or night, in any class. The only difference between first- and second-class travel is that one gets elbowed by a better class of passenger. Yet, in both classes, a significant number of passengers (perhaps at least twenty per each overcrowded railway wagon), can be seen with one hand holding a strap up above for balance (which is unnecessary, because the press of the crowd around the traveler provides perfect stability) and one holding the evening newspaper open to read.

Take a longer train ride, say, the twenty-four-hour Chennai Express from Mumbai's Dadar train station to Chennai's Central Station, and the books emerge from the duffle bags within a few moments of settling in with a clay cup of tea. Or, go to a two-room tenement in a middle-class Mumbai neighborhood, such as Golpitha near the red-light district, and you might see the study area. This is no more than a bar stool near the apartment's only window. The bar stool enables the windowsill to be used as a table for laying out books, pens, and other study materials. The family's readers, adults and children alike, take turns reading and studying at the window. Why at the window? To save electricity, of course. By day, the sun, and by night, the streetlights, provide the needed illumination.

Even the illiterate population is known to "read" newspapers. In the villages, someone who is literate often reads the news to groups of illiterate villagers, although this practice undoubtedly faces increasing competition due to universal TV coverage by satellite.

THE FREEDOM OF THE MEDIA

The media are, in theory, free, because there has never been an official censor except during the Emergency of 1975 to 1977. Since the early days of independence, the media have been owned by large industrial groups. When Nehru began his socialist program, the media were active opponents. In response, the government tried to muzzle the press. Since the media's right to exist was constitutionally protected, the government used other methods, such as denying advertisements to unfriendly newspapers by organizations that were owned by or did business with the state. This included almost all big companies, so it was an effective way to exercise influence.

Another strategy was to fine-tune a newspaper's quota of newsprint, depending on how pliant it was. As a result, over time, most newspapers began to tow the government's line as a strategy for survival. The press releases of the state-owned Press Trust of India provided the bulk of their content. Until the 1990s, private television was disallowed. So, an interesting experience up to the 1980s was to read identical headlines in all the newspapers in the morning and hear the same words later that evening on state-owned television.

In other words, the press, by and large, towed the line of the administration of the day. A few English-language newspapers that were privately owned but independent of conglomerate linkages tended to be more independent-minded than the mainstream press. The *Statesman* (of Kolkata) and the *Indian Express* (of Mumbai) stand out in this regard. The Indian-language newspapers were also more independent than the English press. This was because they relied less on advertising and more on circulation.

The Emergency marked both the low point of press freedom and a turning point. With the exception of the *Statesman* and the *Indian Express*, the English-language press scraped and groveled to accommodate the state during the Emergency. Even the former had to be very careful to escape the censor's eye. In what are now iconic tales of defiance, the *Indian Express* got away with the following message in its obituary section in 1976: "O'Cracy: D.E.M. O'Cracy, beloved husband of T. Ruth, Father of L. I. Berty, father of Faith, Hope and Justice, on June 26."[1] And a library in Calcutta issued a notice in the *Statesman* in December 1975, stating: "On and from 1st January 1976, newspapers will be found in the fiction section."[2]

After the Emergency was lifted and elections were called for, the vernacular press and English-language papers like the *Indian Express* played a key role in Mrs. Gandhi's subsequent electoral defeat. Their success for the first time changed the dependence of the press on the state.

After 1991, the reform of the Indian economy marketized (including the privatization of) larger sections of the economy, thus making the media less dependent on the state for survival. The granting of permission to set up private electronic broadcast channels further increased their independence. By the mid-1990s, it seemed that the media were under no real threat of state control. They were ready to play, it seemed, a central role in the vitalization of civil society and in the development process.

THE POWER OF THE MEDIA

I discovered the power of the media firsthand as an editor at *Business India* magazine, then the country's largest-circulating business magazine, during the early days of the economic reforms. I was responsible for editorials, corporate stories, and the stock markets section of the magazine. Our editorial stance was promarket. In those early days of reform, Indian businesses were still small and their managers were approachable. I found it easy to meet with the CEO of almost any company that our magazine wished to write about.

Writing about stock markets was more challenging. The markets in those days, as I have documented in Chapter 12, were composed of, to put it delicately, ethically challenged individuals. As the editor of all stock market content, I constantly had to confront and manage this issue. For example, shortly after I joined, a colleague returned from a press conference with a bag laden with gifts: a bottle of Indian liquor (its official term was IMFL or Indian-made foreign liquor), a pen set, and some food. I asked him where he had obtained the bag. He turned over the bag to its other side and showed me the name of a firm about to go public with a stock market listing of its shares. He had returned from the pre-IPO media meeting in which the company had handed out a bag like this to all the journalists present. I was appalled, but being new, kept quiet.

Upon further inquiry, I discovered that my colleague's acceptance of the "gift bag," as it was referred to by the advertising agencies that arranged the media event, was common practice. For every media conference, a gift bag for each reporter was, it turned out, a must. The value was at least Rs.2,500—about half the typical journalist's monthly salary in those days.

Since each of our team members attended at least two such IPO meetings each week, the gifts seemed out of line with ethical practice. I argued with my colleagues and, with the intervention of the publisher, got the practice stopped, at least officially. Although many of my fellow journalists argued that the gifts had no influence on their writing, we later found that one of our team had indeed written stories that were influenced by such gifts, so it turned out to be the right thing to do.

An equally difficult problem, interestingly, turned out to be how to refuse the gift. My colleagues argued that if they turned down the gift, the advertising agency would assume that a competitor had paid them off to write a bad story on the agency's client. I decided to call their bluff by attending one such event myself jointly with a more regular attendee colleague and the magazine's photographer.

The soon to-be-listed company, a firm making stainless steel and stainless steel appliances, made an impressive presentation. As we were leaving, my colleague introduced me as his editor to the ad agency representative. The agency man was very warm, accompanied us to the door and, as we left, handed us not one bag, as he was apparently wont to do, but two—one of which, he said, was specially to thank me for coming.

I politely said that it was now company policy that we would not accept gifts. This had the reaction that my colleague had predicted: The agency man, after first pressing me repeatedly to accept, then gave up with bad grace and said that he would have to inform his client that we had refused their gift.

A few days later, the CEO of the firm called me. He asked if there was anything I needed to know about his firm. This was, of course, unusual. I asked him some questions. At the end of the call, he asked for my home address. I asked him why he needed it. He said that he wanted to send me an invitation card for an upcoming corporate event. I should have suspected something, but did not, and so gave him my address.

The next day, my wife, who was home, called and said that a very large parcel had been delivered. It was from the same CEO who had called. When we opened it that evening, we found that it was a full dinner set of stainless steel.

At the office the next day, I carried the heavy gift with some difficulty to the fourteenth floor where we had our offices, to the amusement of the liftman and the reception staff. I proceeded to call the advertising agency's representative and told him what had happened. I told him that I saw a connection between the press event and the CEO's call, and that if he did not immediately collect the gift, I would have to take action (although I had no idea what I might do). The agency man asked for some time and later called back to say that he thought the CEO, of whom he spoke in worshipful terms as a man of great achievement and a pillar of Ahmedabad society, would be deeply offended if he found out. Would I mind keeping the gift this one time and he would ensure such a thing never happened again?

I refused, but we finally agreed on a course of action. He would collect the gift back but determine on his own what to do about it. He reserved the right to inform his client or not. I let it go at that. Later, I got to know his client a little better and found out that he, like all other CEOs, was merely following the advice of his investment bankers on these matters. He was indeed a pillar of Ahmedabad society and a man of achievement. Later, as an investment banker myself, I understood how correct the CEO had been about the importance of following his investment banker's advice—but that is another story.

In 1992, I left *Business India* to head a multinational investment bank. As I went about mining the same contacts to get business for our firm, I discovered the same CEOs were far more reluctant to speak with me. Because I had established direct relations with quite a few and considered myself respected in the field, I was curious to find out what had changed. Was it because I had joined a foreign company? Or was it something else?

The answer came to me a short while later when I met the CEO of a large steel firm (not the same as in the IPO story) to discuss doing business with his company. I had been thinking, meanwhile, of writing a column for *Business India* on business reforms, and mentioned this to the CEO. Immediately, I found his attitude changing; he seemed far keener to speak with me. Puzzled, I asked him frankly, "S__, I notice that CEOs of firms we want to do business with do not seem to want to talk to me as frankly as they used to when I was in the media. I was expecting quite the reverse, since they can now give me information with the confidence that I won't reveal it to the world; indeed, by the standards of practice of the investment banking profession, I cannot reveal it to the world."

He replied, "Earlier I always met you because I was scared that, if I did not, you would write something based on outside and possibly incorrect information. So, I wanted to make sure that you heard what you needed to hear from me. Now, meeting you or not is a commercial decision, so it is less frequent—after all, there are many investment banks that want my business."

I got the message: Earlier, he met me because he was scared of the power of the media. As an investment banker, I could not harm him in any way; in fact, I would want to deal with him even if he was rude—but that is the vitiated nature of the investment banking world, which is, as I noted, another story!

As you can see, the media are unfettered and now a powerful civil society participant in India. Have they used that power well? Some previous examples might suggest that media capture is possible, though less so by government than before. However, as is well known, this is not unusual, even in developed democracies. Unlike these countries, though, there is no other system of checks and balances. Hence, it is possible for the media to also get things wrong and for the results to be damaging, as I documented in Chapter 12 on stock markets.

THE STORY OF *TEHELKA*

The quality of investigative journalism has improved both with time and as the media gained more freedom. As in the United States and other western countries, the media have been the main tool in the hands of the people to report truthfully on current events, expose underlying corruption, and write good investigative stories.

"Operation West End," as it was called, exposed both the power and the limitations of the media. In 2001, the online journal *Tehelka*, headed by two fearless journalists, Tarun Tejpal and Aniruddha Bahal, carried out a sting operation that exposed politicians at the highest levels accepting bribes to approve defense contracts. The public outrage forced the ruling coalition government, headed by the BJP, to collect the resignation of its defense minister, George Fernandes, who was directly exposed by the sting operation, along with several politicians of the BJP.

As a long-time watcher of the media and an erstwhile participant, I was particularly impressed by Tejpal and Bahal's willingness to take on the defense ministry, a byword in India for corrupt practices. While a business journalist, I had sometimes heard fellow nonbusiness journalists mutter to one another that the defense ministry was not worth taking on: It was so powerful and so tied up in intrigue and murky dealings up to the highest that interfering with it could ruin their careers. And yet, here was an apparent success for open and fearless journalism against the defense ministry, something that all journalists in India ought to rejoice in.

Alas, I should have kept my cynicism intact and reined in my optimism. The government launched a fierce counterattack, accusing *Tehelka* of financial irregularities. It jailed some of its journalists and its chief financial supporter. Other investors backed off in consequence, and the site shut down in 2003. A short while later, George Fernandes was reinstated as defense minister.

Worse, a perusal of the other newspapers of the day, beginning with the all-pervasive *Times of India*, showed that none, without exception, had been willing to follow up on *Tehelka*'s expose with their own work. Their reportage on the sting operation was based entirely on work done by *Tehelka*. When *Tehelka* was shut down, they let the story drop. Had they taken it up, it would have been much harder for the state to pursue *Tehelka*.

After *Tehelka* shut down, the issue disappeared from view. *Tehelka*, however, restarted in 2004 and remains a fine example of investigative journalism. In Chapter 5 I documented its role in bringing the Jessica Lall case to retrial. Nonetheless, a golden opportunity to bring to account one of the murkiest government departments has been lost.

I spoke with Bahal when he visited the United States in 2003 to give talks on his work. He was candid about the personal implications of what he had done. He told me, "I doubt whether I will be allowed to do such work again; the government will make sure that I do not." So, it is heartening to note—and undoubtedly a tribute to the government of Manmohan Singh—that Bahal is back at his job, though the defense ministry remains out of reach for investigative journalists. As of this writing, the stung Mr. Fernandes also remains a parlimentarian, having been reelected in 2004. His is a sad if unfinished tale of a once-promising fiery trade-union leader whose career included such genuine achievements as publicly opposing the Emergency and being jailed for it. The inference for the freedom of the media is mixed: Although India's media are as free as they have ever been, it appears that they are not as free as they should be.

WHAT'S RIGHT WITH THE MEDIA AND WHAT'S LEFT TO DO

In Chapter 10 I documented the complicity of the *Sandesh* newspaper in abetting the 2002 Ahmedabad riots. The *Tehelka* story shows what can happen when the government behaves badly. In both cases, it appeared that the state could decide the outcome. On the one hand, *Sandesh* continues to publish its newspaper and has never been officially taken to task for its role in the riots. This is because the government in power sympathizes with its views. *Tehelka*, on the other hand, was shut down because the government wanted revenge for its exposé of government corruption.

Because these are modern-day, post-Emergency stories, it is worth asking if they tell us something about the media beyond the starry-eyed opinion that they are a pillar of Indian democracy. It is clear that the media are vibrant in the sense that media cater to market demand and determine their own priorities. In a negative sense, then, the media are free. No agency can force a television channel or newspaper to publish or otherwise cover a story it does not wish to cover.

It is in the other senses that we should assess the quality of the media. Does it choose to cover the issues of the day with sincerity and depth? Certainly, Operation West End showed the rest of the media in a very poor light. However, the media coverage of the Enron affair, the stock market scam, and the Jessica Lall corruption case, documented in Chapter 5, was intense and valuable.

In general, if there is a crisis that affects the public at large, such as a water shortage, the media provides excellent coverage. In fact, given that India is both a poor country and a large one, there are normally several critical stories every day. When I was the editor of *Business India*, I would sympathize with my colleagues who worked in the daily papers. While we would pick our stories well in advance and work on them over long periods, their task seemed infinitely more demanding. This was because they had far too many important stories to choose from. At any point, some state in the country would be having a political crisis, a health crisis would have broken out in some city, farmers would be protesting high electricity prices, and the stock market would be hitting a record high or tumbling. After all, it is in the nature of a politically active, developing country that it would have more crises and other newsworthy events than a stable, developed country or a dictatorship. News that would make the headlines of a western newspaper would jostle for a paragraph's space with a dozen other items on page three of an Indian newspaper.

This makes Indian media always worth listening to or reading. It is unthinkable, for example, for the Indian media to cover the Chinese famine of 1958 to 1961 the way that the Chinese media covered it, even if the Emergency was on. Then, the Chinese press duped the public by suppressing information about the famine. In the process, as Jean Dreze and Amartya Sen have pointed out, it duped the government as well. According to Dreze and Sen, local leaders competed with one another "to (publish) rosy reports of their alleged success (in managing the famine), outdoing their regional rivals, and at one stage, the Chinese government was convinced that it had a 100 million more metric tons of foodgrains than it actually had."[3]

Though great on reportage, the problem with the media is the lack of investigative work. The few exceptions, such as *Tehelka*, only prove the view that the Indian media are "high on carbs and low on protein." This cannot be due to a lack of education or lack of demand. Nor are the media any longer underpaid or lacking glamour, unlike their situation up to the 1980s. On the contrary, the reverse is the case. Their conservative business owners are probably one reason, but competition should nullify this effect.

Whatever the reasons, there is much that is right with the media and much that is left to do.

CHAPTER 15

Different Approaches
to Development?

SUCCESSFUL COUNTRIES WERE INFLUENCED by certain key idiosyncratic forces in their development. In Asia, Malaysia's Chinese businesses and Korea's large firms' ties with the state are examples, although human-capital development appears to be a more general, precedent force to their economic development. A description of Taiwan's success would have to include the role played by the state in encouraging small firms—in particular, its role in leading the shift to technical-goods exports was critical. In Korea, state policy was directed toward enabling exports by large firms working closely with banks.

After decades of commentary on its idiosyncratic weaknesses, such as in human capital and physical infrastructure, India these days is getting another look. Its growth story is commonly understood to be a three-stage process. In the first stage, starting in 1991, the state got out of business and removed constraints on the private sector. In the second stage, starting in the mid-1990s, the state began facilitating infrastructure through effective regulation. In the new century, a third stage has begun: India is reaping the benefits through the initiative of private enterprise.

Is it really that simple? This final chapter is an attempt to provide a more nuanced view. I shall consider the role of two developmental forces, one of which is little noticed and the other little understood. I refer, respectively, to urbanization and democracy. I shall discuss their role and whether these can be sources of vulnerability in India's growth story.

THE ROLE OF CITIES

The first aspect I consider is the role of cities in a country's development. Cities matter a great deal to a country's economic development. Geographer Walter Christaller's central place theory has proven that a country that lacks at least one great city has never succeeded. Cities enable specialization and the provision of more sophisticated services than is possible with distributed rural populations. Services such as financial markets, sports, film, and education can usually be sustained only in the large cities.

Up to a certain national size, urban areas are few and highly concentrated. In some countries, only a single city really matters for the country's development. Japan, Korea, and the United Kingdom are examples where their leading city accounts for at least 20 percent of national population and product—in Korea, Seoul accounts for 50 percent. If a large, established business from overseas wishes to set up shop in Korea, there is effectively no choice but to do so in Seoul.

However, in populous countries, several large cities are the norm. There is more specialization by city and, therefore, more choice. For instance, politics and business are specialized by city.

Mumbai is as different from Delhi as New York is from Washington, D.C. One pioneers finance and commerce (and is wooed by politicians), the other focuses on politics (and is wooed by business). In both countries, the politically sensitive industries are located in the capital city—industries such as telecommunications, airlines, and defense industries. The industrially sensitive policies, such as securities regulation, are determined in Mumbai and New York, not Delhi or Washington. Since business and politics can be overpowering activities, consuming too much time and energy for those who just want to *do it*, the *it* part is often done elsewhere, whether it be IT in Bangalore or the Silicon Valley or automobile manufacturing in Chennai or Detroit.

In these respects, the United States and India share some similarities. The variety of their cities also stabilizes development in a way that smaller countries cannot hope for. For instance, the cities of the Indian South—Bangalore, Hyderabad, and Chennai—have offset the cyclical stagnation of earlier industrial leaders such as Ahmedabad and Kolkata. This is similar to the role that the cities of the American South and Southwest, such as Atlanta and Houston played in the 1970s and 1980s when the rust-belt cities such as Detroit and Pittsburgh declined.

Despite these urban parallels, there is greater cultural homogeneity across American cities than Indian cities. This is partly because the proportion of the urbanized population is vastly different. The United States is almost completely urbanized and subject to nationally common influences such as television. India, however, has a largely rural, more isolated, population. The rural population retains influence over a nearby urban area through constant migration and political interaction. The urban areas of India are, therefore, more integrated with their rural areas than American cities are with their surrounding rural areas.

An example of these differences is in the way urban residents vote. The ten most populous cities in the United States all voted for

Democratic candidates in the 2004 presidential election. By contrast, in India's 2004 national elections, three of the ten most populous cities voted for the Congress, three for the BJP, one for the Communists, and the rest for regional parties. In all these cases, the cities voted like the villages surrounding them.

The other reason for the lack of homogeneity of thought across Indian cities is that different regions areas often have long histories of their own that have influenced the thinking of their inhabitants. For instance, Delhi's residents include large numbers who trace their roots to Mughal Delhi of the seventeenth century. Their cultural expressions reflect a "Delhi-ness" that is unique.

So, for example, to a resident of Trivandrum, Kerala's capital city, development is intrinsically linked with public action on basic citizens' rights, such as health and education. This is because Trivandrum has witnessed over two centuries of public action in these fields. To his nearby Bangalorean counterpart, just a state away, development occurs when the state gets out of the way and leaves even the provision of education and health services to the private sector. This, in turn, reflects Bangalore's history of British colonial rule. The imperial state chose not to support education and other infrastructure, leaving private initiative to finance schools and roads.

The cultural heterogeneity of urban India should be viewed as a strength, not least for the richness of cultural expressions that it produces. From a developmental viewpoint, I have noted the stabilizing influence of the variation in industrial activity that it enables. Even the different strategies chosen by different cities should be viewed positively. As developmental experts are increasingly realizing, there is no single best approach. It is now recognized that, at the very least, strategies for development ought to be sensitive to differences in local traditions and capabilities. If this means that the Kerala path to development differs from that of Karnataka, it does not mean that one is worse than the other.

VARIATIONS IN DEMOCRACY

A second fundamental issue is the role of democracy in India's development. It is common these days to read that "India is the world's largest democracy" (the phrase gets more than 2 million search results on Yahoo!, 1.2 million on Google). This is true, but it misleadingly conveys the sense that the main difference between Indian democracy and, say, U.S. democracy, is that there are more people around to experience it in India.

In fact, democratic values mean different things in the two countries. One reason is that there are differences in the federal structure: In the United States, power flows upward from the state to the nation's capitol; Indian federalism, on the other hand, means a strong center with limited powers delegated to the states.

This has implications for how decisions on social services are taken, for example. In India, both New Delhi and the states run schools, colleges, and hospitals, whereas in the United States, federally managed institutions are rare. Utility regulation is another important difference. Telecommunications is a *central* subject in India, so regulatory decisions by New Delhi cannot be challenged by the states. This is unlike the United States, where the responsibility for telecommunications is shared between Washington and the states. By contrast, electric power is a *concurrent* subject, shared between New Delhi and the states, just like in the United States.

Because the states generally have more political power in the United States than in India, they are more responsible for outcomes. So those that believe in being business-friendly, for instance, have a greater capacity to be so than an equally business-friendly Indian state. For example, the southern state of Andhra Pradesh prides itself on being pro-business. Yet, its recent initiatives to woo American semiconductor fabricators were successful (it finally persuaded Advanced Micro Devices to supply critical technology to a fabrication plant) only when New Delhi turned supportive. In the United

States, by contrast, Washington, D.C., is typically neutral to inter-state competition for new investment from overseas.

Another difference in the type of democracy is the quality of civil society—that is, the capability of a country's citizens to voluntarily create associations for the public good. In his book *Democracy in America*, published in 1835, Alexis de Tocqueville said:

> In democratic peoples, associations must take the place of the powerful particular persons whom equality of conditions has made disappear. . . . Among the laws that rule human societies there is one that seems more precise and clearer than all the others. In order that men remain civilized or become so, the art of associating must be developed and perfected among them in the same ratio as equality of conditions increases.[1]

About Americans and civil society, de Tocqueville stated:

> Americans of all ages, all conditions, all minds constantly unite. Not only do they have commercial and industrial associations in which all take part, but they also have a thousand other kinds: religious, moral, grave, futile, very general and very particular, immense and very small; Americans use associations to give fêtes, to found seminaries, to build inns, to raise churches, to distribute books, to send missionaries to the Antipodes; in this manner they create hospitals, prisons, schools. Finally, if it is a question of bringing to light a truth or developing a sentiment with the support of a great example, they associate. Everywhere that, at the head of a new undertaking, you see the government in France and a great lord in England, count on it that you will perceive an association in the United States. . . . As soon as several of the inhabitants of the United States have conceived a sentiment or an idea that they want to produce in the world, they seek each other out; and when they have found each other, they unite. From then on, they are no longer isolated men, but a power one sees from afar, whose actions serve as an example; a power that speaks, and to which one listens.[2]

In India, for reasons of its colonial and immediate post-independence history more than culture, there is a near-absence of civil society, as we have discussed. The lack of public action to tackle issues such as corruption and the lack of public discussion of important issues such as secularism, food security, and AIDS makes society vulnerable to the sway of politicians. Indira Gandhi showed the fragility of Indian democracy during the Emergency, but the problem is still evident on a daily basis to the millions of citizens denied basic rights such as food. The country's ability to respond to challenging issues rests solely on the right to vote at elections in a free and fair way. This is only an occasional corrective—powerful for "throwing the scoundrels out" but ineffective for ongoing accountability and midcourse corrections.

Even a free and fair vote can be subject to misuse due to the lack of civil society. Indira Gandhi, for example, used to regularly manufacture artificial crises at election time in order to divert citizens' minds from her governance. She would then use populist rallying cries in order to portray herself as the people's heroine. For instance, prior to the elections of 1971, she accused businesses of being responsible for the country's economic failure. She then launched a much-trumpeted *garibi hatao* (remove poverty) program in response, which she promised would be funded by taxes on the rich. The slogan-mongering won her the election in 1971; but *garibi hatao* was never seriously implemented, nor were taxes on the rich increased. It was all a ruse, it turned out, to win the vote. Meanwhile, there was no civil society that could organize to hold her accountable to her promises or even expose her prior policies to public scrutiny during a subsequent vote.

Ultimately, the political system loses out when civil society is weak. This is because politicians have a strong incentive not to keep their promises. One cannot entirely blame politicians for this. They seek votes from an electorate that is hardened to the point that it will not believe them. In the absence of civil society, there is no group that will be their advocate and stand up for their promises through public scrutiny of their work in other areas.

In the United States, the typical politician spends a lifetime preparing for national office—through college politics, local politics, and state politics. He thus establishes a paper trail of accountability that is eagerly scrutinized by civil society when he stands for higher office. In India, the voting public frequently knows little about a politician standing for parliament for the first time. Voters might not see the candidate's name until it appears on the rolls as a candidate. There is no group to act as an intermediary on the public's behalf. This allows candidates with no known record in public office to win—something unthinkable in the United States. In one state election in Uttar Pradesh, so little-known was the candidate of a particular party that he was serving a jail term when he won. Having obtained bail, he came to the public announcement of his victory straight from prison!

The only way to get elected is through tendering, with each successive election, an ever-more extravagant promise. So, the politician who may believe that electric power ought to be fairly priced is forced by his competitors to consider a subsidy because they argue that the poor ought to pay less than the rich. He ends up campaigning for its free provision to the farmers and housewives in order to get their votes.

There are already three states in India—Andhra Pradesh, Tamil Nadu, and Punjab—where farmers receive free power for running their agricultural operations. The reform-minded chief minister of Andhra Pradesh lost the election on this issue in 2004. He refused to countenance the provision of free power, while his opponents in the Congress Party lobbied vigorously for it. Throughout this process, there were no organizations that, through public action, could have worked to discuss the issue, convince the public that free power was not sustainable, and urge politicians to cease from such destructive policy. The press is a lively commentator, of course, but its power is limited by its inability to undertake public action.

INDIA VS. CHINA

Outsiders are wont to say that India differs significantly from its great neighbor to the east, China. More unkindly for India, there have been several articles in the recent past with titles such as, "Is China a Success While India is a Failure?" According to commentators like Edward Friedman, whose 2004 article ran with that title (he is, however, skeptical about calling China a success), for many Chinese, it is a matter of Confucianism versus Hinduism. As Friedman writes, "The Chinese assumption is that Confucianism is sober, rational, and practical, and Hinduism is mystical, irrational, and otherworldly, which is why China succeeds and India fails."[3] As Friedman and others have pointed out, however, it is probably wise to be skeptical about some of the claims for China's success because the statistics could be false or misleading. India does worse than China on development indicators, such as infant mortality, but it has not had any famines since independence, unlike China, which has had at least three.

From an urban development viewpoint, India loses out in the *skyline test*. The number of skyscrapers that dot Shanghai, Beijing, or even Shenzhen far exceed India's leader, Mumbai. One could argue that "real" India and China are in the villages, where skylines do not matter. But that misses a key point: The skyline test symbolizes China's far greater progress in building a business-friendly society.

Also, as is well-known, India is evidently a democracy, judged at least by the power of the people to change government, and China is not. The question is whether the economic climate and democracy might be connected. This used to be a favorite critique of Indian democracy during the 1980s and 1990s, when China's economy flew and India's was grounded. It is less heard now that India also does well, yet there are good reasons to believe that there is a connection. It is not as simple as concluding that India has difficulty pulling together as a nation because of its poverty. That is, democracy magnifies the stresses of its poor population, while China's dictatorship muffles these stresses and chooses to focus on growth. This may be true, but has always been true, so it cannot explain India's current progress. Similarly, one may not easily conclude that India is so ethnically divided that a dictatorship makes more sense, whereas China is ethnically much more homogeneous, so that its people will pull together and progress, regardless of whether China has a dictatorship or a democracy.

The real difference between Indian and Chinese governance is in how the rules are made, as the following tale illustrates. When I was working with the Indian government on venture capital reform in the years 1999 to 2001, I discovered how archaic Chinese venture capital rules were. These rules, somewhat similar to earlier Indian rules, restricted the avenues of investment and forms of financing. There were no tax pass-throughs and no simple organizational forms such as limited partnerships that would enable a venture capitalist to raise either angel or institutional capital. I concluded that China would never be able to raise significant venture capital unless its rules changed.

Some weeks later, when a Chinese venture capital group visited Stanford University, I was on hand to meet it and discuss what I was doing in India to change the rules.

The group consisted of about twenty Chinese-speaking venture capitalists. All of them, to my surprise, were serving bureaucrats who had been deputized by their local governments to run a venture capital firm. The Chinese government, they explained, had realized the importance of venture capital over the past year and decided to do something about it. As a first pass, it had immediately allocated $200 million among twenty newly formed venture capital firms, all state-owned, and asked them to travel to the Silicon Valley and other locations around the world to understand how venture capital was raised and invested.

I was surprised by such *dirigisme,* or state control of the economy, in China of 2001. I would have thought that, just as we were doing for India, China would be studying global practices and would then come out with a sensible set of rules that fit into its legal and corporate system. In the case of venture capital, there was adequate evidence that a private-sector-led investment process was best practice, although the sources of funds—in the absence of developed pension institutions or capital markets—could partly come from the state. Yet here was the Chinese state setting up state-run firms to decide what to invest in and funding them to do so.

I explained to the visitors what I was working on for India and pointed out that their approach was faulty. This had to be done delicately, since I was telling our visitors that they were the wrong persons to be venture capitalists. Instead, I said, venture capitalists had to grow out of an ecosystem that enabled successful entrepreneurs to turn into providers of capital. The state's role ought to be to further the ecosystem by spending on public education, building infrastructure, and perhaps providing some access to capital. The audience listened politely and even applauded when I finished, which made me wonder if the translator had chosen to be overly tactful when translating.

Later, I had a chance to talk to the team leader, who was the only one of the team to speak English. I asked if my point had gotten through. He nodded, noting that he and the team were very grateful for my talk, as it had helped them to become aware of the Indian approach. I naturally, then, queried him: "Why don't you do the same with China? After all, I'm merely adapting U.S.- and other developed-country-rules to the Indian legal system and to India's stage of development."

His reply led to my second surprise of the evening. He said:

If we follow your approach, we will never come up with rules, because that is not how we work. We always frame our rules after we have our own experiences that tell us what works. With your approach, we won't have any experience of what works and what does not. Instead, we have decided to begin with this experiment right away. We will also shortly be supporting several private venture capitalists with funds to invest in new ventures. That way, we will have at least two competing experiments on the ground. We might later add some more business models. In fact, that is what we are in Silicon Valley for: We want to understand all the ways in which venture capital is invested here, who does it and what skills they have. Then we will try them all and see which work. Finally, we will design rules to support those that seem to show the greatest evidence of success.

I asked him if he was worried about the cost of failure. He looked at me in surprise. He was not at all worried, he said, adding, "At most, we will lose a few hundred million dollars from this experiment by the time we learn what works and what does not. That is not much compared to the benefit."

It took me some time to grasp the implications of this, but when I had, I concluded that I had learned something very useful that day: There are two ways to achieve best practices in a country playing catch-up. The Indian approach of "studying-before-adopting" is grounded in a basic concern about losing any money at all. This is because the loss will lead to the project being deemed a failure. The failure will then immediately be attributed to the minister or bureaucrats who led the project. They will end up losing prestige and career prospects. Further, by the time failure occurs, enough entrenched interests will have been created to make policy reversal difficult. Hence, the way reforms are done in India is that a proposed policy is always first tested intellectually. Because most policies have both upside and downside risks, those that seem relatively immune to downside risks (whether to the treasury's purse or to careers) will be pursued first. Sometimes, nothing is done—the fabled paralysis by analysis.

The Chinese approach is to try several methods at costs that are low relative to the potential from a success. The bureaucrat can do this because he and his boss, the minister, are protected from the consequences of failure by the absence of a ballot box. This approach is evident in a range of fields, ranging from village enterprises to planning a city, and may be termed a Chinese style of *learning by doing*.

Which approach is better? On the one hand, the Chinese approach gets a system off the ground more quickly. Extensive experimentation is more likely to yield a successful model than the Indian approach of a single good effort. On the other hand, the Indian approach has the merit that if, through good thinking, the right approach is chosen the first time around, it will lead to a solid, low-cost success.

As it happened for venture capital, the Indian approach was right the first time around, and the Chinese floundered for a few years. So, by 2004, India had already crossed a billion dollars of venture capital money invested each year, while China was less than a half billion. But, as may be expected, once they got it right, the Chinese venture capital industry became a success, and by 2005 had caught up with and even overtaken the Indian venture capital industry. Interestingly, a review of the current venture capital system in China shows that the state-run venture capital funds have mostly shut down. However, some of the startups that they funded went on to get later-stage funding from private venture capitalists and were successful.

What this demonstrates is that changing one's political representatives regularly, as India allows, can make for little change in policy even while, in China, the security provided by the single-party system has done wonders for the rate of change.

How can India remedy the deficiencies of its democracy, something that no one in the country would give up even for China-like rates of growth? Alas, the answer lies in a key difference in India's democracy from the United States that was discussed earlier: the need for civil society. Even in the promarket United States, the Washington Consensus approach is rarely adopted. Like India, the approach is to *study-then-adopt*. The difference is that extensive consultation is done. Before a new rule comes into force, the American method is to consult as many stakeholders as possible. Think tanks, universities, and lobbying groups will all typically participate in such a project. The motive of these civil-society organizations is that their success and future funding is determined by the extent and success of their participation.

The result is that the quality of thinking that goes into rule formation is sophisticated and the chances of failure are low. After that, if there is failure, the bureaucrat and politician are, of course, held responsible, but less so because they can point to the consultative process for evidence of the quality of their efforts.

By contrast, in India, getting the public to respond to such consultative processes is very difficult. Bureaucrats are not used to it and will sometimes ignore public depositions, while the public does not have the associations to participate effectively on its behalf. Hence, the answer to the question posed in the earlier paragraph is, in concept, simple: India needs to become more democratic, not less democratic. In practice, the near absence of civil society makes consultation difficult.

Nevertheless, there are some rules of the game at which India excels vis-à-vis China. A simple, though comprehensive, list of things at which India does relatively well includes respect for property rights, the building of effective regulatory and legal institutions, and the management of pervasive risks (such as crop failure). Of these, it has done best in creating independent, empowered regulation in many areas, including the macroeconomy and financial markets. It is also well ahead in property rights, broadly defined to include intellectual property rights, but also to include the right of a private entity to provide all kinds of services. In China, the regulation of professional services is weak, and access to providing a range of services, such as telecommunications and airline services, is excluded for the private sector.

Of course, having the institutions in place does not mean that their progress is irreversible. This is the second difference from China, where its centralized autocracy enables progressive, sequential reform. Although Indian policy makers are fond of proclaiming that reform and liberalization of the economy is always happening, so that there is always forward progress (even while conceding that the pace might differ, depending on the political environment), the reality is that rules change.

A Fortune 500 technology firm from Silicon Valley found that this worked to its detriment after it began a large project to connect villages with broadband in a certain district in Andhra Pradesh around 2002. At that time, the chief minister of Andhra Pradesh (mentioned at the beginning of the chapter), was the all-powerful and charismatic leader of his state. In order to gain his favor, the firm agreed to connect villages in his electoral constituency using long-distance wireless technology based on the popular Wi-Fi standard. The chief minister agreed to support the project with digitized content, such as information on jobs, payment of water taxes, and other government services. A year later, the project was launched with fanfare, connecting several dozen villages. A year after that, a visit to the site by my research assistant for a project I was doing on rural use of technology revealed that the sites were in disrepair. By 2005, the project had been abandoned.

The reason for the failure was that the chief minister's party lost the local elections in 2004, although he won his seat. The new government lost no time in withdrawing support for what was now an opposition party's project. The firm also lost favor with the state.

It is, of course, not the case that all the rules of the game are subject to change. Certain institutions, such as an independent central bank and industrial delicensing are here to stay. Their institutionalization, like all changes to the rules in the 1990s, was initially a response to India's fiscal and foreign-exchange crisis of 1990. The public sector was politically weakened by these changes; and the government, in response to the terms of a bailout by the International Monetary Fund (IMF), agreed to them. By the time that the proponents of public sector "rule" regained political power, the private sector had entered sufficiently so that its political power matched the public sector, making the change irreversible.

In general, the key indicator for what is permanent and what is temporary about the rules is the ingress of private corporate interests into a sector. Thus, private telecommunications firms are deeply entrenched in providing telephone services. One predicts, therefore, that reforms achieved will stay and new reforms will be made. However, the power sector is still the preserve of state-owned interests: Reform in this sector will be choppy in consequence.

INDIA'S FUTURE

India's future, as I have sought to show in this chapter, is dependent on much more than just its democratic tradition or its relatively recent turn toward private enterprise. Some of the additional factors we discussed, such as its urban diversity, will stand it in good stead in the years ahead. Others, such as its form of democracy, may sometimes turn against its development.

Two decades ago, a newspaper commentator noted that India, under Rajiv Gandhi, could not yet see the light at the end of the tunnel but, at least, the tunnel had finally come into view. In 1991, a bureaucrat-turned-politician named Manmohan Singh took India into that tunnel with an understanding of the risks. As the finance minister, he began a series of economic reforms that were to fundamentally change India. The risks were immense, as India was then a nation that was fiscally bankrupt and socially divided.

By the time Singh returned to political governance in 2004, this time as the prime minister, the economic reforms he had initiated had begun to pay off. It had taken over a decade, but India had become one of the world's fastest-growing countries by 2004. Its incredible journey has since continued. At its heart is an awareness of real freedom. Not just the freedom to vote politicians in and out of office—this has been necessary, but hardly sufficient. The real freedom is to be able to invest one's time in the acquisition of knowledge and then to put that knowledge to use as one wants. With the possession of this power, the freedom that was promised at the stroke of midnight on August 14, 1947, is finally being tasted. The enterprise and energy of its people have begun to convert this once poorest of countries.

A reporter once asked Singh if his reforms would lead to a prosperous India. He replied that his hope was that India would not enter the twenty-first century as one of the world's poorest nations. From that modest hope, India has indeed come a long way.

NOTES

Chapter 1

1. Howard B. Schaffer, "U.S. Interests in South Asia," in Rafiq Dossani and Henry S. Rowen, eds., *Prospects for Peace in South Asia* (Stanford, CA: Stanford University Press, 2005), pp. 328–329.

Chapter 2

1. Vaasanthi, *Cut-outs, Caste and Cine Stars: The World of Tamil Politics* (New Delhi: Penguin Books, 2006).

Chapter 3

1. www.aiadmkindia.org, accessed March 4, 2007.

Chapter 4

1. Approach Paper to the Sixth Plan, quoted in R. Balashankar, *Golden Era of Indian Telecommunications* (New Delhi: Department of Telecommunications, Government of India, 1998), p. 30.

Chapter 5

1. Rebecca Mark, quoted in Swaminathan Anklesaria, "You Could Not Take India for a Ride, Rebecca Mark," *Times of India*, February 16, 2002. http://timesofindia.indiatimes.com/articleshow/1197901.cms, accessed May 24, 2007.

2. United Nations Development Programme, "Human Development Report," 2006. p. 13.

Chapter 6

1. Thomas B. Macaulay, "Minute on Indian Education," Feb. 2, 1835. www.geocities.com/bororissa/mac.html, accessed May 24, 2007.

Chapter 7

1. World Development Indicators, wbln0018.worldbank.org/psd/compete.nsf/f14ea5988b0eec7f852564900068cbfd?OpenView&Start = 1, accessed October 21, 2006.

2. Government of India Ministry of Human Resource Development, *Technical Education Quality Improvement Project of the Government of India* (New Delhi: Ministry of HRD, 2001).

3. Stephen E. Siwek and Harold W. Furchtgott-Roth, *International Trade in Computer Software* (Westport, CT: Quorum Books, 1993), p. 140.

4. George Otto Trevelyan, *Cawnpore* (1865, reprinted Boston: Adamant Media Corporation, 2001), p. 23.

5. Interview with author.

6. Jean Dreze and Amartya Sen, "India and China," in Jean Dreze and Amartya Sen, *India: Development and Participation* (Oxford: Oxford University Press, 1996), p. 3.

Chapter 9

1. Rafiq Dossani and Martin Kenney, "The Next Wave of Globalization: Relocating Service Provision to India," *World Development* 35, no. 5 (2007), pp. 772–791.

2. Siwek and Furchtgott Roth, p. 140.

3. Interview with author.

4. Interview with author.

5. Interview with author.

6. Interview with author.

Chapter 10

1. Interview with K. R. Narayanan in "Manav Samskriti," quoted in the Hindu online newspaper www.hindu.com, March 4, 2005. www.hindu.com/2005/03/04/stories/2005030408911100.htm, accessed May 24, 2007.

2. Vajpayee's public speech during an election campaign in Goa,

April 12, 2002, reported in the Hindu newspaper, www.hinduonnet.com/
fline/fl1909/19090280.htm, accessed May 24, 2007.

3. Syeda Hameed, Ruth Manorama, Malini Ghose, Sheba George,
Farah Naqvi, Mari Thekaekara, "How Has the Gujarat Massacre Affected
Minority Women? The Survivors Speak," *Citizen's Initiative*, Ahmedabad,
April 16, 2002. Cac.ektaonline.org/resources/reports/womensreport.htm,
accessed May 24, 2007.

4. Javed Ameer, quoted by Anjum Rajabali, personal e-mail to the
author, March 22, 2002.

5. Harsh Mander, "Cry, The Beloved Country: Reflections on the
Gujarat Massacre." http://www.sacw.net/Gujarat2002/Harshmandar2002
.html, accessed June 13, 2007.

6. Hameed, et al. "How Has the Gujarat Massacre Affected Minority
Women?"

7. Ibid.

8. Nicole Leistikow, "Indian Women Criticize 'Fair and Lovely'
Ideal," *Women's Enews*, April 28, 2003. www.womensenews.org/article
.cfm/dyn/aid/1308/context/archive, accessed May 24, 2007.

9. http://www.hll.com/brands/fairnlovely.asp, accessed Dec 28, 2006.

10. William W. Hunter, *The Indian Mussalmans* (1871, reprinted
New Delhi: Rupa & Co., 2002), p. 161–162.

11. Ibid.

12. Urvashi Butalia, *The Other Side of Silence* (New Delhi: Penguin
Books, 1998), p. 87.

13. William H. Sleeman, *Rambles and Recollections of an Indian
Official* (1844, reprinted Teddington, UK: Echo Library, 2006), p. 45.

14. Thomas B. Macaulay, "Minute on Indian Education," Feb. 2,
1835. www.geocities.com/bororissa/mac.html, accessed May 24, 2007.

15. Veer Savarkar, *Hindutva* (1925, reprinted New Delhi: Hindi Sahi-
tya Sadan, 2003).

16. Acton, John E. E. D., "Nationality," *Home and Foreign Review*
(London, 1862), reprinted in John N. Figgis and Reginald V. Laurence,
eds., *The History of Freedom and Other Essays* (London: Macmillan,
1907), p. 300.

17. Eric Hobsbawm, *Nations and Nationalism since 1780: Programme, Myth, Reality* (Cambridge: Cambridge University Press, 1992),
p. 130.

18. Christophe Jaffrelot, *India's Silent Revolution: The Rise of the
Lower Castes in North India* (London: Hurst and Co., 2003).

19. Government of India National Task Force on Information Technology and Software Development, 1998. www.ilo.org/public/english/employ ment/skills/hrdr/init/ind_1.htm#Part%201, accessed May 24, 2007.

20. Tarquin Hall, *Salaam Brick Lane: A Year in the New East End* (London: John Murray, 2006).

21. Sukrat Desai, "Hoping to Make Peace, Muslims Welcome BJP Campaign," *Yahoo! India News*, March 5, 2005, http://in.news.yahoo .com/040305/43/2bu6h.html, accessed January 27, 2007.

Chapter 13

1. Jean Dreze and Amartya Sen, "India and China," in Jean Dreze and Amartya Sen, *India: Development and Participation* (Oxford: Oxford University Press, 1996), p.129.

2. Mike Davis, *Late Victorian Holocausts: El Niño Famines and the Making of the Third World* (London: Verso Books, 2001), p. 31.

3. "Green Revolutions: an Overview," Christopher J. Baker, in Tim P. Bayliss-Smith and Sudhir Wanmali, eds., *Understanding Green Revolutions: Agrarian Change and Development Planning in South Asia: Essays in Honour of B.H. Farmer* (Cambridge: Cambridge University Press, 1984), p. 48.

4. V. K. Ramachandran, "On Kerala's Development Achievements," in Jean Dreze and Amartya Sen, eds., *Indian Development: Selected Regional Perspectives* (Oxford: Oxford University Press, 1998), pp. 295–296.

5. Atul Kohli and Rani Mullen, "Growth and Poverty in India," in Atul Kohli, Chung-in Moon, and George Sørensen, eds., *States, Markets and Just Growth: Development in the Twenty-First Century* (Tokyo: United Nations University Press, 2003), p. 201.

6. Barrington Moore, *Social Origins of Dictatorship and Democracy: Lord and Peasant in the Making of the Modern World* (Boston: Beacon Press, 1966), quoted in Atul Kohli and Rani Mullen, "Growth and Poverty in India," p. 199.

7. U. R. Anantha Murthy, *Samskara*, translated into English from the original Kannada by A. K. Ramanujan (New Delhi: Oxford University Press, 1965), p. 145.

8. Rafiq Dossani and V. Ranganathan, "Farmers' Willingness to Pay for Power: Conceptual Issues, Survey Results and Implications for Pricing Reform in India" *Energy Economics* 26 (2004), pp. 359–369.

Chapter 14

1. *Indian Express,* Mumbai edition, June 27, 1976

2. *Statesman,* Calcutta edition, December 31, 1975.

3. Jean Dreze and Amartya Sen, "India and China," in Jean Dreze and Amartya Sen, *India: Development and Participation* (Oxford: Oxford University Press, 1996), pp.132–133.

Chapter 15

1. Alexis de Tocqueville, *Democracy in America* (1840, reprinted New York: Signet Classics, 2001), p. 201.

2. Ibid., p. 198.

3. Edward Friedman, "Is China a Success While India is a Failure," *World Affairs,* 167 no. 2, (Fall, 2004), p. 59.

INDEX

ABCD (American-born Confused Desi), 187
Abdullah, Sheikh, 35
Acton, John E. E. D., 178, 186
Adobe India, 128, 144
advocacy state, 101
agriculture
  future, democracy and, 238–241
  independence and removal of tax burden, 222
  moneylender's role, 226–228
  policies, 231–233
  subsidiaries for, 224
  taxation, 220–221
Ahmed, Fakhruddin Ali, 33
Ahmedabad, 153–156, 158, 162–168, 184
All India Anna Dravida Munnetra Kazhagam (DMK), 40
All India Radio, x
Allahabad University, 104
Ambedkar, B. R., 169–171
American India Foundation, 196
Anand, 240
Andhra Pradesh, 50, 52, 57, 180, 229, 230, 259, 262, 269
Arada Systems, business model, 135
army in Pakistan, 20
Asian American Hotels Owners Association, 190
Athena Semiconductors, 136
Atlanta, 190
attrition rates for employees, 94, 147

automobile producers, 65
Ayodhya agitation, 53

babudom (bureaucracy), 10
Babur, 164
Bahal, Aniruddha, 250, 251
Bahujan Samaj Party, 40
Baker, Christopher, 222
Bangalore, 107, 115, 144, 151, 257, 258
  digital and ethnic divide, 148–149
  engineering salary, 137
  software industry growth, 116–117
Bangladesh, 35
Bank of America, 143
banking, 269–270
  nationalization, 224
  small loan program, 69
Bara Din, 162
"below poverty line" certificate, 235
Bengal
  famine of 1943, 222
  Muslims in, 166
best practices, determining, 266–267
Bharatiya Janata Party (BJP), 39, 53, 58, 174
  defeat in 2004, 186
Bhatia, Sabeer, 192–193, 196
Bihar, 23
Birla Institute of Technology and Sciences, 192
body shopping, 112
Boeing, 120
Bombay, *see* Mumbai

Bombay Stock Exchange (BSE), 44–45, 199, 216
 foreign brokers' application to, 214–215
Brahmins, 162
brain drain, 123
 vs. brain gain, 124
bribes, 64, 69–70
brinksmanship, 60
British rule, 18–19
 patronage system of, 220–222
Broadcom, 128, 136
bureaucracy, 63
 change in thinking, 45–46
 integrity breakdown, 27
 of Mughals, 19
 reinstitutionalization, 43
Burroughs, 111–112
Business India, 246, 253
business models, innovation in, 127–130
Butalia, Urvashi, 166

C programming language, 115
cable TV, 50
Calcutta, *see* Kolkata
Calendar Reform Committee, 19
California, Sikhs as landowners, 188
call centers, 93
 growth in, 95
caste system, 162–163
 Dalits (untouchables), 23
 see also Dalits (untouchables)
 and malnutrition, 219
 obsession with, 186
 opposition to discrimination, 40
 progress against discrimination, 4
 repression of lower, 23
cell phones, 7, 49, 79
central place theory, 256
centralism, 31
 budget decisions, 42
centralist government, of Nehru, 25
Chandrampet, 50

Chatterjee International Center, 72
Chennai (formerly Madras), 2–3, 257
 politicians, 3–4
children, rural conditions, 219
China, 96, 109–110
 vs. India, 263–270
 literacy rate, 243
 massive industrialization, 8
 urban infrastructure, 233
Chinese, professional associations, 195
Christaller, Walter, 256
Cisco, 151
cities, *see* urban areas
Citigroup, 111
civic responsibility, 156–158
civil code, 175–176
civil society movements, 42–43, 268
civil society, quality of, 260–261
coalitions, 38, 39–41
 decision making in, 41–46
 and Muslims, 180
 region-based, and budgets, 42
Cochin in Kerala, 220
Cold War, 26–27
colonialism, 178
communications, face-to-face, 146
Communist Marxist Party, 39, 174
competition
 for faculty, 105
 public vs. private sector, 64
computer sciences, graduate degrees in, 97
computers in India, 113
 see also information technology
Confucianism, 263
Congress Party, 18, 21, 28, 170, 174
 Nehru and, 25–26
 R. Gandhi on, 38
 rural votes, 34, 223
Controller for Capital Issues, 117
corruption, 27–28, 63–81
 causes, 69–70

in civic life, 65–68
continuing, 77–81
cost of, 71
fear of, in higher education, 103
Council of Scientific and Industrial
Research, 98
Credit Suisse, 143
custom service, Indian software as,
110–112

Dabhol project, 76
Daksh, IBM acquisition, 143
Dalal Street, 199
Dalits (untouchables), 4, 23, 163,
169–171
Congress and, 176
oppression, 178
as slum occupants, 179
Dalrymple, William, 177
data-mining industry, 130
deinstitutionalization, by I. Gandhi,
226
Delhi, 36, 257
High Court, 78
democracy, ix, 21
and agriculture future, 238–241
variations, 259–262
Democracy in America (Tocqueville), 260
Desai, Meghnad, 186
desi, 187
Deutsche Bank, 143
Dev Ahilyabai University, 101
developing countries, two-track politics in, 41
dialects, x
discrimination, 183
diversity of India, x
division of labor model (DOL), 128
Diwali, 161
dowry premium, 68
Dravida Movement, 186

Dravida Munnetra Kazhagam, 40
Dreze, Jean, 107, 253

economic change, cell phone affordability as measure of, 8
economic class divisions, English language and, 86
economic ecosystems, 138–143
economic rationality, 42
economic stagnation, and crises,
28–29
economies of scale, 118
EDS, 143
education
budget priority, 98
change in content, 96
costs, 5, 7
and freedom, 106–108
rural, 237–238
tutoring, 131
electric-power sector, 33, 48–49
Emergency (1975 to 1977), 10
and press freedom, 245
employment projects, villagers' need
for information on, 235
engineers
of Chinese origin, 193–194
migration to U.S., 191–193
salaries, 137, 141
English bilingualism, 88
English language, 12–15
in-house training, 94
quality of, 85
seeping in of, 89–90
Enron, power generation plant,
75–76
entrepreneurship, 110, 121, 138, 145
trust in, 195
epidemics, 71
ethno-linguistic-fractionalization
index (ELFI), x
expectations for business, 3
Ezekiel, Nissim, 13

face-to-face communication, 146
faculty, 103, 105
Fair & Lovely facial cream, 163–164
faith, politicization of, 180
famines, 221, 222–223
Fanaa (movie), 183
farmers, 219
    suicide rate for, 22
federalism, 39–40, 259
    implications, 48
Fernandes, George, 250, 251
fertilizer, rural subsidies for, 229
fiber-optic backbone network, 51
five-year plans for investment, 26
follow-the-sun (FTS) model, 127
food-grain crop failures, absence of,
    47–48
foreign brokers, applications to Bom-
    bay Stock Exchange, 214–215
foreign capital, need for, 26
Foreign Exchange Regulation Act of
    1973 (FERA 1973), 201
foreign investment after 1991, 74–75
foreign policy of India, 59
freedom, 271
    and education, 106–108
Friedman, Edward, 263
Furchgott-Roth, Harold W., 124

Gandhi, Indira, 10, 27, 31, 32, 68,
    174, 261
    and agriculture, 223–224
    assassination, 35
    legal verdict on charges of misus-
        ing state machinery, 33
    reelection 1980, 34
Gandhi, Mohandas, 9, 17
    views on secularism, 169
Gandhi, Rajiv, 29, 32, 36, 175
    on Congress Party, 38
    corruption in defense program, 37
    historians' view of, 37–38

loan mela (loan festival) project,
    68
Garibi Hatao ("Remove Poverty")
    strategies, 38
General Insurance Corporation of
    India, 204
Ghosh, Amitava, 13
gift bags for reporters, 246–248
Global Entrepreneurship Monitor,
    121, 138
global office, India as, 142–143
global partnerships, 2
globalization, 197
God, Western concept vs. Eastern re-
    ligions, 160
Goldman Sachs, 143
Google, 90
governance standards
    India vs. China, 263–264
    for Indian universities, 100–106
government offices, 28
government services, rural popula-
    tion need for, 234–235
grain output, per capita, 232
Great Britain, disengagement from
    colonies, 19–20
Green Revolution, 2, 224–225
gross domestic product, services as
    proportion, 47
guilt, over corruption, 72
Gujarat, 53, 183, 190, 237
gun-control laws, 157

Hall, Tarquin, *Salaam Brick Lane*,
    185
hardware,
    government discouragement of im-
        ports, 113
    IBM open standards, 111
health care, in rural areas, 220
heritable assets, phone lines as, 67
Hewlett-Packard, 115
Hewlett-Packard GlobalSoft, 144

high-opportunity entrepreneurship, 138
Himachal Futuristic Communications Limited (HFCL), 76–77
Hindi, 84
  and English, 13
Hindu temple, mosque destruction and replacement with, 53
Hinduism, 263
Hindu-Muslim riots of 1984, 184
Hindus
  burning of, on train, 154
  origins of rivalry with Muslims, 164–165
  see also caste system
Hindustan Motors, 65
Hindustani, 13
Hindutva movement, 39, 42–43, 53–54
Hobsbawm, Eric, 178
honesty, and stockbrokers, 204
Hotmail, 192
Houston, 190
Hunter, William, 166
Hyderabad, 257
hydroponics, 226–227
hygiene standards, 219

IBM
  acquisition of Daksh, 143
  decision to leave India, 113
  open standards for hardware, 111
IBM India, job applicants, 141
illegal immigrants, 190
illiteracy, 9
immigration to U.S., 188–191
independence of India, 9, 17–18, 19–20
  religion and politics during movement, 168–171
  and taxes on agriculture, 222
India
  vs. China, 263–270
  future of, 270–271
  growth process, 255
  national identity, 9–12
  official languages, 13
  world relations, x
India Express (Mumbai), 245
Indian Institutes of Management (IIMs), 98, 99–100, 103
Indian Institutes of Technology (IITs), 97
Indians, living overseas, 47
India-U.S. relations, 1–2
Indore, 7–8, 106, 133
The Indus Entrepreneurs (TiE), 83, 194
Industrial Credit and Investment Corporation of India, 204
Industrial Development Bank of India, 204
industrial development, R. Gandhi and, 36
industrial production, quota system, 64
industrial quotas, liberalization of, 208–210
industrialization, in China, 8
industry, interaction between university and, 97
information disclosure, 116
information technology, 93
  globalization of Indian industry, 144
  infrastructure inadequacy, 97
  new challenges for industry, 144–148
  rural use potential, 233
Information Technology Action Plan, 182
Infosys, 117
  employee count, 119
  job applicants, 142
infrastructure, 109
in-house training, 94

innovation, in business models,
 127–130
insider trading, 207–208
Insilica, 134, 135–136
International Monetary Fund, 43, 270
Internet, 234
 for social services, 236
isolation-within but globalization-
 outside phenomenon, x

Janata Party, 39
Jayalalitha, Jayaram, 180
Jeffrelot, Christophe, 179
Jinnah, Muhammad Ali, 171, 172
JPMorgan Chase, 143
Jurvetson, Steve, 192

Karnataka, 115
Kashmir, 35, 54–56
 National Conference Party in, 55
 rigged local program, 37
Kashmiriyat movement, 42
Kaul, P. D., 76
Kenney, Martin, 123
Kerala, ix, 98, 177, 223
 Communists in, 39
 land redistribution, 225
 social economic condition, ix
Ketera Technologies, 133, 134
Khan, Amir, 183
Kharagpur, 98
knowledge economy, 83
Kodnani, Maya, 154–155, 185
Kohli, Atul, 41, 224
Kolkata (formerly Calcutta), 34
 building codes, 71–72
 money-market broker fraud,
 210–212
Korea, 255
Krepon, Michael, 60
Kshatriya (warrior) caste, 162
Kumar, Raj, 148

labor, demand for skilled, 94
labor arbitrage, 112
labor unions, 33
Ladaphone project in Mexico, 51
land ownership, 222, 229
 need for change, 21
land reform, I. Gandhi and, 225–226
languages, x
 Hindi, 84
 Hindi and English, 13
 native tongue, 90
 states based on, 173
 see also English language
learning by doing style, 267
licensed firms, 200
Life Insurance Corporation of India,
 204, 205–206
literacy, 25
literacy rate, 243
literature, by Indians, 13
loan mela (loan festival) project, 68
local community, dominance of, x

Macaulay, Thomas, 85, 167–168
Madhya Pradesh, 7, 101
Madras, *see* Chennai
Maglio, Paul, 146
Maharashtra, 41
Mahmud of Ghazni, 164
mainstreamed immigrants, 191,
 196–198
majoritarianism, 4, 24
Malabar in Kerala, 220
malnutrition, and caste system, 219
management education, 99
managers, 125–126
Mander, Harsh, 155–156
manufactured goods, queues for,
 66–67
Mark, Rebecca, 75
market economy, 29
Marketics Technologies, 130
Markowitz, Harry, 99

Massachusetts Institute of Technology, 98
master's degree graduates, in computer sciences, 97
matrix model, 129
MBA students, 104
media, 243–253
  assessing quality of, 252
  freedom of, 244–246
  gift bags for reporters, 246–248
  investigative journalism, 250–251
  power of, 246–250
  and violence, 156–158
Meerut, 37
Mehta, D. R., 45
Mehta, Harshad, 211–212
Mexico, *Ladaphone* project, 51
middle class, queues for manufactured goods, 66–67
migration, Muslims and non-Muslims, 20
Ministry of Communications, 43
Ministry of Panchayati Raj Institutions (Village Governance Institutions), 48
Mishra, Pankaj, *Butter Chicken in Ludhiana*, 13
Modi, Narendra, 153, 181, 185
Mohalla Ekta Committees (Locality Unity Committees), 158
moneylenders, and agriculture, 226–228
monogamy, 176
Moore, Barrington, 225
Morgan Stanley, 143
mosque, destruction and replacement with Hindu temple, 53
motivation, for company entry in India, 147
Mphasis, 143
Mughals, 18–19
Mukherji, Ayan, 146
Mullen, Rani, 225

multilingual character of India, 84–85
multinational corporations (MNCs), 124, 125
  importance of, 150–152
  Indian promotions in, 139
  restrictions on, 201
  subsidiaries, 151
Mumbai (formerly Bombay), 71, 158, 175, 243, 257
  money-market broker fraud, 210–212
  October Dussehra festival, 15
  professional skills in, 3
  slum dwellers, 179
  software industry in, 116
  toilets in, 79
Murthy, Narayana, 47
Murthy, U. R. Anantha, *Samskara*, 226
Muslim League, 172
Muslims, 163
  in Ahmedabad, 153–156
  British discrimination against, 165–166
  economic decline, 165, 174
  in north and south India, 173
  origins of rivalry with Hindus, 164–165
  and Pakistan, 20
  progrom of, 36
  restrictions on employment, 174–175
  role within Congress, 171
  self-sufficiency within ghetto, 175
  as slum occupants, 179
  status in 1880s, 167

Nano City, 193, 196
Narayanan, K. R., 154, 157
nation, India as, xi
National Conference Party, in Kashmir, 55
National Informatic Center (NIC), 233

national language, attempt to legislate, 14
National Stock Exchange (NSE), 44,
199, 215–217
nationalism, 169
Nationalist Congress Party (NCP), 41
nationalization, of bank, 224
national-regional coalition, 39
native tongue, 90
Nehru, Jawaharlal, 10, 18, 173
and agricultural development, 223
commitment to democracy, 21
concern over fragmentation risk,
24–25
on India's role in world affairs, 26
and Kashmir, 35
on land reform, 21–22
nation-building project, 28
popularity, 35
quota system, 64
socialist economic policy, 35
Nehru, Motilal, 170
Network Solutions, 143
networks, importance of, 193–195
newspapers, x, 243
9/11 terrorist attacks, 57
nongovernment organizations, 52
nonresident Indians (NRIs), 138–
139, 187
Indian attitudes toward, 196
management skills, 125
mixed loyalty, 198
returning, 123–127
nonviolence, M. Gandhi and, 17
Northwestern University, 100
nuclear fuel, 58
nuclear testing, 35, 57

octroi, 68
Office Tiger, 143
Old Guard, 68
Orissa famine, 221

OTCEI (Over the Counter Exchange
of India), 215
outsourcing, 2
Over the Counter Exchange of India
(OTCEI), 215

Pakistan, 20, 60, 171, 172
India relations with, 54
patent registrations, 97
Pathan, Nazir Khan, 185
patronage system, 231
of British Raj, 220–222
peat moss, importing, 227
People's Democratic Party, 55
personal law, 175–176
Ph.D.'s, in computer sciences, 97
Philippines, 109
pluralism, 21
and tolerance, 158–162
pneumonic plague, 71
police
do-nothing orders, 183–184
effectiveness of, 157
and mob violence, 156
politicians
promises, 261
voters' knowledge of, 262
politics, during independence movement, 168–171
polygamy, 176
postal service, 236
poverty, 5–8, 9, 25
Nehru rule and, 10
perception of, 4
power
for farmers, 262
outages, battery backups for, 133
subsidies for, 229
Premier Automobile Company, 65
Premji, Azim, 47
press
see media
Press Trust of India, 245

primary education, priority for budget, 98
private education, 47
  vs. state institutions, 101–102
  universities, 105
private enterprise, 26
process excellence, global standards for, 120
programmers, sending overseas, 113–114
project management, 114, 118
public sector
  and bribes, 64
  education expenditures, 96
  employment, 99
  expansion, 38
  overstaffing, 67
public works, quality of, 28
Punjab, 20, 34–35, 56, 262

queues for manufactured goods, 66–67
quota system for industrial production, 64
  end of, 74–77

rainfall, shortage, and farming conditions, 221
Rajasthan, 177
rakaabi believer, 160
Ramachandran, M. G., 180, 223
Ramadorai, S., 111–112, 121
Ramakrishna, G. V., 44–45, 215
Ramanujan, A. K., 226
Ranga Reddy, 52
Ranganathan, V., 230
Ranvir Sena, 23
Raza, Atiq, 149, 150
reading, 243
receptionists, virtual, 131
regional parties, interests, 40
regionalism, 59–61
regionalization, 186

region-based coalitions, budget decisions, 42
regulation of stock exchanges, 199–200
regulator state, 101
Rekhi, Kanwal, 107
religion, 15
  during independence movement, 168–171
  see also Hindus; Muslims
religious software, 106–107
remote communication, 146
rent system, 21
research, 97, 140
reservation policies, 24
risk capital, obtaining, 117
rote learning skills, 104
R.R. Donnelly, 143
rule by coterie, 37
rules, change in, 269
rural population
  daily caloric consumption, 22
  education, 237–238
  elite, 232
  poor voting rates, 239–240
  stability, 23
Rural Telecom Foundation (RTF), 52
Rushdie, Salman, 13

Salaam Brick Lane (Hall), 185
salaries
  engineers, Bangalore vs. Silicon Valley, 137
  professionals in Mumbai, 158, 160
Salcedo, Javier, 63
Salisbury, Robert, 221
Salve, Harish, 78
Samskara (Murthy), 226
Sandesh, 252
Sangh, Rashtriya Swayamsevak, 36
Sanscrit, literary value of, 167–168
Sanskrit, 13
SAP, 129

SAP Labs India, 144

Saurashtra, 88

Savarkar, Veer, 172

Sayeed, Kashmiri M.M., 55

Schaffer, Howard, 1

Scindia Steamship, 211–212

secondary education, priority for budget, 98

sectarian conflict, 171–176
  sources of, 162–168

sectarian harmony, prospects for, 178–186

secularism, 168
  risk from debating, 186

Securities and Exchange Board of India (SEBI), 44, 117, 203, 210, 213

Sen, Amartya, 19, 107, 186, 219, 221, 253

senior management, premium vs. discount for work in India, 95

separation of church from state, 168

services economy, 8–9
  language in, 87
  proportion to GDP, 47

services from India, 109

Shah, Raj, 134

Sharma, Manu, 78

Sharpe, William, 99

short supply, 66

Sikhs
  as California landowners, 188
  deaths following Gandhi assassination, 36
  migration to U.S. and Canada, 187–188

Silicon Valley
  division of labor in, 134
  engineering salary, 137
  Indians' success in, 195

Silicon Valley Indian Professionals Association (SIPA), 194–195

Sindh (Pakistan), 20

Singh, Manmohan, 43, 251, 270–271

Sino-Indian War of 1962, 35

Siwek, Stephen E., 124

Six Sigma program, 120

skilled labor, demand for, 94

skin color, 163–164

skyline test, 263

Sleeman, William, 167

Slovenia, 136

slums, 3

small-town India, English language in, 91

social services, Internet for, 236

Software and Technology Parks of India (STPI), 139

software industry
  development shift to India, 118–121
  domestic beginnings, 114–116
  Indian exports, 112

South Asia, nuclear weapons, 60

Soviet Union, collapse, 29

soybean trading, 7

specialization, cities and, 256

Sri Lanka, 61

stagnation, 2

stand-up comics, 13

startups
  for Indian market, 136–137
  role of, 130–137

state of emergency (1975), 32–33

state-owned enterprises (SOEs), 33

states
  bureaucracy, 3
  funding for religious places of worship, 172
  institutions, vs. private education, 101–102
  political power, 259

Statesman (Kolkata), 245

steering state, 101

sterilizations, forced, 10

stockbrokers, as jobbers, 209

stock exchanges, 44–45
  beginnings of trading, 200–204
  foreign participants, 212–214
  insider information, 207–208
  liberalizations impact, 208–210
  making money, 204–208
  "price-recorder," 207
  regulation, 199–200
  state-sponsored, 216
study before adoption, 266
subnationalism, 53–54, 170, 172
subsidiaries, for agriculture, 224
subsidies, 228–229, 232
sufi shrines, 177
suicide rate, for farmers, 22, 232
Surat, 71
Swatantra Party, 39

Taiwan, 255
talent, depth of, 3
Tamil Nadu, 4, 24, 40, 180, 262
  oppression of lowest castes, 23
tantra, 162
Tata, Ratan, 47
Tata Consultancy Services, 91
Tatkal Phone Service, 66
taxation, agricultural, 220–221
taxi drivers, income, 5
TCS, 111–112
  Boeing contract, 120
  employee count, 119
technical work, quality of, 96–101
technology, 233–236
Tehelka (online journal), 250–251, 252
Tejas Networks, 135, 137
Tejpal, Tarun, 250
telecommunications
  bidding for licenses, 76–77
  cost of, 113
  growth in, 49
  regulation, 259

telephone
  company losses from, 50
  see also cell phones
Telsima, 135–136
Telugu Desam, 40
terror, 154
Texas Instruments, 115, 142
The Indus Entrepreneurs (TiE), 83, 194
Thidal, Periyar, 186
time differentials, taking advantage of, 127
Tocqueville, Alexis de, *Democracy in America*, 260
tolerance, 160
  Indian form of, 168
  and pluralism, 158–162
  in practice, 177–178
total responsibility model (TR), 128
tourists, immigration to U.S. as, 190
townships, 33
trade unions, 33
  disruptions from, 34
Trevelyan, George, 103
TRG, 130–131
Trivandrum, 258
Tutor Vista, 131
two-glass roadside café, 4
two-nation theory, 172

undernutrition, 219
United Nations, 54
  Human Development Report for 2006, 79
United States
  corporate involvement in India, 56–57
  embassy in India, 96
  newspapers, 243
  position of Indian access to nuclear fuel, 58
  trend toward demainstreaming, 198

United States (*continued*)
universities as model for India, 100
war on terror, 59
universities, 140, 142
interaction between industry and,
97
Unix operating system, 115–116
untouchables (Dalits), 4, 23, 163,
169–171
Congress and, 176
oppression, 178
as slum occupants, 179
urban areas
migration to, 179
role in country's development,
256–258
slum dwellers, 179
variety in, 257
voting patterns, 257–258
urban elite, 9
Urdu, 13
US India Political Action Committee,
196
Uttar Pradesh, 37, 40, 43, 171, 182,
262
English in, 89–91

Vajpayee, Atal Behari, 154
Varanasi, 5
vasectomies, forced, 33
venture capitalists, 45, 137
in China, 264–265, 267
knowledge of technology markets
in India, 139
Vijayaditya, Dr., 235
Village Governance Institutions (Ministry of Panchayati Raj Institutions), 48

violence, 17–18
voting
by caste, 180
poor rural population, 239–240
rural and urban, 10, 12
urban areas, 257–258

wages
gap between American and Indian,
95
increase in, 93–94
low, and bribes, 70
West Bengal, 39
land redistribution, 225
Western India Automobile Association sports club, membership, 66
Wipro, 146
employee count, 119
WNS, 130
women
sexual assaults, 155–156
social status, 219
as stockbroker, 209–210
workstations, 115
world affairs, Nehru view on India's
role, 26
World Bank, statistics on poverty, 4
World War I, 19
worship, 160

Yahoo!, 127
India Development Center (IDC),
128–129
Yew, Lee Kuan, 59

zamindari system, 19, 21

ABOUT THE AUTHOR

Dr. Rafiq Dossani is a senior research scholar at the Shorenstein Asia-Pacific Research Center of Stanford University and is responsible for directing its South Asia Initiative. He teaches courses in the politics, religion, and development of South Asia. A specialist on sectoral policy reform, he has advised the Indian government on telecommunications, venture capital, energy, and rural access to information technology.

Prior to joining Stanford University, Dossani worked for the Robert Fleming investment banking group, first as CEO of its Indian operations and later as head of its San Francisco operations. He has also been a deputy editor of *Business India*, India's largest circulating business magazine.

He has degrees from St. Stephen's College, Delhi, the Indian Institute of Management at Calcutta, and Northwestern University, Evanston.